SUPPOSING THE SUBJECT

Each volume of this annual series will contain original essays from leading theorists focusing on one topic of immediate cultural and political concern. While experts from a variety of fields will contribute to each volume, the avowed aim of the series is to demonstrate the fundamental psychoanalytic character of the issues raised and the solutions required. Against the narrowing and reduction of psychoanalysis to a specialized vocabulary, which so often takes place in cultural studies, the project of these volumes is to enlarge the scope of psychoanalysis by equating it, more properly, with its concepts, no matter what term designates them. From the perspective of this enlargement, our modernity – including its 'postmodern' inversion – will be shown to be more thoroughly defined by psychoanalysis than was previously thought, and the strategies for thinking our current conditions will be rigorously rehauled.

SUPPOSING THE SUBJECT

edited by
JOAN COPJEC

VERSO
London · New York

First published by Verso 1994
© Verso 1994
All rights reserved

Verso
UK: 6 Meard Street, London W1V 3HR
USA: 29 West 35th Street, New York, NY 10001-2291

Verso is the imprint of New Left Books

ISBN 1-85984-980-6
ISBN 1-85984-075-2 (pbk)

British Library Cataloguing in Publication Data
A catalogue record for this book is available from the British Library

Library of Congress Cataloging-in-Publication Data
Supposing the subject / edited by Joan Copjec.
    p.   cm. – (S)
  Includes bibliographical references and index.
  ISBN 1–85984–980–6. – ISBN 1–85984–075–2 (pbk.)
  1. Subject (Philosophy) 2. Psychoanalysis and philosophy.
I. Copjec, Joan. II. Series: S (London, England)
BD223.S96   1994
126–dc20   94–22052 CIP

Typeset by York House Typographic Ltd, London W13
Printed and bound in Great Britain by
Biddles Ltd, Guildford and King's Lynn

CONTENTS

INTRODUCTION

JOAN COPJEC

This inaugural volume should make plain from the start
the project of the S series. In subsequent volumes we will
focus, as here, on one topic of immediate cultural and
political concern, which will be addressed in original essays
written by leading theorists specifically for each volume.
But while a range of expertise across disciplines will always
be sought, the avowed aim of the series is to demonstrate
the crucial significance of psychoanalysis to the
formulation and analysis of the issues discussed. That is,
besides aiming to contribute in a rigorous and considered
way to timely issues, the series – recognizing the
precarious status of psychoanalysis in our contemporary
world – wants to reaffirm the critical power of Freudian
theory, and to intervene against the forces that seek to
debase it.

The precariousness of psychoanalysis is attributable to
the constantly intensifying demand for return – for gain –
that characterizes today's societies. The calculus of gain to
which we are obliged ever more vigilantly to submit is
grounded in notions of unfailing reciprocity and
recognition. These notions dictate that every expenditure
can and must be duly recorded in some symbolic register
from which no entry is ever erased. The eventual profit
expected from every notable expenditure is guaranteed by
the complete survival – the record – of all past
expenditures, to which the current one can simply be
added, counted as 'everything plus one' – that is, as pure

gain. The strong belief driving our information age – that everything can be/is recorded, that nothing exists outside this historical register – serves this capitalist logic of gain.

Conversely, what this logic cannot abide is the notion that something might be permanently lost, utterly irretrievable for all time; this is precisely why its foundational concept of *foreclosure* makes psychoanalysis such anathema within capitalism. Although certain notions of psychoanalysis, interpreted in limited ways – secondary repression and the return of the repressed; the retrieval of the past through the overcoming of resistances, for example – have been not only tolerated but embraced, foreclosure (and concepts stemming from it), which marks the fact that some originary, irredeemable loss structures our reality, some libidinal fraction always remains as leftover to spoil any total investment in this reality, is a concept that can only be greeted with disdain. Thus, while Freud once noted that the unconscious was the perfect capitalist slave, his description is accurate according to a logic that would be inadmissible to proponents of a social structure whose primary goal was profit. For the pleasure that the unconscious sets to work accumulating is a surplus pleasure which has no use for material reward or even well-being; it contributes nothing to the subject's inclination towards survival. This less-than-useless surplus pleasure cannot, therefore, enter the calculus of capitalism except to undermine it.

To speak of the insidiousness of these notions of reciprocity and recognition that underwrite this calculus is to acknowledge the ways in which they often enter unnoticed in our thinking, the very subtlety by which they inform our ideas. One of the tasks of this series will be to expose the operations of notions such as these, and to bring the consequences of our unacknowledged adoption of them to light. But one such instance needs to be mentioned at the outset, since it currently poses one of the most clamorous challenges to psychoanalysis: I refer to the phenomenon of 'new historicism.' What is new about this brand of historical research, which has baptized itself with this distinguishing epithet, is its abandonment of a conception of the continuity of history in favour of a conception of its displacements and ruptures, its radical discontinuity. Although it may at first appear that this deference to discontinuity betokens new historicism's commitment to a disparagement of our belief in the complete survival of the past – after all, we note, its constant refrain is that history is not retrieved, nor even retrievable, but constructed – its unwavering adherence to the tenet that there is nothing outside history, nothing that is not historicizable, countermands our preliminary impression by installing elsewhere a notion of the impossiblity of irrecoverable loss. Its stolid denial of any 'transcendence', of any notion that there is a beyond *internal* to historical reality, or that there is something that will forever remain inarticulable in any historical text,[1] is what leads new historicism to isolate each historical moment from the one preceding and following it, and to reduce it to its contemporaneity with itself – that is, to an account of what was conceivable at any particular moment, to what it was possible to think at a certain time. Attempting to construct the actual, effective conditions of the past, new historicism turns out, in the end, to be as 'presentist' as the histories it critiques. Its absolute abhorrence of anachronism – which, arguably, exceeds the scrupulosity of its legitimate distrust of presentist, teleological accounts of history – is, rather, a symptom of the aversion of new historicism to the notion of a loss that can never be made good.

For the incomplete – and permanently so – accessibility of any moment to itself, its partial absence from itself, forbids historicism's motivating premise: that the past must be understood in its own terms. This is a simple impossibility: *no historical moment can be comprehended in its own terms*; the circuit of self-recognition or coincidence with itself which would enable such comprehension is deflected by an investment that cannot be recuperated for self-knowledge. This impossibility causes each historical moment to flood with alien, anachronistic figures, spectres from the past and harbingers of the future. Historicity is what issues from this inevitable and constitutive misapprehension of ourselves – from what Freud would call the latency of historical time with regard to its own comprehension. This notion of latency must not be positivized, as though something lay dormant but already formed in the past, and simply waited to emerge at some future time; this would indeed be a continuist notion. Instead, latency designates our inaccessibility to ourselves, and hence our dependence on others – on other times as well as other subjects.

Yet historicism encourages us to believe that every era is wrapped only in itself, that it is desirable and possible to isolate one from another. That historicists have set themselves so implacably against psychoanalysis is not, then, such a marvel. Attacking psychoanalytic theory as always too belated (or too antiquated, as historians of the postmodern present have been known to do) to be of any relevance to historical research; confining the period of the efficacy of psychoanalysis to the narrow temporal corridor of Freud's 'invention' of it; and seeing its genesis as fully accounted for by its immediate historical conditions, historicists betray more than a simple intolerance for what they take to be the anachronism of psychoanalytic interpretations of the pre- (or post-) nineteenth century; they betray a vertiginous dread of the groundlessness of history. Unable to countenance the fact that historicity as such is grounded in this very groundlessness or gap between history and its own self-knowledge, historicists refuse to countenance the apparitions, spectres of the future and past, which necessarily haunt every present.[2]

Before this historical and effective marginalization, many psychoanalytic theorists have elected to retreat, either by abandoning the terrain of history to historicism (on the grounds, tacitly proposed, that they are concerned with different matters), or by making their own theory more anodyne, refashioning its categories to the point where they begin to resemble historicist ones (the reinterpretation of the concepts of sexual difference, the symbolic, and – most prominently – the subject are discussed in this volume). The S series will proceed from the position that historicity must not be ceded to historicists by psychoanalysis, which provides a much more compelling and complex account of the operations of this process. This does not mean that we will not wish to pursue analyses of the historical conditions of the possibility of Freudian theory; in fact we hope, in so doing, to restore to the theory some of the political and philosophical content that has so far gone largely unmarked. But we will also assume that historical conditions alone do not provide sufficient cause for the emergence of an event, that it is always necessary to assume another cause (of a second order) which motivates these conditions to function as aetiological account of the event. We will want, then, to demonstrate how psychoanalysis – being a theory of this other, 'second-order' cause – can be a theory of historical events that predate its own appearance.

Part of the marginalization and reduction of Freudian theory has been the result of its equation – not simply by its detractors; by its defenders as well – with its vocabulary, to the exclusion of any serious consideration of or work on its concepts. Too many critics and supposed practitioners believe that psychoanalytic thinking is evidenced by the mere use of words such as *ego*, *id*, *resistance*, *sublimation*, *personality disorder*, and their like. Distinguishing words from concepts, the S series will attempt to excavate psychoanalytic concepts wherever they are at work, even in texts that employ no psychoanalytic vocabulary, and will remain wary of what Gaston Bachelard[3] called the 'spontaneous ontology of words' – in this case, of being duped by the mere presence of words from a select lexicon into thinking that a text is engaged in a reasoning of the psychoanalytic sort. Thus, Kant or Hegel, or any number of theorists who are not normally taken to be psychoanalytic thinkers, will be accepted as precisely that in these volumes.

Since concepts are not determinate packets of ideas, but are always inevitably unfinished, we will assume that their proper deployment in every instance entails a further determination of them, an increase and a shifting of their content. This means that fidelity to Freud will never be able to be calculated in advance by any prior knowledge, and certainly not by any previously established signs of recognition. One's faithfulness to psychoanalytic theory provides its own measure through an active filling out of its concepts, a fulfilling of their undetermined destiny. The true inheritors of Freudian theory, who construct it through this *labour of fidelity*, distinguish themselves from those who believe that it is necessary to surpass or go beyond Freud, in that for the former Freud is understood to contain, unawares, his own uncharted beyond, which is neither simply outside him nor definitively realizable.

For this reason, the devotion of this first volume to the concept of the subject is significant in that Freud does not himself use the term *subject*; it is under the word *unconscious* – and through a conceptualization of it – that he will elaborate a theory of what we are calling 'the subject'. To state it somewhat differently: in psychoanalysis the subject is not hypostatized, but hypothesized – that is, it is only ever *supposed*: we never actually encounter it face to face.

We have, in fact, for a long time now – since the beginnings of modern science – been dwelling in the graveyard of the subject. For modern science, as we know, established itself on a thorough exclusion of the subject, an effacement of all authorial traces from every text deemed to be scientific. In recent years these exclusions have been renewed by waves of 'sappers' who have reassured us, over and over again, that nothing of the subject remains alive in our modern world. Structuralism, deconstruction, historicism – so many of our contemporary discourses have announced the death of the author, the ends of man, the deconstruction, atomization and demise of the subject, that one cannot help but be struck by the very thoroughness of its effacement.

Psychoanalysis has theorized and named exclusion as radical as this: it calls it *foreclosure*. What is absolutely, thoroughly, eliminated from the symbolic will never, like the repressed, return there, but it does return in the real. In other words, psychoanalysis argues that the subject, eliminated from all its own statements, deconstructed, appears in the real, or: the subject discovers itself *in* its very effacement, *in* its own modern graveyard. This is the secret solidarity between science and psychoanalysis, the reason why the latter historically follows the former.

The reader will encounter in the chapters that follow a detailed account of this logic of real rather than symbolic return, which can be made to refute the Heideggerian charge that the concept of the subject belongs to an old metaphysical project bound up with representation and intent on picturing the world to the self: the real return of the subject is radically unassimilable to that other logic of gainful return – of reciprocity and recognition. Heidegger's complaint that the subject is merely a metaphysical notion also meets in these chapters with a more direct counterargument, which resupplies the notion of the subject with the cosmopolitical content which was originally its own, but which subsequent criticisms have chosen to ignore. The subject is defined, from the beginning and at its core, as a 'citizen of the world', with an ethical and practical, not merely an ontological, vocation. The reader will also be able to detect an implicit response to the frequently advanced accusation that the notion of citizenship which underwrites the emergence of modern, bourgeois society is patriarchal in nature, that it excludes any consideration of sexual difference; here we are presented with an argument that proposes that this notion *requires* us to assume a sexual differentiation of the universal citizen.

But do not expect to find a consistent or mutually reinforcing line of argument within this volume. The goal of the series is not consensus, but a commitment to thinking through the questions posed by the issues in focus. For this reason, contributions were sought from theorists noted for their problematization of some of the very positions I have just outlined. Nor were contributors charged with 'supposing' the subject in the strictly logical sense I have described – that is, they were not explicitly asked to consider the subject as a logically supposed (and thus necessarily empty), rather than directly encountered, entity. They were simply invited to muse, in a directed way, on the place of the subject in contemporary discourse. What results from analyses of issues ranging from queer theory to recent disturbances in the area of national identity is a diverse and heteroclite gallery of subjects – hysterical, perverse, transsexual, homosexual, fascist, British, anxiety-ridden – and quite solid evidence that reports of the demise of the subject have been so exaggerated that we have good reason to suppose its continued vitality.

Notes

1. Here we might note that historicism, whose own beginnings can be located in the nineteenth century, participates in 'a kind of puritanism in relation to desire', which, as Jacques Lacan argues (*The Ethics of Psychoanalysis* , ed. Jacques-Alain Miller, trans. Dennis Porter, London: Routledge, 1992, p. 303), occurred historically at the moment when the 'universal spread of the service of goods' became an ambition.

2. One of the richest texts on this subject is Claude Lefort's 'Marx: From One Vision of History to Another' (*The Political Forms of Modern Democracy*, Cambridge, MA: MIT Press, 1986). There Lefort demonstrates the ways in which Marx's analysis of the historical specificity of capitalist forms is invaded by such ghosts. Though Marx argues firmly that human beings become *labourers*, properly so-called, only within capitalist society, he retroactively employs this category in order to analyse precapitalist forms of human activity. Thus, in Marx, 'precapitalist forms are not simply those that the observer identifies in empirical times, . . . they constitute a whole whose distinctiveness capitalism enables us to see' (p. 142). Additionally, while bourgeois society constituted itself out of a dissolution of all traditional forms, it nevertheless dissimulated the unprecedented nature of its existence by masquerading in forms of the past. Accordingly, Marx occupies himself with an account of this upsurging of the past, not merely of the novelty of the bourgeois present.

3. Gaston Bachelard's considerable contribution to a noncontinuist history of science has, unfortunately, remained obscure to those who know him only by his later reveries on the metaphors of language.

1 SUBJECTION AND SUBJECTIVATION

ÉTIENNE BALIBAR

I will begin by sketching out a problematic, or research programme, on which I have been working for some time now, which aims at resuming and recasting the notion of a *philosophical anthropology*. For reasons which, I hope, will become clear later, I suggest that such a programme ought to begin with a critical discussion, both historical and analytical, of the notions of *man*, the *subject* and the *citizen*, which together delineate the ambivalent order of subjection and subjectivation.

My presentation will be divided into three parts:

1. A brief recall of previous discussions around 'philosophical anthropology', including Heidegger's critique of that notion.
2. A critique of Heidegger's critique, focusing on the importance of the onto-political category of the 'citizen' in the debate.
3. An outline of what a renewed philosophical anthropology could be: it is there that subjection and subjectivation properly come into play.

Allow me, first, some schematic considerations on the past controversies that surround the very notion of a 'philosophical anthropology'. At certain moments they have been quite harsh; at others they have played a decisive role in shaping twentieth-century philosophy,[1] overdetermined though by various other developments: on one side, the theoretical effects of successive philosophical 'turns' (epistemological, ontological, linguistic); on the other, the progressive shifting of the very meaning and use of the term *anthropology* in the field of the so-called human sciences, from the once prevailing notion of a physical or biological anthropology towards a social or cultural or historical and, more recently, cognitive anthropology.

Indeed, the great debate on 'philosophical anthropology', which remains the source of many of the issues that might be raised today around this notion, took place in Germany in the late 1920s and early 1930s, taking the form of a multilateral confrontation between the prominant representatives of *Lebens-philosophie*, the neo-Kantian and the newly born phenomenological currents. It was crossed by references to evolutionist biology, to the great 'crisis of values' after the First World War and the Socialist revolutions, to what one would describe as the long process of secularization of the Image of the World and Man itself, which began in the sixteenth century and led to a problematic victory of intellectual, social and technical rationality in the twentieth.

It seems likely that the expression 'philosophical anthropology' was coined by Wilhelm Dilthey himself, whose aim was to reorganize philosophy in a historicist perspective around such notions as successive psychologies and modes of comprehension in human history. Ernst Cassirer, another repres-entative of the Kantian tradition, though quite opposed to Dilthey's vitalist or 'irrationalist' standpoint, did not explicitly use the term *philosophical anthropo-logy* in his pioneering studies of the 1920s (*The Philosophy of Symbolic Forms; Individual and Cosmos in the Philosophy of the Renaissance*)[2] but he did express its programme by combining two directions of investigation: he analysed the 'symbolic' (we might also say 'logical', or 'signifying') structures of representa-tion, whether scientific, moral or aesthetic, which inscribe 'reason' or 'rational-ity' in the history of culture; and, conversely, he investigated from a historical perspective the philosophical problem of 'Man', or 'human essence', in its relation to the World, to God, to his own 'conscience'. Here, it is mainly a question of tracing all the implications of the great successive ruptures which, from classical antiquity onwards, following an irresistible though not neces-sarily linear progression, have established 'Man' as the centre of its (or his) own universe.

The year 1928 marks a crucial turn in this discussion: it sees the simultaneous publication of two books, which explicitly cite 'philosophical anthropology' as their central goal. One was written by Bernhard Groethuy-sen, a socialist-leaning historian and philosopher of culture, and a pupil of Dilthey. The other, which remained uncompleted because of its author's premature death, was written by the Catholic philosopher Max Scheler, one of Husserl's first and most distinguished students, though profoundly influenced by Nietzsche, Dilthey and Bergson (in short, by the *Lebensphilosophie*), and very hostile to the shifting of phenomenology towards the problematics of consciousness.

According to Groethuysen, 'philosophical anthropology' is above all a reconstruction of the great dilemma running throughout the history of philosophy, which opposes the philosophers of interiority – for whom the answer to the question of human essence has to be looked for in the *gnôthi seauton* ('know thyself'), in intimate self-consciousness – to the philosophers of exteriority, who seek to analyse in a positive way the position of Man in the cosmos, *phusis* and *polis*. Whereas, according to Scheler, 'philosophical anthropology' is a typology of *Weltanschauungen*, which combines in a specific manner the perception of nature and the hierarchy of ethical values, ranging from the ancient universe of myth to the modern universe of the will to power, and places them above 'resentment', religious faith and progressive Enlightenment.

As early as 1927, however, in the introductory paragraphs of *Being and Time* – and, in a more developed manner, in his 1929 book on Kant – Martin Heidegger had radically challenged all these attempts: not only did he reject the identification of philosophy and anthropology, thus challenging the notion that the basic questions of philosophy were anthropological, but, more radically, he denied the very possibility of asking the question of the nature or essence of Man without enclosing philosophy in an unsurpassable meta-physical circle. Certainly, this would not lead Heidegger in his turn to suggest that the anthropological question be handed over to a more 'positive' discipline. On the contrary, it was a question of showing how, while defining itself as 'anthropology', philosophy would find itself trapped in the same dogmatic horizon as the 'human sciences', unable to overcome the dilemmas of subjectivism and objectivism. This led Heidegger to discuss at length the old Kantian formulation, which proposes that the system of transcendental philosophical questions concerning the conditions of the possibility of know-ledge, of morals, of the very teleology of reason, be summarized in the one critical interrogation: 'What is Man?' But whereas other readers and followers of Kant understood this question as asking for a *foundation* of critical philosophy (admittedly a 'human' or 'humanist' one), Heidegger himself read it as an indication of the *limits* of the critical problematic in the Kantian style: the limits beyond which critical philosophy either falls back into dogmatism (not a theological, but a humanist dogmatism), or sets about deconstructing any notion of 'foundation', thus interrogating the very form of metaphysical questions.

But the core of the representation of Man as the 'foundation' of his own thoughts, actions and history, has, for three centuries at least, not been simply a valorization of human individuality and the human species as the bearer of the universal, it has been the representation of *Man as* (a, the) *subject*. The essence of humanity, of being (a) human, which should be present both in the universality of the species and in the singularity of the individual, both as a reality and as a norm or a possibility, is *subjectivity*. Metaphysics (which from this point of view, and in spite of the depth and novelty of the questions asked by Kant, includes transcendental philosophy) relies on a fundamental equation – we might also read it as the equation of foundation as such:

$$\text{Man} = \text{(equals) Subject}$$
or:
The Subject is (identical to) the *Essence of Man*

This is why – and later Michel Foucault, notably, would take up this question again – the privileged theoretical object of modern metaphysics, starting with critical philosophy and ending, not surprisingly, with anthropology, is endlessly to reflect on the 'empirico-transcendental doublet', the difference between empirical individuality and that other eminent subjectivity which alone bears the universal, the 'transcendental Subject'. But we should also remark, following Heidegger, that this fundamental equation, which summarizes the philosophical definition of 'the essence of Man', can also be read *the other way round*: as an equation that provides the clue to *all questions of essence*, to the 'metaphysical questions' in general.

Why is this the case? Because the equation 'Man = Subject' is not *any* essential(ist) identity. It is the equation which has replaced the old onto-theological equation: 'God = (the) Being' (which you can also read: God is the Supreme Being, or God is Being as such) to become the archetype of every metaphysical attribution of an essence, by means of which the normative form of the universal is supposed to inscribe itself in the very substance, the very singularity of the individual. This allows us to understand why, when Heidegger introduces the concept of Dasein as originary reference for philosophy, while indicating in a very ambivalent and perhaps perverse manner (as a puzzle, or a trap for philosophers), that the Dasein at the same time 'is and is not' the subject, 'is and is not' Man with respect to the being of its (his) existence, the theoretical effect he produces is deconstructive and destructive *on both sides*. It deconstructs and destroys the concept of the Subject, but it also deconstructs and destroys the concept of the essence (or, if you like, the concept of 'concept' in its traditional constitution). *If* there were something like an 'essence of Man', that essence could *not* be 'the Subject' (nor could it be the Object, of course), i.e. a universal being immediately conscious of itself (himself), given to itself (himself), imaginarily isolated from the existential context and contents which form its being-to-the-world, to human situations. But neither can we consider the Dasein, which substitutes the Subject, as an 'essence', although it appears as a generic concept of existence. It is rather the name, the always still provisional term by means of which we try to explain that proper philosophy begins when the questions about 'essences' are overcome.

Allow me to pause here. To put it briefly, I think that Heidegger's argumentation, which I have greatly simplified, is irreversible. It did not put an end, as we know, to the projects of 'philosophical anthropology'. But, consciously or not, it became a model and a warning for all twentieth-century philosophers who, especially after the Second World War, ventured to provide alternatives for philosophical anthropology or theoretical humanism, or simply tried to describe their limits.[3]

Though this critique is, as I say, irreversible, cannot be bypassed, it is itself riddled nevertheless with strange limitations and lacunae, with historical prerequisites which are extraordinarily fragile. We must examine them if we want to decide whether or not the question can be re-opened, possibly on quite new bases, different from those that ultimately trace back to the grand adventure of German Idealism, of which Heidegger appears as the ultimate (though heretical) representative.

The most immediate and striking mistake in Heidegger, although one not frequently recognized, concerns the very history of the notion of (the) *subject* in philosophy, provided we take it literally. Why is it not easily recognized? Obviously, because Heidegger, with some personal nuances, shares it with the whole modern philosophical tradition, from Kant to Hegel to Husserl to Lukács. This entire tradition considers and repeatedly asserts that it is with *René Descartes* that philosophy became conscious of 'subjectivity' and made 'the subject' the centre of the universe of representations as well as the signal of the unique value of the individual – an intellectual process which, it is claimed, typifies the transition from Renaissance metaphysics to modern science, within the general framework of the assault against ancient and medieval cosmology and theology. *Before* Descartes, it is merely a question of looking at the contradictory *anticipations* of the concepts of subject and subjectivity. *After* Descartes – that philosophical 'sunrise', as Hegel put it – it is a matter of finding the subject there, of *naming* and acknowledging it: this is the first of its successive philosophical figures, which together form the properly modern metaphysics of the subject.

But this story, however broadly accepted,[4] is materially wrong. It is a mere retrospective illusion, which was forged by the systems, the philosophies of history and the teaching of philosophy in the nineteenth century. Neither in Descartes nor even in Leibniz will you find the category 'subject' as an equivalent for an autonomous self-consciousness (a category which itself was invented only by John Locke),[5] a reflexive centre of the world and therefore a concentrate of the essence of man. As a matter of fact, the only 'subject' that the 'classical' metaphysicians knew was that contained in the scholastic notion of *subjectum*, coming from the Aristotelian tradition, i.e. an individual bearer of the formal properties of the 'substance.' Therefore, the more they rejected the substantialist ontology, the less they spoke of the 'subject' (which is, indeed, the case with Descartes, Spinoza and Locke, among others).

If this is the case, you will ask, *when* should we locate the 'invention of the subject' in the modern philosophical sense, at what place in history and in which truly revolutionary work? On this point there can be no doubt: the 'subject' was invented by Kant through a process that took place in the three *Critiques*. These three major works (1781, 1786, 1791) are immediately disposed around the great revolutionary event, this time in the political sense of the term. I will return to this point. It is Kant, and nobody else, who calls properly 'subject' (*Subjekt*) that universal aspect of human consciousness and conscience (or rather the *common ground* of 'consciousness' and 'conscience') which provides any philosophy with its foundation and measure.

Now, this reference to the Kantian text immediately allows us to correct another distortion in Heidegger's critique of philosophical anthropology, which nowadays has become all the more visible. *What was the context* that led Kant to systematize the table of the 'critical questions' of transcendental philosophy in order to connect them explicitly or implicitly to the question 'What is Man?' (i.e. the virtual programme of 'philosophical anthropology'). This context has less to do with a speculative elaboration of the reflections on the Subject than with a very pragmatic *Ausgang*, or 'way out', of speculation, in the direction of 'concrete' questions of human life. These are the 'cosmic' questions[6] of the 'world' or of the 'mundane' (*weltliche*), not the 'scholastic' ones (which, according to Kant's terminology, are of interest not for the amateur, but only for the professional theoretician). On this point Kant is quite explicit: the practical questions of the world are those that connect knowledge and duty, theory and morals, with the existence of *humanity* and the very meaning of its history. The questions of and about the 'world' therefore, are not *cosmological*, they are *cosmopolitical*. To ask 'What is Man?' for Kant is to ask a concrete question, a question which is therefore more fundamental than any other, because it immediately concerns the experience, knowledge and practical ends of Man as a *citizen of the world*. Indeed the Kantian *question* already involves and predetermines a formal *answer*: 'Man' is a (the) citizen of the world; his 'essence' is nothing other than the horizon within which all the determinations of that universal 'citizenship' must fall. The only thing that remains to do, then, is to elaborate and clarify the meaning of all this.

This remarkable formulation is not the exclusive property of Kant.[7] At a decisive historical moment, at the very turning point of the 'bourgeois revolutions', we find it combining, within the intimate structure of philosophical language itself, two quite different series of conceptual paradigms. It indicates: (1) that the *human subject* is able concretely to meet the essence of its 'humanity' only within a *civic*, or *political*, horizon in the broad sense of the term, that of a 'universal citizenship', which implies epistemological, ethical and aesthetic rationality,[8] and (2) that the 'citizen' belonging to any human institution and *subjected* to it, but particularly to the legal state (and probably more precisely the legal national state), can 'belong' to that institution and state as a *free and autonomous subject*[9] *only* inasmuch as every institution, every state, is conceived as a partial and provisional representative of *humanity*, which in fact is the only absolute 'community', the only true 'subject of history'.

We have now arrived at the core of the question 'What is Man?' in Kant – namely, its civic and cosmopolitical content, which is inseparable from its metaphysical content. And we see that it is precisely *this* (including its idealistic/ utopian aspect) that Heidegger would ignore. Not only is he not really concerned with the fact that the 'man' at issue in Kant is a 'citizen of the world' in the *political* sense (or in the *moral-political*, therefore also the *juridical* sense of the term)[10] (unless he believes that this is a purely empirical and pragmatic matter, not a 'transcendental' one), but he does not see that the very proposition which *equates* the 'subject' and the 'essence of man', before and after Kant, relies on a *third term*, an 'essential mediation', by no means accidental, namely *the citizen*. This citizen may become symbolically universalized and sublimated, but never ceases to refer to a very precise *history*, where it is a question of progress, conflict, emancipation and revolutions. The result, which does not arrive by chance, is that at the very moment when Heidegger submits metaphysics and its anthropological derivations to the most radical questioning, he proves totally unable to see that the history of metaphysics, being intimately connected with the question 'What is Man?', is also originally intricated with the history of politics and political thought. No wonder, then, that he later engages in discussing the meaning of the Aristotelian 'definition' of Man as 'that speaking animal', 'that living being which disposes of *logos*', i.e. language, reason and discourse, *without* ever mentioning its counterpart, which in fact says the same thing: not *zôon logon ekhôn*, but *zôon politikon tē phusei*, 'the being naturally living by and for the city', or the 'political animal'. This means that Heidegger will not even suspect *the originary unity of ontology, politics and anthropology*, except in so far as he denounces it as a particularly blind form of forgetting the sense of Being.

Suppose, now, that we take careful note of that shortcoming of Heidegger and correct it. We can then resume, on new bases, the problem of philosophical anthropology *without* completely losing the benefit of the Heideggerian critique of any essentialist conception of the 'subject'. Among the problems that immediately arise, there is precisely that of 'the subject' as *representation*: how was it historically constituted? What were the breaks, the *ruptures* in this process, which could be referred to successive figures of the citizen and citizenship? I have two theses about this, each of which would, of course, require longer explanations.

My first thesis is this: the whole history of the philosophical category of the 'subject' in Western thought is governed by an *objective* 'play on words', rooted in the very history of language and institutions. This play on words comes from the Latin, whence it passes to the Romance languages (including English), while remaining latent, repressed as it were, in the German language. This is a remarkable effect of the concrete universality of Latin in Western civilization, being at the same time the classical language of law, theology and grammar.

Of which 'play on words' am I speaking? Simply the fact that we translate as *subject* the neutral, impersonal notion of a *subjectum*, i.e. an individual substance or a material substratum for properties, but we *also* translate as *subject* the personal notion of a *subjectus*: a political and juridical term, which refers to *subjection* or *submission*, i.e. the fact that a (generally) human person (man, woman or child) is *subjected to* the more or less absolute, more or less legitimate authority of a superior power, e.g. a 'sovereign'. This sovereign being may be another human or supra-human, or an 'inner' sovereign or master, or even simply a transcendent (impersonal) *law*.[11]

This historical play on words, I insist, is completely objective. It runs throughout Western history for two thousand years. We *know* it perfectly, in the sense that we are able immediately to understand its linguistic mechanism, but we *deny* it, at least as philosophers and historians of philosophy. Which is all the more surprising, since it could provide us with the clue to unravelling the following enigma: why is it that the very *name* which allows modern philosophy to think and designate the *originary freedom* of the human being – the name of 'subject'[12] – is precisely the name which *historically* meant suppression of freedom, or at least an intrinsic limitation of freedom, i.e. *subjection*? We can say it in other terms: if freedom means freedom *of the subject*, or subjects, is it because there is, in 'subjectivity', an originary source of spontaneity and autonomy, something irreducible to objective constraints and determinations? Or is it not rather because 'freedom' can only be the result and counterpart of liberation, emancipation, *becoming* free: a trajectory inscribed *in* the very texture of the individual, with all its contradictions, which starts with subjection and always maintains an inner or outer relation with it?

Here then, is my second thesis. In the history of the 'problem of Man', as 'citizen' and as 'subject', at least two great breaks have taken place, which, certainly, were not simple events, but nevertheless marked irreversible thresholds. Philosophical reflection, in its most determining level (which I would call *onto-political*), remains dependent on these two historical breaks.

The first one was accomplished with the 'decline of the ancient world', or if you like when a transition took place, say, between Aristotle and Augustine, which meant the emergence of a *unified* category of subjection or *subjectus*, including all categories of personal dependence, but above all the interpretation of the subject's subjection as (willing) *obedience*, coming from inside, coming from the soul. In this respect obedience does not mean an inferior degree of humanity, but on the contrary a superior *destination*, whether terrestrial or celestial, real or fictitious. This allows subjection to appear as the condition, or even the guarantee of future salvation. But of course, the other side is that any 'citizenship', any immanent transindividual or collective freedom, becomes relative and contingent. The ancient structure fades away, the one that Aristotle had once developed in an exemplary manner: man as a citizen, that is, being 'naturally' or 'normally'[13] a *politès*, but only in a given sphere of activity, the 'public' sphere of reciprocity and equality with his fellow men, who are like him – who *look* like him – placing aside and indeed *below* him the various anthropological types of dependent and imperfect beings: the woman, the child (or pupil), the slave (or labourer), and placing symmetrically aside and *above* him the ideal types of the teacher, the hero, the god (or the divine beings). Now that this ancient figure has been destroyed, the figure of the *inner* subject emerges, who confronts a transcendent law, both theological and political, religious (therefore also moral) or imperial (monarchical) – because he *hears* it, because in order to be able to hear it, he has to be *called* by it.[14] This subject is basically a *responsible*, or an *accountable*, subject, which means that he has to respond, to give an account (*rationem reddere*) of himself, i.e. of his actions and intentions, before another person, who righteously interpellates him. Not a Big Brother, but a Big Other – as Lacan would say – always already shifting in an ambivalent manner between the visible and the invisible, between individuality and universality.

The crucial point here is this: the 'subject', for the first time bearing that name in the *political* field where it (he) is subjected *to* the sovereign, the lord, ultimately the Lord God, in the *metaphysical* field necessarily *subjects himself to himself* or, if you like, performs his own subjection.[15] *Ancient* man and *medieval* man (who will survive in our days in the guise of the 'voice of conscience') both have a relation to subjection, dependency and obedience. But the two structures radically differ in that, if you consider the man-citizen of the Greek *polis*, you will find that his autonomy and reciprocity, his relationships of equality, are incompatible with the outer subjection typical of woman, the slave, even the child, or the disciple who is learning under a master. Whereas, if you consider the Christian man, made of spirit and flesh, who is also subjected to Caesar, the imperial sovereign, who is confronted with the sacrament and the state, the ritual and the Law, you will find that his subjection is the very condition of any reciprocity.[16]

I will call *unilateral speech* the mechanism of subjection corresponding to ancient citizenship (but probably by no means restricted to it), which is both suppressed in the public sphere of the city and required as its prerequisite: for it has to do with that amazingly uneven and asymmetrical relationship towards the *logos*, which Aristotle describes in the cases of man and woman (wife), master and slave (servant), even father and son (or teacher and student: in Aristotle the paternal authority is basically a 'pedagogical' or 'educative' one) – all relationships in which one person is always *talking* while the other is always *listening*, whereas in the civic space (on the civic stage) the *same* individuals alternately talk and listen – in short, they engage in a dialogue – just as they alternately command and obey.[17] As for the completely different mechanism of subjection, which characterizes the situation of the *subjectus* or *subditus*, obedience to the Law, this is no longer a matter of unilateral speech: I will call it instead the *inner voice* (or interiorized voice), that of a transcendent authority which everyone is bound to obey, or which always already compels everyone to obey, including the rebels (they certainly do not escape the *voice* of the Law, even if they do not surrender to it) – because the foundation of authority is not located *outside* the individual, in some natural inequality or dependency, but *within* him, in his very being as creature of the verb, and as faithful to it.

We might comment at length on this difference, which never ceased to work within philosophy, and probably other discourses as well, but let us indicate the second basic historical threshold. We crossed it when secular and would-be democratic societies were constituted. Better said, when the principle of a secular and democratic social organization was declared, namely during the 'revolutions' at the end of the eighteenth and the beginning of the nineteenth centuries, in North America, France, Latin America, Greece and elsewhere.

As we know, the whole trajectory of historical idealism, from Kant to Marx onwards, which pictures humankind as subject and end of its own collective movement, is a reaction to that event and its contradictory effects: being inseparably a discursive or intellectual *and* a political event (which changed the very concept of 'politics'), as well as a metaphysical event.

I shall take as a main reference here the very text of the French *Déclaration des droits de l'homme et du citoyen*, which does not mean that the complexity of the event can be enclosed within the limits of this singular initiative of the French revolutionaries, since it clearly exceeds the 'property right' of one people.

Why is it that this new event becomes irreversible, not only in the political order, but also, inseparably, in the order of ontology? The very title of the *Déclaration* makes it manifest: because it poses a universal equation, which does not have any real anticipation in history, between Man as such and a new citizen defined by his 'rights', better said, by his conquest and collective defence of his rights, without any *pre-established* limitation. Allow me to imitate a famous philosophical formulation: just as a century before, there had been a philosopher who dared to formulate the provocative sentence, *Deus sive Natura* [God means 'Nature' (universally)], there are now practical philosophers who formulate something like the no less provocative (and possibly obscurely related) sentence, *Homo sive Civis* [Man means 'Citizen' (universally)].

What does this mean, precisely? Formally speaking, that man ceases to be a *subjectus*, a subject, and therefore his relationship to the *Law* (and the idea of law) is radically inverted: he is no longer the man *called before the Law*, or to whom an inner voice dictates the Law, or tells him that he should recognize and obey the Law; he is rather the man who, at least virtually, 'makes the Law', i.e. constitutes it, or *declares* it to be valid. The subject is someone who is responsible or accountable because he is (a) legislator, accountable for the *consequences*, the implementation and non-implementation of the Law he has himself made.

Here we must choose on which side we stand. A long historical and philosophical tradition (the one I was referring to when I said earlier that Heidegger had put a heretical end to the adventures of Idealism) has explained to us that the men of 1776 and 1789, the men of liberty and revolution, became 'citizens' because they had universally won access to *subjectivity*. Better said: because they had become conscious (in a Cartesian, or Lockean, or Kantian) way, of the fact that they were indeed free 'subjects', always already destined to liberty (by their 'birthright'). I choose the opposite interpretation: it seems to me that these men, and their followers, were able to begin thinking of themselves as free subjects, and thus to identify liberty and subjectivity, *because* they had abolished the principle of their subjection, their being subjected or subject-being, in an irreversible if not irresistible manner, while conquering and constituting their political citizenship. From now on, there could exist no such thing as 'voluntary servitude'. Citizenship is not one among other attributes of subjectivity, on the contrary: it *is* subjectivity, *that form* of subjectivity that would no longer be identical with subjection for anyone. This poses a formidable problem for the citizens, since few of them, in fact, will achieve it completely.

Now, what kind of 'citizen' is this? It cannot be only the citizen of some particular state, some particular nation, some particular constitution. Even if we do not accept the idealized notion of the Kantian 'cosmopolitical right', we can still maintain that it alludes to a universal claim, possibly to an absolute one. We could try to formulate it in this way: to equate man and citizen universally does not mean that only the legal citizens *are men* (i.e. human beings),[18] or that men as such participate in humanity only within the conditions and boundaries of their official citizenship. We know it means that the humanity of human individuals becomes determined by the inalienable character of their 'rights'. We also know that this amounts to saying in effect that, while rights are always *attributed to individuals* in the last instance, they are achieved and won[19] *collectively*, i.e. politically. In other terms, this equation means that the humanity of man is identified not with a *given* or an essence, be it natural or supra-natural, but with a *practice* and a task: the task of self-emancipation from every domination and subjection by means of a collective and universal access to politics. This idea actually combines a logical proposition: no liberty without equality, nor equality without liberty; an ontological proposition: the property of the human being is the *collective* or transindividual construction of his *individual* autonomy; a political proposition (but what is not already political in the previous formulations?): any form of subjection is incompatible with citizenship (including those forms which the revolutionaries themselves did not dare to challenge – slavery, the inequality of genders, colonization, exploited labour, perhaps above all these forms); and finally an ethical proposition: the value of human agency arises from the fact that no one can be liberated or emancipated *by others*, although no one can liberate himself *without others*.[20]

I shall now conclude by posing very briefly two questions. We started with a philosophical investigation, which may have seemed a little scholastic: what does 'philosophical anthropology' mean? What might its programme be after the discussions that took place at the beginning of this century and the devastating critique of Heidegger?

First then: If it is true that *man, subject, citizen* – all these terms being connected through historical analysis rather than essentialist conceptualization – remain for us the key signifiers of philosophical anthropology, must we arrange their figures in an evolutionary, linear process? This is not necessarily the case. I spoke of irreversible thresholds. Before medieval political theology had combined obedience to the Prince and obedience to God, the *subjectus* could not be given a unitary figure. Before the French Revolution and, generally speaking, the democratic revolutions equated man and citizen, it was not really possible to think of *rights* in a universal manner as opposed to privileges, or to do so without defining them as counterparts of obligations, services and duties. However, that a *new* form emerges does not imply that the ancient one simply disappears. So we see that the modern identity of man and citizen did not lead to the pure and simple negation or *Aufhebung* of the subjection to the Law, as an 'inner' voice. It has led, rather, to a new twist, a new degree of interiorization (interiority, intimacy) or, if you like, repression, along with a new 'privacy' of the moral sentiments. On the other hand, if there are inaugural thresholds or historical events, this does not mean that they arise out of the blue, without historical preconditions. Therefore a 'philosophical anthropology' along these lines must also be an investigation of repetition, recurrence and evolution as they mingle within history, i.e. of historicity as such.

Second: clearly, a critical rethinking of the philosophical debate *pro et contra* philosophical anthropology leads quite naturally to emphasizing a theme, better said a programme: that of enquiring on the *forms of subjection*. Borrowing from Michel Foucault, I would speak of an enquiry into the forms of *subjectivation* inasmuch as they correspond to certain forms of *subjection* – yet another fundamental 'play on words' . . . unless it is always the same. But to mention Foucault immediately leads to the following question. Following the permanent traces they have left in philosophical tradition, we spoke of *two* basic forms or figures of subjection: the one I described as 'unilateral speech' and the one I described as 'inner voice' (or inner calling). But why should we think that there are only two such figures? Why not search for others, from which other ways of stitching together the questions of man, subject and citizen would follow? Either in the past: figures of withering away (but does an anthropological figure, a figure of subjection, ever wither away?); or in the present: figures of constitution, possibly of becoming dominant. Was not this what Foucault would have suggested when he wrote on *norms*, 'discipline' or 'bio-power'? But before him, although in a different way, would not Marx also have provided us with similar hints when he returned in his theory from political alienation to human alienation, and from there to the structural 'fetishism' of merchant and capitalist societies, which goes along with the *use* of man and citizen in the valorization of objects, and their contradictory freedom as legal subjects? Probably there are more than simply *two* ways of displaying the dialectics of subjection and subjectivation. Maybe there is no 'end of history', no 'end of the story'.

Notes

1. On 'continental' philosophy, above all; on 'insular' philosophy the influence of this debate has admittedly been weaker.
2. The much less interesting *An Essay on Man* was written later in 1941, when Cassirer had emigrated to the United States.
3. The term *theoretical humanism* was introduced by Louis Althusser in the 1960s to describe and criticize the roots of every 'philosophical anthropology', including the 'Marxist' variants. This marks a shift from the Heideggerian critique, while it retains, at the same time, the basic idea that the two problems of the 'essence of man' and of 'subjectivity' are inseparable. I will discuss this relationship elsewhere.
4. See, for example, Richard Rorty's brilliant *Philosophy and the Mirror of Nature* (Princeton, NJ: Princeton University Press 1979), especially the first two chapters.
5. See my essay, 'L'invention de la conscience: Descartes, Locke, Coste, et les autres', forthcoming in *Traduire les philosophes*, Actes des journées de l'université de Paris – I, January–March 1992, Publications of the Sorbonne.
6. See the chapter in the *Critique of Pure Reason* called 'Architectonics of pure reason'. It is also in this text that Kant lists the three famous transcendental questions, namely: What can I know? What must I do? What can I hope? But it is only in his later *Course on Logic*, edited by one of his assistants, that he explicitly proposes summarizing them by means of the single question, 'What is Man?' The importance of this addition was hardly suspected until the twentieth-century debate.
7. Was it not Tom Paine who referred to himself in this way? But during this period he was not alone in moving in the 'cosmopolitan' direction.
8. Indeed, as Hannah Arendt observed, this means that Kant, formally speaking, retrieved the Aristotelian 'definition' of man as *zôon politikon*, although immediately to imply that the true *polis* should no longer be identified with any particular 'city-state', but only with the 'world city' as such. To trace back such an idea to the Stoics, via the Christian theologians and the political economists among others, is beyond the scope of this chapter.
9. Such a formulation can be traced back at least to the sixteenth century and *Les six livres de la République* by Jean Bodin, one of the first and leading theoreticians of the modern nation state. On this, along with other aspects of the history of the concept of 'the subject', see my 'Citizen Subject', in *Who Comes After the Subject?*, ed. E. Cadava, P. Connor and J.-L. Nancy (New York and London: Routledge 1991).
10. In *Kant and the Problem of Metaphysics*, Heidegger depicts the 'cosmic' nature of 'Man' and the 'cosmopolitan' character of the Kantian question 'What is Man' as *metaphysical* notions. Typically, what interests Heidegger in the Kantian notion of the 'cosmopolitical' is not the 'political', but the 'world', the *cosmos*.
11. There is no doubt that the 'subject' – namely, the one who is subjected – has to be 'personal' (though not necessarily 'individual'). Whether the 'sovereign' or the one *to whom* the 'subject' is subjected also has to be personal is much less clear: this is a basic theological question which I will leave aside here.
12. Everyone knows that the main characteristic of 'morality' in Kant's philosophy is that it provides the subject with its own essential 'autonomy'. The moral subject is 'autonomous', whereas the 'non-moral' or 'pathological' subject is 'heteronomous': but, in the Kantian view, this amounts to saying that *the subject as such* is 'autonomous'. (Therefore, to speak of an 'autonomous subject' is *essentially* redundant, whereas the 'heteronomy of the subject' marks a contradiction, a departure of the subject from its proper essence. All this amounts to an explanation of why the 'essence of man' is 'to be a subject': this expresses an

imperative as well as a given, or a given that immediately gives rise to an imperative.)

13. Two possible translations of the Greek *tē phusei*.
14. The German tradition uses the word *Beruf* for this 'calling'.
15. These two phrases: 'to be subjected ultimately to the Lord God', and 'to be subjected to (nobody but) oneself', are basically equivalent; they refer to the same 'fact', viewed from opposite angles.
16. Such a pattern will, of course, become secularized in later political philosophy and ideology; see, notably, the way the necessary 'mediation' is instituted in Hobbes by the supreme authority of the state in order to create the conditions for a social (or civic) equality.
17. What Aristotle does not describe, because he is so rationalistic, are the *looks*, the *visual* and hallucinatory counterparts of this unilateral speech, which he so acutely defines in the *Politics* (mainly in Book I) and the *Nicomachean Ethics*.
18. Although there is a very strong tendency to do so, as Hannah Arendt noted when she remarked, in vol. II ('Imperialism') of *The Origins of Totalitarianism*, that in the modern world 'apatrids' (people without a definite citizenship) are hardly considered human.
19. Or *vindicated*, to borrow from Mary Wollstonecraft's beautiful title.
20. Recall the 'Preambulum' of the Statutes of the First International, written by Marx, a good Jacobin in this respect: 'The emancipation of the labouring classes will be the work of the labourers themselves.'

2 SEX AND THE EUTHANASIA OF REASON

JOAN COPJEC

This is what concerns me: a growing sense that in
theorizing sex we are engaged in a kind of 'euthanasia
of pure reason'.[1] I borrow this phrase from Kant, who
used it to label one of two possible responses to the
antinomies of reason, that is, to the internal conflicts of
reason with itself. Reason, he said, falls inevitably into
contradiction whenever it seeks to apply itself to
cosmological ideas, to things that could never become
objects of our experience. Faced with the apparent
unresolvability of these conflicts, reason either clings
more closely to its dogmatic assumptions or abandons
itself – and this is the option for which Kant reserved
his impassioned put-down – to a despairing scepticism. I
will suggest that the attempt to contemplate sex also
throws reason into conflict with itself, and will here
declare my opposition to the alternatives we face as a
result, particularly to the latter, only because – in critical
circles, at least – this is the one that currently claims our
attention.

Judith Butler's strongly argued *Gender Trouble:*
Feminism and the Subversion of Identity[2] is an excellent
contemporary example of this second alternative. The
uncontestable value of this book lies in the way it deftly
shakes off all the remnants of sleepy dogmatism that
continue to adhere to our thinking about sexual
identity. The notion of sex as an abiding, a priori
substance is fully and – if careful argument were

enough to prevail – finally critiqued. Without in any way wishing to detract from the real accomplishments of this book or the sophistication of its argument, I would like to challenge some of its fundamental assumptions on the grounds that they may not support the political goals the book seeks to defend. The problem, as I see it, with this exemplary book is that its happy voidance of the dogmatic option simply clears a space for the assertion of its binary opposite, if not for the 'despairing scepticism' about which Kant warned us, then of scepticism's sunny obverse: a confident voluntarism. Having successfully critiqued the metaphysical notion that sex is a substance inscribed at the origin of our acts, our discourse, Butler defines sex as a 'performatively enacted signification . . . one that, released from its naturalized interiority and surface, can occasion the parodic proliferation and subversive play of gendered meaning' (p. 33). In other words, Butler proceeds as though she believes that the deconstruction of the fiction of innate or essential sex is also, or must lead to, a rejection of the notion that there is anything constant or invariable about sexual difference; that sex is anything but a construct of historically variable discursive practices into which we may intervene in order to sow 'subversive confusion'. All kinds of practices construct masculinity and femininity as discrete entities, and there is no denying the effectiveness, the reality of this construction, she argues. But if sex is something that is 'made up', it can also be unmade. What is done, after all, can always be undone – in the order of signification, at least. What is familiar, naturalized, credible can be made strange: defamiliarized, denaturalized, 'incredibilized'. Negated.

First complex of questions: Are the alternatives offered here – sex is substance/ sex is signification – the only ones available? And if not, what else might sex be?

What Butler is primarily intent on undoing is 'the stability of binary sex' (p. 6), since she takes it to be the effect of practices seeking to install a compulsory heterosexuality. It is the very *twoness* of sex, the way it divides all subjects absolutely into two separate, mutually exclusive categories, that serves the aims of heterosexism. Now, this argument makes no sense unless we state its hidden assumption that two have a tendency to one, to couple. But from where does this assumption spring? From the conception of the binary terms, masculinity and femininity, as complementary. That is, it is only when we define the two terms as having a reciprocal relation, the meaning of the one depending on the meaning of the other, and vice versa, that we incline them – more strongly, compel them – towards union, albeit one that is sustained through violent antagonism. For the complementary relation is, in Lacan's terms, an imaginary one: it entails both absolute union and absolute aggression.

Second complex of questions: Must sexual difference be conceived only as an imaginary relation? Or, is there a different way to think the division of subjects into two sexes, one that does not support a normative heterosexuality?

The stability of the male/female binary is not undone, however, simply by chipping away at the barrier that separates them, calling into question the neatness of their division. If the categories of woman, femininity, feminism cannot ultimately hold, Butler – taking a frequently advanced contemporary position – tells us, this is also due to the fact that these categories are crossed by all sorts of others – race, class, ethnicity, etc. – which undermine the integrity of the former list of categories. The very heterogeneity of the category of woman is evidenced in the opposition to feminism by women themselves. There will never, and can never, be a feminism unified in its politics.

Third complex of questions: Can sexual difference be equated with other categories of difference? Is one's sexual identity constructed in the same way, does it operate on the same level, as one's racial or class identity; or is sexual difference a different kind of difference from these others?

Fourth complex of questions: Is the heterogeneity of the category of women, the very failure of feminism to enlist all women, similar to the failure to enlist all men in a single cause? Is the fractiousness of feminism attributable solely to racial, professional, class differences? Why can't feminism forge a unity – an all – of women?

What is sex, anyway? My first question is also the one that initiates the inquiry of *Gender Trouble*. Echoing Freud's contention that sexual difference is not unambiguously marked either anatomically, chromosomally or hormonally, i.e. questioning the prediscursive existence of sex, Butler automatically assumes, as I noted earlier, that sex must be discursively or culturally constructed. But Freud himself eschewed the limitation of these alternatives; he founded psychoanalysis on the refusal to give way either to 'anatomy or convention',[3] arguing that neither of these could account for the existence of sex. While sex is, for psychoanalysis, never simply a natural fact, it is also never reducible to any discursive construction, to sense, finally. For what such a reduction would remain oblivious to is *the radical antagonism between sex and sense*. As Lacan put it, 'Everything implied by the analytic engagement with human behaviour indicates not that meaning reflects the sexual, but that it makes up for it.'[4] Sex is the stumbling-block of sense. This is not to say that sex is prediscursive; we have no intention of denying that human sexuality is a product of signification, but intend, rather, to refine this position by arguing that sex is produced by the internal limit, the failure of signification. It is only there where discursive practices falter – and not at all where they succeed in producing meaning – that sex comes to be.

Butler, of course, knows something about the limits of signification. She knows, for example, that there is no '*telos* that governs the process' (p. 33) of discourse, that discursive practices are never complete. This is why she makes the claim that '*woman* itself is a term in process, a becoming, a constructing that cannot rightfully be said to originate or end' (p. 33).

So far so good – we find nothing here with which we would want to quarrel. The error, the subreption, occurs only in the next step, where the argument no longer concerns only the term *woman*, but becomes instead an argument about woman as such. For the thesis of the book is not that the meaning of the term *woman* has shifted, and will continue to shift, throughout history, but that it is 'never possible finally to become a woman' (p. 33), that one's sexual identity is itself never complete, is always in flux. In other words, Butler concludes from the changing *concepts* of women something about the *being*, the *existence* of women. I will argue that her conclusion is illegitimately derived: we cannot argue that sex is incomplete and in flux because the terms of sexual difference are unstable. This is first of all a *philosophical objection*; to argue, as Butler is careful to do, that reason is limited is precisely to argue that reason is unable to move conclusively from the level of the concept to the level of being; it is impossible to establish the necessity of existence on the basis of the possibilities created by concepts.

To say that discourse is ongoing, always in process, is to acknowledge the basic and by now much taken for granted fact that within discourse there are no positive terms, only relations of difference. One term acquires meaning only through its difference from all the others – ad infinitum, since the final term is never at hand. Put another way, the statement that discourse is ongoing simply acknowledges a *rule of language*, which prescribes the way we must proceed in determining the value of a signifier. We would not be wrong to call this prescription a *rule of reason* – reason, since Saussure, being understood to operate not through the modalities of time and space, as Kant believed, but through the signifier. But his very rule entangles us in a genuine contradiction, an antinomy, such as troubled Kant in *The Critique of Pure Reason*. To be brief (we shall return to these points later), this rule of language enjoins us not only to believe in the inexhaustibility of the process of meaning, in the fact that there will always be another signifier to determine retroactively the meaning of all that have come before, it also requires us to presuppose 'all the other signifiers', the total milieu which is necessary for the meaning of one. The completeness of the system of signifiers is both demanded and precluded by the same rule of language. Without the totality of the system of signifiers there can be no determination of meaning, and yet this very totality would prevent the *successive* consideration of signifiers which the rule requires.

Kant argues that there is a legitimate solution to this contradiction, but first he attacks the illegitimate solutions which function by denying one of the poles of the dialectic. Saussure's displacement of his own notion of 'pure difference' by the more 'positive' notion of 'determinant oppositions' is a type of illegitimate solution which may be referred to as the 'structuralist solution'.[5] Emphasizing the 'synchronic perspective' of the linguist and his community, Saussure eventually decided to give priority to the contemporaneous system of signifiers operating at some (hypothetical) frozen moment: the present. Forgetting for his own purposes his important stipulation that meaning must be determined retroactively, that is, forgetting the diachronic nature of meaning, he ultimately founded the science of linguistics on the systematic totality of language. Thus, the structuralist argument ceased to be that the final signifier S_2 determines that which has come before S_1, and becomes instead: S_2 determines S_1 *and* S_1 determines S_2; that is, reciprocal oppositions stabilize meanings between coexistent terms and differential relations no longer threaten the transvaluation of all preceding signifiers.

A certain 'poststructuralist' response to this structuralist thesis has taken an antithetical position by simply ignoring the requirement for the completion of meaning. Butler's position in *Gender Trouble* fits into the second category of response to the antinomic rule of language; it notes merely that signification is always in process, and then concludes from this that there is no stability of sex. Kant would argue that her error consists in illegitimately 'attribut[ing] objective reality to an idea which is valid only as a rule' (*CPR*, p. 288), that is, in confusing a rule of language with a description of the Thing-in-itself, in this case with sex. But this is misleading, for it seems to imply that sex is something that is beyond language, something that language forever fails to grasp. We can follow Kant on this point only if we add the proviso that we understand the Thing-in-itself to mean nothing but the impossibility of thinking – articulating – it. When we speak of language's failure with respect to sex, we speak not of its falling short of a prediscursive object, but of its falling into contradiction with itself. Sex coincides with this *failure*, this inevitable contradiction. Sex is, then, the impossibility of completing meaning, not (as Butler's historicist/deconstructionist argument would have it) a meaning that is incomplete, unstable. Alternatively, the point is that sex is the structural incompleteness of language, not that sex is itself incomplete. Butler's argument converts the progressive rule for *determining* meaning (the rule that requires us to define meaning retroactively) into a *determined* meaning. The Kantian/psychoanalytic argument, like this other, wants to desubstantialize sex, but it does so in a different way. First, it acknowledges rather than ignores the contradiction of the rule of reason. Then it links sex to the conflict of reason with itself, not simply to one of the poles of the conflict.

This constitutes a more radical desubstantialization of sex, a greater subversion of its conception as substance, than the one attempted by the Butler position. For sex is here not an *incomplete* entity, but a totally empty one – i.e. it is one to which no predicate can be attached. By linking sex to the signifier, to the process of signification, Butler makes our sexuality something that communicates itself to others. While the fact that communication is a process, and thus ongoing, precludes a complete unfolding of knowledge at any given moment, further knowledge is still placed within the realm of possibility. When, on the contrary, sex is *disjoined* from the signifier, it becomes that which does not communicate itself, that which marks the subject as unknowable. To say that the subject is sexed is to say that it is no longer possible to have any knowledge of *him* or *her*. *Sex serves no other function than to limit reason, to remove the subject from the realm of possible experience or pure understanding.* This is the meaning, when all is said and done, of Lacan's notorious assertion that 'there is no sexual relation': sex, in opposing itself to sense, is also, by definition, opposed to relation, to communication.[6]

This psychoanalytical definition of sex brings us to our third complex of questions, for, defined not so much by discourse as by its default, sexual difference is unlike racial, class or ethnic differences. While these differences are inscribed in the symbolic, sexual difference is not: only the failure of its inscription is marked in the symbolic. Sexual difference, in other words, is a real and not a symbolic difference. This distinction does not disparage the importance of race, class or ethnicity; it simply contests the current doxa that sexual difference offers the same *kind* of description of the subject as these others do. Nor should this distinction be used to isolate considerations of sex from considerations of other differences. It is always a sexed subject who assumes each racial, class or ethnic identity.

Why insist, then, on the distinction? The answer is that the very sovereignty of the subject depends on it, and it is only the conception of the subject's sovereignty that stands any chance of protecting difference in general. It is only when we begin to define the subject as *self-governing*, as subject to its own laws, that we cease to consider her as *calculable*, as subject to laws already known, and thus manipulable. It is only when the sovereign incalculability of the subject is acknowledged that perceptions of difference will no longer nourish demands for the surrender of difference to processes of 'homogenization', 'purification' or any of the other crimes against otherness with which the rise of racism has begun to acquaint us.

This does not mean that we would support a conception of the subject as pre-existent or in any way transcendent to the laws of language or the social order, a subject who calculates, using the laws of language as a tool to accomplish whatever goal she wishes. The subject who simply does or believes as she wishes, who makes herself subject only to the law she *wants* to obey, is simply a variation on the theme of the calculable subject. For it is easy to see that one is quickly mastered by one's sensuous inclinations, even as one seeks to impose them.

The only way to resolve this particular antinomy – the subject is *under* (i.e. the determined effect of) the law/the subject is *above* the law – is to demonstrate that, as Étienne Balibar has put it,

> [s]he is neither only above, nor only under the law, but *at exactly the same level as it* . . . Or yet another way: there must be an exact correspondence between the absolute activity of the citizen (legislation) and [her] absolute passivity (obedience to the law, with which one does not 'bargain,' which one does not 'trick') . . . in Kant, for example, this metaphysics of the subject will proceed from the double determination of the concept of right as freedom and as compulsion.[7]

To claim that the subject is at *the same level as the law* is not equivalent to claiming that she *is* the law, since any conflation of subject with law only reduces her, subjects her absolutely *to* the law. At the same level as and yet not the law, the subject can only be conceived as the failure of the law, of language. *In* language and yet *more than* language, the subject is a cause for which no signifier can account. Not because she transcends the signifier, but because she inhabits it *as limit*. This subject, radically unknowable, radically incalculable, is the only guarantee we have against racism. This is a guarantee that slips from us whenever we disregard the non-transparency of subject to signifier, whenever we make the subject coincide with the signifier rather than its misfire.

To my first philosophical objection to the Butler definition of sex one must add not only the above ethical objection, but a psychoanalytical one as well. I have noted that there was a crucial difference between Butler's and the psychoanalytical position on sex. I want now to go further by exposing the 'total incompatability' of the two positions. I choose this phrase in order to echo the charge raised against Jung by Freud, whose characterization of the former's stance in regard to the libido is germane to our discussion. This stance, Freud says, 'pick[s] out a few cultural overtones from the symphony of life and . . . once more fail[s] to hear the mighty and powerful melody of the [drives]'.[8] Freud is accusing Jung of evacuating the libido of all sexual content by associating it exclusively with cultural processes. It is this association that leads Jung to stress the essential plasticity or malleability of the libido: sex dances to a cultural tune. Freud argues, on the contrary, that sex is to be grasped not on the terrain of culture, but on the terrain of the drives, which – despite the fact that they have no existence outside culture – are not cultural. They are, instead, the other of culture and, as such, are not susceptible to its manipulations.

Sex is defined by a law (of the drives) with which, to return to Balibar's phrase, 'one does not "bargain," which one does not "trick."' Against the Jungian and contemporary critical belief in the plasticity of sex, we are tempted to argue that from the standpoint of culture, *sex does not budge*. This is to say, among other things, that *sex, sexual difference cannot be deconstructed*, since deconstruction is an operation that can be applied only to culture, to the signifier, and has no purchase on this other realm.[9] To speak of the deconstruction of sex makes about as much sense as speaking about foreclosing a door; action and object do not belong to the same discursive space. Thus we will argue that while the subject – who is not pinned to the signifier, who is an effect, but not a realization of social discourses – is, in this sense, free of absolute social constraint, he or she is nevertheless *not* unconditionally free to be a subject any which way: within any discourse the subject can only assume either a male or a female position.

The Jungian, and contemporary 'neo-Jungian', position remaining deaf to the 'melody of the drives' does not recognize this compulsory dimension of sex, its inescapability. Focusing merely on the cultural 'free' play of the signifier, this position disjoins freedom from compulsion: it is for this very reason *voluntarist*, despite all its own precautions, despite all the steps taken to inoculate itself against this charge. *Gender Trouble*, for example, is not careless on this point. The book's conclusion anticipates and attempts a defence against the accusation of voluntarism, which it knows awaits it. Redefining the notion of agency, the final chapter aims to locate the subject 'on the same level as' language, neither above it (where the naive notion of agency would place it) nor below it (where it would be positioned by a determinist notion of construction). What is missing, however, and what thus leaves Butler defenceless before the charge she tries to sidestep, is any proper notion of the unsurpassable limit, the impossibility that hamstrings every discursive practice. Even when she speaks of compulsion and failure, she says:

> If the rules governing signification not only restrict, but enable the assertion of alternative domains of cultural intelligibility, i.e., new possibilities for gender that contest the rigid codes of hierarchical binarisms, then it is only *within* the practices of repetitive signifying that a subversion of identity becomes possible. The injunction to *be* a given gender produces necessary failures . . . The coexistence or convergence of

[different] discursive injunctions produces the possibility of a complex reconfig-
uration and redeployment . . . (p. 145)

What we are provided with here is a description of the *effect* of the inherent
failure of discourse – a riot of sense in which one meaning constantly collides
with another; a multiplication of the possibilities of each discourse's meaning –
but no real acknowledgement of its cause: the impossibility of saying
everything in language. We repeat, Freud taught us, because we cannot
remember. And what we cannot remember is that which we never experienced, never had the possibility of experiencing, since it was never present as
such. It is the deadlock of language's conflict with itself that produces this
experience of the inexperiencable (which can neither be remembered nor
spoken); it is this deadlock which thus necessitates repetition. But the
constraint proper to repetition is occluded in the sentences quoted above; and
so, too, is sex. Sex is that which cannot be spoken by speech; it is not any of the
multitude of meanings that try to make up for this impossibility. In eliminating
this radical impasse of discourse, *Gender Trouble*, for all its talk about sex,
eliminates sex itself.

Sex does not budge, and it is not heterosexist to say so. In fact, the opposite
may be true. For it is by making it conform to the signifier that you oblige sex to
conform to social dictates, to take on social content. In the end, Butler, wanting
to place the subject on the same level as language, ends up placing her *beneath*
it, as its realization. Freedom, 'agency', is inconceivable within a schema such as
this.

The Phallic Function

Let me now confront the objections I know await me. I have been presenting
the psychoanalytical position using arguments borrowed from critical philosophy. And yet the subject posed by this philosophy – sometimes referred to as
the 'universal' subject, as opposed to the concrete individual – seems, by
definition, to be *neuter*, to be *un*sexed, while the subject of psychoanalysis is,
equally by definition, always sexed. How, then, does the sexually differen-
tiated subject enter the framework of critical philosophy? By what route have
we arrived at what will no doubt appear to be the oxymoronic conclusion that
the 'universal' subject is *necessarily* sexed?

But why, we may ask in our turn, is it so readily assumed that the
philosophical subject must be neuter? From our perspective it is this
assumption that seems unwarranted. What grounds it, those who hold it

suppose, is the subject's very definition as constitutionally devoid of all positive characteristics. From this we may infer that those who desexualize the subject regard sex as a positive characteristic. Everything we have said so far boils down to a denial of this characterization. When we stated, for example, that sexual difference is not equatable with other kinds of difference, we were saying that it does not positively describe the subject. We could put it this way: *male and female, like being, are not predicates, which means that rather than increasing our knowledge of the subject, they qualify the mode of the failure of our knowledge.*

We have been defining the subject as the internal limit or negation, the failure of language – this in order to argue that the subject has no substantial existence, that it is not an object of possible experience. If this subject is thought to be unsexed, it is not only because sex is naively assumed to be a positive characteristic, but also because failure is assumed to be singular. If this were true, if language – or reason – had only one mode of misfire, then the subject would in fact be neuter. But this is not the case; language and reason may fail in one of two different ways. The distinction between these modalities of misfire – between the two ways in which reason falls into contradiction with itself – was first made by Kant in *The Critique of Pure Reason* and employed again in *The Critique of Judgement*. In both works he demonstrated that the failure of reason was not simple, but foundered on an antinomic impasse through two separate routes: the first was mathematical, the second dynamical.

Many have attempted to locate sexual difference in Kant's texts, but what they were in fact looking for was sexual bias or sexual indifference. Some have discerned in the descriptions of the beautiful and the sublime, for example, a differentation of a sexual sort. These critics have, if I may say so, been looking for sex in all the wrong places. I am proposing that sexual differences can, indeed, be found in Kant, not in an accidental way, in his use of adjectives or examples, but, fundamentally, in his distinction between the mathematical and the dynamical antinomies. That is to say, *Kant was the first to theorize, by means of this distinction, the difference that founds psychoanalysis's division of all subjects into two mutually exclusive classes: male and female.*

I intend then, for the rest, to interpret psychoanalysis's sexuation of the subject in terms of Kant's analysis of the antinomies of reason. More specifically, my focus will be on the formulas of sexuation proposed by Lacan in his *Seminar XX: Encore*. In this seminar Lacan reiterates the position of psychoanalysis with regard to sexual difference: our sexed being, he maintains, is not a biological phenomenon, it does not pass through the body, but 'results from the logical demands of speech'.[10] These logical demands lead us to an encounter with a fundamental bedrock or impasse when we inevitably stumble on the fact that 'saying it all is literally impossible: words fail'.[11]

Moreover, we are now in a position to add, they fail in two different ways, or, as Lacan puts it in *Encore*, 'There are two ways for the affair, the sexual relation, to misfire . . . There is the male way . . . [and] the female way.'[12]

The formulas of sexuation, as they are drawn in 'A Love Letter', the seventh session of the seminar, look like this:[13]

$$\exists x \, \bar{\Phi} x \qquad\qquad \bar{\exists} x \, \Phi x$$
$$\forall x \, \Phi x \qquad\qquad \bar{\forall} x \, \Phi x$$

Each of the four formulas is a simple logical proposition and, like all propositions, has both a *quantity* and a *quality*. The quantity of a proposition is determined by the quantity of its subject term; the symbols $\forall$ and $\exists$ are quantifiers, i.e. they indicate the quantity of the subject term. $\forall$, the universal quantifier, is shorthand for words such as *every, all, none*; but it is important to note that proper nouns are also considered universals. $\exists$, the existential quantifier, stands for words such as *some, one, at least one, certain, most*. The quality of a proposition is determined by the quality of its copula, either affirmative or negative. The affirmative is unmarked, while the negative is marked by a bar placed over the term.

Since the symbol Φ is already familiar to us from Lacan's other texts, a translation of the propositions is now possible:

There is at least one x which is not submitted to the phallic function.	There is not one x which is not submitted to the phallic function.
All x's are (every x is) submitted to the phallic function.	Not all (not every) x is submitted to the phallic function.

The left side of the schema is designated the male side, while the right side is female. The first thing to notice is that the two propositions that compose each side appear to have an *antinomical* relation to each other, that is, they appear to contradict each other. How have these apparent antinomies been produced, and how do they come to be designated by the terms of sexual difference? Before answering these questions, we need to know a little more about the formulas.

Lacan abandons two of the terms of classical logic which we used in the description above; instead of *subject* and *predicate*, he uses the terms *argument* and *function*. This substitution marks a conceptual difference: the two classes, male and female, are no longer formed by gathering together subjects with similar attributes as was the case with the older terms. The principle of sorting is no longer descriptive, i.e. it is not a matter of shared characteristics or a common substance. Whether one falls into the class of males or females depends, rather, on where one places oneself as argument in relation to the function, that is, which enunciative position one assumes.

What legitimates Lacan's abandonment of some of the terms, and even some of the premises of classical logic is the function – the phallic function – that appears in each of the four propositions. This function, and particularly the fact that it does appear on both sides of the table, has been at the centre of controversy since Freud first began elaborating his theory of feminine sexuality. Feminists have always revolted against the notion that the phallus should be made to account for the existence of both sexes, that the difference between them should be determined with reference to this single term. They have deplored what they have understood to be a reduction of difference to a simple affirmation or negation: having, or not having, the phallus. But this complaint strikes out against the wrong target, for the peculiarity, or singularity, of the phallic signifier is due precisely to the fact that it ruins the possibility of any simple affirmation or negation. It is the phallic signifier that is responsible for the production on each side of the table not of a simple statement, but of two conflicting statements. Each side is defined both by an affirmation and a negation of the phallic function, an inclusion and exclusion of absolute (non-phallic) *jouissance*. Not only is the notorious 'not-all' of the female side – not all are submitted to the phallic function – defined by a fundamental undecidability regarding the placement of woman within the class of things submitted to phallic rule, but the male side embraces a similar undecidability: the inclusion of *all* men within the domain of phallic rule is conditioned by the fact that *at least one* escapes it. Do we count this 'man escaped' among the all, or don't we? What sort of a 'man' is it whose *jouissance* is not limited to the male variety? And what sort of an 'all' is it that is missing one of its elements?

So you see, there is no use trying to teach psychoanalysis about undecidability, about the way sexual signifiers refuse to sort themselves into two separate classes. It is no use preaching deconstruction to psychoanalysis, because it already knows all about it. Bisexuality was a psychoanalytical concept long before it was a deconstructionist one. *But the difference between deconstruction and psychoanalysis is that the latter does not confuse the fact of bisexuality – i.e. the fact that male and female signifiers cannot be distinguished absolutely – with a denial of sexual difference.* Deconstruction falls into this confusion only by

disregarding the difference between the ways in which this failure takes place.
Regarding failure as uniform, deconstruction ends up collapsing sexual
difference into sexual indistinctness. This in addition to the fact that, on this
point at least, deconstruction appears to be duped by the pretension of
language to speak of being, since it equates a confusion of sexual signifiers with
a confusion of sex itself.

This, in brief, is the lesson of the formulas of sexuation; it is a lesson learned
from Kant, as I will now show in greater detail. First, however, we need to say a
little more about the phallic function, which is the source of all this
undecidability. Its appearance – on *both* sides of the table – indicates that we
are concerned with speaking beings, beings, according to Lacan's translation
of the Freudian concept of castration, who surrender their access to *jouissance*
on entering language. This not only restates what we have been arguing all
along – it is the impasses of *language* that create the experience of the
inexperiencable, the unsayable – it also exposes the foolishness of that reading
of Lacan's theory of sexual difference which asserts that it strands woman on a
dark continent, outside language. Each side of the table describes a different
impasse by means of which this question of the outside of language is raised, a
different manner of revealing the essential powerlessness of speech. But while
the phallic function produces on each side a failure, it does not produce a
symmetry between the sides.

The Female Side: Mathematical Failure

We are not going to begin our reading, as is customary, on the left, but rather
on the right, or female, side of the formulas. As opposed to the fairly common
prejudice that psychoanalysis constructs the woman as secondary, as a mere
alteration of the man, the primary term, these formulas suggest there is a kind
of priority to the right side. This reading of the formulas is consistent with the
privilege given the mathematical antinomies by Kant, who not only deals with
them first, but also grants the mathematical synthesis a more immediate type
of certitude than its dynamical counterpart. In Kant's analysis, it is the
dynamical antinomies (the 'male side' of the formulas in our reading) that
appear in many ways secondary, a kind of *resolution* to a more fundamental
irresolvability, a total and complete impasse manifested by the mathematical
conflict. One of the things we will want to attend to while investigating the
differences between these two modes of conflict is the way the very notions of
conflict and solution shift from the first mode to the second. (Finally, however,
this notion of the priority of one of the sexes or antinomies over the other must
be regarded as a mirage. Rather than two species of the same genus, the sexes

and antinomies should be read as two positions on a Möbius strip.) There is an unmistakable asymmetry between the mathematical and the dynamical antinomies: on moving from one to the other we seem to enter a completely different space. Rather than remaining baffled by this difference, as so many of Kant's commentators have been, rather than ascribing it to a confusion of thought, we will try, with the help of Lacan, to draw out the logic that sustains it.

What is a mathematical antinomy? How would we describe the conflict that defines it? Kant analyses two 'cosmological ideas' which precipitate this variety of conflict; we shall discuss only the first, since it is this one which seems to us to correspond to the antinomy found on the 'female side' of the formulas of sexuation. The first antinomy is occasioned by the attempt to think the 'world', by which Kant means 'the mathematical total of all phenomena and the totality of their synthesis' (*CPR*, p. 237); that is to say, the universe of phenomena such that it is no longer necessary to presuppose any other phenomenon that would serve as the condition for this universe. Reason aims, then, at the unconditioned whole, the absolute all of phenomena. This attempt produces two conflicting propositions regarding the nature of this all – a thesis: the world has a beginning in time, and is also limited in regard to space; and its antithesis: the world has no beginning and no limits in space, but is, in relation both to time and space, infinite.

After examining both arguments, Kant concludes that while each successfully demonstrates the falsity of the other, neither is able to establish convincingly its own truth. This conclusion creates a sceptical impasse from which he will have to extricate himself, since one of the basic tenets of his philosophy, which opposes itself to scepticism, is that every problem of reason admits of a solution. The solution he arrives at is the following. Rather than despairing over the fact that we cannot choose between the two alternatives, we must come to the realization that we need not choose, since both alternatives are false. That is to say, the thesis and antithesis statements, which initially appeared to constitute a *contradictory* opposition, turn out upon inspection to be *contraries*.

In logic, a contradictory opposition is one that exists between two propositions of which one is the simple denial of the other; since the two together exhaust the entire range of possibilities, the truth of one establishes the falsity of the other, and vice versa. Contradiction is a zero-sum affair. The negation, which bears on the copula, leaves nothing beyond itself; it completely annihilates the other proposition. A contrary opposition, on the other hand, is one that exists between two propositions of which one does not simply deny the other, but makes an assertion in the direction of the other extreme. The negation, which bears this time only on the predicate, does not exhaust all the possibilities, but leaves behind something on which it does not pronounce. For this reason *both* statements may simultaneously be false.

In order to make this logic less abstract, Kant resorts to an uncharacteristically pungent example, which successfully illustrates what is at stake in the mathematical antinomies. He opposes the statement 'Bodies smell good' to a contrary, 'Bodies smell bad' in order to show that the second does not simply negate the first (for which 'Bodies are not good-smelling' would have been sufficient), but goes on to posit another smell, this time a bad one. While it is not possible for both of these propositions to be true – since fragrance and stench cancel each other out – it is possible for both to be false – since neither takes into account another possibility, that bodies may be odourless.

To illustrate this logical point in a different way, we might note that it is the structure of contrary opposition that produces the 'When did you stop beating your wife?' joke. The form of the question, while seeming to allow the addressee to supply any answer he chooses, in fact allows him only to choose among contraries. It does not allow him to negate the accusation implicit in the question.

Kant avoids the sceptical impasse by refusing to answer the question 'Is the world finite or infinite?' and by negating instead the assumption implicit in the question: the world *is*. As long as one assumes that the world exists, the thesis and antithesis of the cosmological antinomy have to be regarded as contradictory, as mutually exclusive and exhaustive alternatives. One is thus forced to choose. But once this assumption is shown to be ill-founded, neither alternative need be taken as true; a choice is no longer necessary. The solution to this antinomy, then, lies in demonstrating the very incoherence of this assumption, the *absolute impossibility* (*CPR*, p. 294). (Kant's words) of the world's existence. This is done by showing that the world is a self-contradictory concept, that the absolute totality of an endless progression is inconceivable by definition.

How can this be? If the world is an object of experience, as those so eager to determine its magnitude suppose, then the conditions of the possibility of experience must be met in conceiving it. Thus, the essential bankruptcy of the idea of the world will be made visible by the demonstration of its inability to meet these formal conditions. These conditions specify that a possible object of experience must be locatable through a progression or regression of phenomena in time and space. The concept of an absolute totality of phenomena, however, precludes the possibility of such a *succession* because it is graspable only as the *simultaneity* of phenomena. The rule of reason that requires us to seek after conditions is therefore abridged by the conception of the rule's total satisfaction, that is, by the conception of the world. Adherence to the rule and the complete satisfaction of the rule are, it turns out, antinomic. The world is an object that destroys the means of finding it; it is for this reason illegitimate to call it an object at all. A universe of phenomena is a true contradiction in terms; *the world cannot and does not exist.*

Having demonstrated the impossibility of the existence of the world, Kant can then dismiss both the thesis and the antithesis statements. This is indeed what he does when he states his solution twice, first in a negative and then in an affirmative form. 'The world has no beginning in time and no absolute limit in space' is the negative solution; it denies the thesis without going on, as the antithesis does, to make a counter-assertion. There can be no limit to phenomena in the phenomenal realm, for this would require the existence of a phenomenon of an exceptional sort, one that was not itself conditioned and would thus allow us to halt our regress, or one that took no phenomenal form, i.e. that was empty: a void space or a void time. But clearly these self-contradictions admit of no real possibilities. No phenomena are exempt from the rules of reason that alone make them objects of our experience. Or, *there is no phenomenon that is not an object of possible experience* (or not subject to the rule of regress): $\overline{\exists} \, x \, \overline{\Phi} \, x$.

Kant then goes on to dismiss the antithesis by stating that 'the regress in the series of phenomena – as a determination of the cosmical quantity – proceeds *indefinitum* (*CPR*, p. 294). That is, our acknowledgement of the absence of a limit to the set of phenomena does not oblige us to maintain the antithetical position – that they are *infinite* – rather, it obliges us to recognize the basic *finitude* of all phenomena, the fact that they are inescapably subject to conditions of time and space and must therefore be encountered one by one, indefinitely, without the possibility of reaching an end, a point where all phenomena would be known. The status of the world is not infinite but indeterminate. *Not-all phenomena are a possible object of experience*: $\overline{\forall} \, x \, \Phi \, x$.

The solution offered by Kant's critical philosophy must be stated twice in order to guard against any possible misunderstanding. For the simple statement that there is no limit to phenomena will imply to those given to transcendental illusions that the world is limitless. While the simple statement that not all phenomena can be known will imply that at least one phenomenon escapes our experience.

Now, it should be obvious that the formulas we have produced from Kant's two statements regarding the solution of the first mathematical antinomy formally reduplicate those that Lacan gives for the woman, who, like the world, does not exist. But how can this parallel between woman and world be sustained? How is it that Lacan can speak of the non-existence of woman? Our response must begin with Lacan's own explanation: *'in order to say "it exists", it is also necessary to be able to construct it, that is to say, to know how to find where this existence is'*.[14] You will be able to hear the Kantian tones in this explanation, but you should hear in it as well echoes of Freud, who argued that in order to find an object, you must also be able to re-find it. If the woman does not exist, this is because she cannot be re-found. At this point my explanatory restatement of Lacan's not very well understood dictum will seem no less opaque than its original. My intention, however, is to clarify this explanation as I proceed through the explication of the dynamical antinomies, and by this further to establish the links between Kant and Freudian psychoanalysis.

For the moment let us continue to attend to the purely Kantian tones of Lacan's statement. Lacan is undoubtedly arguing that a concept of woman cannot be constructed because the task of fully unfolding her conditions is one that cannot, in actuality, be carried out. Since we are finite beings, bound by space and time, our knowledge is subject to historical conditions. Our conception of woman cannot run ahead of these limits and thus cannot construct a concept of the whole of woman. But how does this Kantian position differ from the one articulated by Butler and others? Is our position really so much at odds with the one that now so often poses itself against every universalism: there is no general category of woman or of man, no general category of the subject; there are only historically specific categories of subjects as defined by particular and diverse discourses? What is the difference between our interpretation of 'the woman does not exist' and the following one: we are misguided when we make claims for the existence of the woman, for

> the category of 'women' is normative and exclusionary and invoked with the unmarked dimensions of class and racial privilege intact. In other words, the insistence upon the coherence and unity of the category of women has effectively refused the multiplicity of culture, social, and political intersections in which the concrete array of 'women' are constructed. (Butler, p. 14)

Here it is being suggested that the universal category of woman contradicts, and is contradicted by, current work investigating the class and racial differences among women as they are constructed by various practices. The logic of the argument is Aristotelian; that is, it conceives the universal as a positive, finite term ('normative and exclusionary'), which finds its limit in another positive, finite term (particular women or 'the concrete array of "women"'). The negation of the all, then, produces the particular. The condemnation of the 'binarism of sex' which is launched from this position firmly grounds itself in a binary logic, which conceives the universal and the particular as exhaustive possibilities.

Kant had something else in mind when he argued that the mathematical antinomies demonstrated the limits of reason. His point – which bears repeating – is that our reason is limited because *the procedures of our knowledge have no term, no limit. What limits reason is a lack of limit.* This insight is compromised – not confirmed – whenever we conceive the not-all on the side of extension;[15] i.e. whenever we conceive the negation of the world, or of universal reason and its pretension to be able to speak of all phenomena, as simply implying that all we may properly know are finite, particular phenomena. For in this case, we simply supply reason with an *external* limit by supposing a segment of time, the future, which extends beyond and thereby escapes reason. This eliminates from reason its *internal* limit, which alone defines it.

Recall that Kant maintained that the first antinomy provided indirect proof of 'the transcendental ideality of phenomena'. Here is Kant's summary of the proof:

> If the world is a whole existing in itself, it must be either finite or infinite. But it is neither finite nor infinite – as has been shown, on the one side by the thesis, on the other side, by the antithesis. Therefore the world – the content of all phenomena – is not a whole existing in itself. It follows that phenomena are nothing, apart from our representations. (*CPR*, p. 286)

Kant's logic would appear to be flawed if the negation contained in the penultimate statement were taken as a *limitation* of all phenomena, or of the world, to particular phenomena. It is possible to pass to his conclusion only if one takes the penultimate statement as an *indefinite judgment*.[16] That is, what is involved here is not the negation of a copula such that 'all phenomena' is completely cancelled or eliminated, leaving its complement – some or particular phenomena – to command the field; but rather the affirmation of a negative predicate. Which is to say: Kant is urging that the only way to avoid the antinomies in which the idea of world entraps us is to affirm that the world is not a possible object of experience without pronouncing beyond this on the existence of the world. This conceives reason as limited by nothing but its own nature (its dependence on the merely regulative idea of totality), as *internally* limited.

This is the very crux of the difference between the Kantian position and the historicist one; or, we should say, between the Kantian–*Lacanian* position and the historicist one, since Lacan adopts a similar stance with regard to the woman. When he says, 'The woman is not-all', he demands that we read this statement as an *indefinite judgment*. Thus, while he does indeed claim, as his readers have often been horrified to observe, that the idea of the woman is a contradiction of reason, and that she therefore does not exist, he also claims, and this has not been as readily observed, that her existence *cannot* be contradicted by reason – nor, obviously, can it be confirmed. In other words, he leaves open the possibility of there being something – a feminine *jouissance* – that cannot be located in experience, that cannot, then, be said to exist in the symbolic order. The ex-sistence of the woman is not only *not* denied, it is also not condemnable as a 'normative and exclusionary' notion; on the contrary, the Lacanian position argues that it is only by refusing to deny – or confirm – her ex-sistence that 'normative and exclusionary' thinking can be avoided. That is, it is only by acknowledging that a concept of woman *cannot* exist, that it is structurally impossible within the symbolic order, that each historical construction of her can be challenged. For, after all, nothing prohibits these historical constructions from asserting their universal truth; witness the historical assertion that a general, transhistorical category of woman *does not* exist. The truth of this assertion is simply not available to a historical subject.

Let us be clear that one of the consequences of the Lacanian argument is that it, too, like historicism, calls into question the collectibility of women into a whole. It thus also regards all efforts at a coalition politics as problematic. But unlike the historicists, Lacan sees the collectibility of women as imperilled, not by the external collisions of different definitions, but by the internal limit of each and every definition, which fails somehow to 'encompass' her. Lacan's position opens out onto a beyond which it is impossible to confirm or deny.

Judging from the feminist brouhaha that has surrounded the reference to this beyond, we can safely assume that it needs further explanation and defence. It has frequently been taken to consist of one more relegation of the woman to the outside of language and the social order, one more attempt to banish her to some 'dark continent' (as if any form of life had ever been found to survive within the dead structures of language!). We must therefore be more explicit about just what is meant by the 'failure of the symbolic' with respect to the woman, what is signalled by the indefinite judgment. The symbolic fails to constitute not the *reality*, but more specifically the *existence* of the woman. To be more precise: what fails, what becomes impossible, is the rendering of a judgment of existence. As long as it can be demonstrated that world or woman cannot form a whole, a universe – i.e. that there is no limit to phenomena or language, no phenomenon that is not an object of experience, no signifier whose value does not depend on another – then the possibility of judging whether or not these phenomena or these signifiers give us information about a reality independent of us vanishes. In order to be able to declare that a thing exists, it is necessary also to be able to conclude otherwise – that it does not. But how is this second, negative judgment possible if there is no phenomenon that is not an object of our experience, i.e. if there are no metaphenomena that escape our experience and are thus able to challenge the validity of those that do not? The lack of a limit to phenomena (and to signifiers) precludes precisely this: a metalanguage, without which we are restricted to endless affirmation, that is, to affirming without end – and without being able to negate any – the contingent series of phenomena that present themselves to us. There is, as Freud said of the unconscious, no 'no' where no limit is possible. And as with the unconscious, so here, too, contradiction is necessarily ignored, since everything has to be considered equally true. There are no available means of eliminating inconsistency where nothing may be judged false.

So, whereas historicist feminists currently propose that we regard the aggregation of 'female subject positions' as the solution to the 'riddle of femininity', that is, that we acknowledge the *differences* in these various constructions of woman and the non-necessity of their relation to each other in order finally to lay to rest the question of what a woman is, Lacan proposes that this 'solution' is a datum in need of explanation. *Why* is it – Lacan requires us not to rest content with the observation, but to inquire further – *why* is it that woman does not form an all? Why is it that we must see in the discursive constructions of women a series of differences, and never encounter among them woman as such? Lacan answers that the woman is not-all because she lacks a limit, by which he means: she is not susceptible to the threat of castration; the 'no' embodied by this threat does not function for her. But this may be misleading, for while it is true that the threat has no purchase on the woman, it is crucial to note that the woman is the consequence and not the cause of the non-functioning of negation. She is the failure of the limit, not the cause of the failure.

In sum: woman is there where no limit intervenes to inhibit the progressive unfolding of signifiers, where, therefore, a judgment of existence becomes impossible. This means that everything can be and is said about her, but that none of it is subject to 'reality testing' – none of what is said amounts to a confirmation or denial of her existence, which thereby eludes every symbolic articulation. The relation of the woman to the symbolic and to the phallic function is considerably complicated by this argument. For it is precisely because she is totally, i.e. limitlessly, inscribed within the symbolic that she is in some sense wholly outside it, which is to say: the question of her existence is absolutely undecidable within it.

From this we are obliged to recognize that the woman is indeed a product of the symbolic. But we must also recognize that in producing her, the symbolic does not function in the way that we are accustomed to think it does.

Ordinarily we think of the symbolic as synonymous, in Lacanian terms, with the Other. The Other is, however, by definition that which guarantees our consistency and, as we have seen, there is no such guarantee where the woman is concerned. She, or the symbolic that constructs her, is fraught with inconsistencies. We are thus led to the conclusion that the woman is a product of a 'symbolic without an Other'. For this newly conceived entity Lacan, in his last writings, coined the term *lalangue*. Woman is a product of *lalangue*.

The Male Side: The Dynamical Failure

If we were to play by the rules of historicism, we would have to argue that, like the woman, the man does not exist, that no general category of man is instantiated in the multiplicity of male subject positions which every era constructs. Thus, a nominalist argument, like a kind of theoretical solvent, currently manages to dissolve the categories of man and woman alike. According to Lacan, however, we *cannot* symmetrically argue that the man does not exist. We have, if the left-hand side of the sexuation table is to be believed, no problem in locating him, in proclaiming his existence.

This statement may come as a surprise, and not only to historicists. For our discussion had led us to assume that the rule of reason, which impels us to seek after a totality of conditions, must forever render any judgment of existence impossible. We are therefore unprepared for the conjuring away of this impossibility, which seems to be implied by the confirmation of the existence of man. A similar surprise is regularly expressed by Kant's commentators, who wonder at the sudden ease with which a resolution of the dynamical antinomies is found. Where thesis and antithesis of the mathematical antinomies were both deemed to be false because both illegitimately asserted the existence of the world (or the composite substance), the thesis and antithesis of the dynamical antinomies are both deemed by Kant to be true. In the first case, the conflict between the two propositions was thought to be irresolvable (since they made contradictory claims about the same object); in the second case, the conflict is 'miraculously' resolved by the assertion that the two assertions do not contradict each other. If it were merely a matter of the thesis, one would have no difficulty in accepting this argument: the thesis 'Causality according to the laws of nature is not the only causality operating to originate the phenomena of the world. A causality of freedom is also necessary to account fully for these phenomena' concedes the importance of natural causality and merely insists on a supplement of freedom. It is, however, not so easy to bring the antithesis in line with Kant's denial of contradiction. The statement 'There is no such thing as freedom, but everything in the world happens solely according to the laws of nature' manifestly resists or negates the thesis. If we are to accept Kant's argument that both statements are simultaneously true, we are going to have to do so *despite* the clear contradiction. In short, we will have to avail ourselves of a non-Aristotelian logic – just as we did with the mathematical antinomies.

We shall not be concerned in what follows with the specifics of Kant's arguments about the cosmological ideas of freedom and God so much as with the way the second set of antinomies overcomes the impasse presented by the first set. We must also note that the left-hand, or male, side of the formulas of sexuation repeat the logic of Kant's resolution: 'There is at least one x that is not submitted to the phallic function' and 'All x's are submitted to the phallic function' are both taken to be true, despite the fact that the antithesis's claim to inclusiveness is obviously falsified by the thesis, i.e. the all of the antithesis is negated by the thesis.

And yet Kant says that the antithesis is *true*; he confirms the existence of the all, the universal, just as Lacan confirms the existence of the universe of men. Since the existence of the universe was regarded in the case of the woman as impossible because no limit could be found to the chain of signifiers, it would be smart to assume that the formation of the all on the male side depends on the positing of a limit. But this resolution is more easily surmised than supported, since we were presented on the female side with good reasons for believing that the positing of a limit was impossible, that there could be no metaphenomena, no metalanguage. We cannot, on the male side, depart from the well-established rule of reason – nor do we.

In fact, the limit on the 'sinister', or dynamical, side does not produce the possibility of metalanguage, but simply covers over its lack. This is accomplished by adding to the series of phenomena (or signifiers) a negative judgment regarding what cannot be included in the series. The phrase 'there is no such thing as freedom', which appears in the antithesis of the third antinomy (to take this one as an example), serves precisely this function, the function of limit. By means of this negative judgment, the inconceivability of freedom is conceptualized and the series of phenomena ceases to be open-ended; it becomes a closed set, since it now includes – albeit in negative form – that which is excluded from it: that is, it now includes *everything*. You will note that this *everything* appears as a consequence in the second phrase of the third antinomy's antithesis: 'but everything in the world happens solely according to the laws of nature.' Suddenly the world, which was prohibited from forming in the mathematical antinomies, comes into being on the dynamical side.

In speaking of this imposition of a limit as an addition, as a *supplementation* of natural causality, we have in fact presented the thesis version of what takes place. But another, equally accurate, equally true description is offered by the antithesis. According to this version, what is involved in the shift from the female to the male side is a *subtraction*. Recall Kant's complaint that the thesis and antithesis of the mathematical antitheses both overstepped their official functions, since they both 'enounce[d] more than [was] requisite for a full and complete contradiction' (*CPR*, p. 285); that is, both said *too much*. A surplus, because illegitimate, affirmation of existence burdened each statement. On the dynamical side, this surplus is *subtracted* from the phenomenal field and – we can look at it this way – it is this subtraction that installs the limit. The removal or separation of freedom from the realm of mechanical causality is what dissolves the radical inconsistency, the absolute impasse, on the dynamical side. Where the mathematical field was defined by the homogeneity of its elements (which were all phenomena, objects of experience) and the inconsistency of its statements (since none could be counted false), the dynamical field is defined by the heterogeneity of its elements (the result of the *separation* of the two types of causality, sensuous and intelligible, into different realms) and – what? What is it that corresponds on this side to the inconsistency on the other? Incompleteness.[17] That is, the all forms on the dynamical side, but it is missing an element: freedom. The initial cause cannot be tolerated by, or disappears from, the mechanical field that it founds.[18] Which means that on this side, it will always be a matter of saying *too little*.[19]

In Lacan's formulas, the parallels between the two sides are more visible, since the same symbols are used throughout. Thus we can see that the question of existence is carried over directly to the dynamical side. That is to say, the surplus declarations of existence which caused the conflict on the female side are silenced on the male side because it is precisely existence – or being – that is *subtracted* from the universe that forms there. This is how one should read Lacan's placing of the existential quantifier as the limit of the all, which is ruled by the universal quantifier. If, therefore, a world (operating solely according to the laws of nature) or universe (of men) can be said to exist on the dynamical or male side, we must not forget that it is merely a conceptual existence that is being claimed for it. Being as such escapes the formation of the concept of world. The universe that forms is thus defined by a certain impotence, since everything can be included therein *except* being, which is heterogeneous to the conceptual world.

That thesis and antithesis – $\exists x \, \bar{\Phi} x$ and $\forall x \, \Phi x$ – must both be stated and judged to be simultaneously true is explained, then, by the paradoxical status of the limit, which cannot be understood as entirely missing or as entirely included in the set of men. For, as Kant taught us, if one were to say that a man existed, one would add absolutely nothing to this man, to the concept of man.

Thus we could argue that this concept lacks nothing. And yet it does not include being and is in this sense inadequate, since the concept cannot include the fact that the thing named by it does in fact exist.

This brings us back to the question of 'reality testing', which we raised earlier. We had promised that this procedure, which was ruled out as impossible on the female side, would finally come into play on the male side. We continue to maintain this, though this is clearly the occasion to clarify what reality testing *is* in Freudian terms. There is no more appropriate place to begin than Freud's essay on 'Negation', since that text is framed in almost the same terms as we, after Kant and Lacan, have been framing our discussion. When Freud makes the comment 'With the help of the symbol of negation, thinking frees itself from the restrictions of repression and enriches itself with material that is indispensable for its proper functioning',[20] we should be reminded immediately of the dynamical antinomies. For the symbol of negation is precisely the limit that allowed Kant, in the dynamical antinomies, to assert a knowledge of 'everything in the world', where, in the mathematical antinomies, he was forced to admit that reasoning on the world fails. In the dynamical antinomies, Kant, too, gives himself material, an object of thought, even though, in the earlier conflict, reason was denied the possibility of any such object and was condemned merely to 'dispute about nothing' (*CPR*, p. 283).

What does Freud say about the process of reality testing? He says, first, something he has been saying since the *Project* (1895) and that he said most memorably in the *Three Essays on a Theory of Sexuality* (1905): the finding of an object is the re-finding of it. Here, the aim of reality testing 'is not to find an object in real perception which corresponds to the one presented, but to *re-find* such an object, to convince oneself that it is still there'.[21] He says also that one of the problems that presents itself to this process is that

> the reproduction of a perception as a presentation is not always a faithful one; it may be modified by omissions, or changed by the merging of various elements. In that case, reality-testing has to ascertain how far such distortions go. But it is evident that a precondition for the setting up of reality-testing is that objects shall have been lost which once brought real satisfaction.[22]

Contrary to the common misperception, reality testing is not described here as a process by which we match our perceptions against an external, independent reality. In fact, it is the permanent *loss* of that reality – or real: a reality that was never present as such – which is the precondition for determining the objective status of our perceptions. Not only is the real unavailable for comparison with our perceptions, but, Freud concedes, we can assume that the latter are always somewhat distorted, inexact. What, then, accounts for the distinction between subjective and objective perceptions? What intervenes to transform the welter of conflicting, distorted phenomena into the conviction that our experience is objective? The answer, which should now be half-guessed, goes something like this. To the multitude of our perceptions something is added which is not a new perception, new sensible content; instead, this addition is intelligibile and contentless: a negative judgment, which marks the limit of our perceptions and hence the loss of the object that 'brought real satisfaction'. The negative judgment excludes this object from thought – or, more precisely, the exclusion of this object makes thought possible. Which means that the term *exclusion* is not entirely accurate in so far as it may tend to imply a non-relation between the real object and the object of thought, while Freud suggests a definite relation between these two terms. For fleeting perceptions seem to acquire the weight of objectivity only when they are weighted or anchored by the excluded real object. That is, it is only when our perceptions come to refer themselves to this lost object of satisfaction that they can be deemed objective. Referring themselves to the object, they come to be understood as manifestations of it. So, the object is excluded from perceptions, but not simply, since it now functions as that which is 'in them more than them': the guarantee of their objectivity. If Freud prefers to name the process of reality testing by the redoubled verb *re-find* rather than *find*, this is not only because the lost object can never be directly found and must instead be re-found in its manifestations, but also because it is found a number of times, again and again, in a multitude of perceptions which, however different they are from each other (the distortions, the modifications), must nevertheless be counted as evidence of the same inaccessible reality which they are all – the whole phenomenal universe – powerless to contain. Thus, while guaranteeing that perceptions designate some objective, independent reality, the negative judgment maintains – must maintain – this reality as ungraspable; for if it were to assume a phenomenal form, it would become merely another perception, in which case the universe of thought would collapse.

To return to our discussion of sexual difference, there should now be no confusion about the fact that if the man, unlike the woman, can be claimed to exist, his ex-sistence, or being, remains inaccessible nevertheless, since it escapes the conceptual or symbolic field in which his existence takes shape. If the differences among men may be disregarded, and one man can be substituted for another because they are manifestations of the same thing, what this thing is is still unknown and must remain so. Correlatively, no man can boast that he embodies this thing – masculinity – any more than any concept can be said to embody being.

All pretensions to masculinity are, then, sheer imposture, just as every display of femininity is sheer masquerade. Through his desubstantialization of sex, Lacan has allowed us to perceive the fraudulence at the heart of every claim to positive sexual identity. And he has done this equally for men and for women. Which is not to say that he has treated them symmetrically or conceived of them as complements of each other. A universe of man and women is inconceivable; one category does not complete the other, make up for what is lacking in the other. Were one to believe in the possibility of such a universe, one would believe in the sexual relation, with all its heterosexist implications.

But Lacan does not. On the contrary, he shows us exactly why the heterosexist assumption – which may be formulated thus: men love women and women love men – is not a legitimate proposition. For it presupposes that a universal quantifier, an *all*, modifies both *men* and *women*, and this is precisely what the formulas contest. While the universe of women is, as we have argued at length, simply *impossible*, a universe of men is possible only on the condition that we except something from this universe. The universe of men is, then, an illusion fomented by a *prohibition*: do not include everything in your all! Rather than defining a universe of men that is complemented by a universe of women, Lacan defines man as the prohibition against constructing a universe and woman as the impossibility of doing so. The sexual relation fails for two reasons: it is impossible and it is prohibited. Put these two failures together, you will never come up with a whole.

Sexual Difference and the Superego

This argument has given itself just two tasks: to challenge the assumptions about sex harboured, often in common, by historicist and deconstructionist positions; and to clarify the alternative offered in Lacan by making explicit his debt to critical philosophy. It would require much more time and space than I have here to develop the implications of this alternative theory of sexual difference. But I do not want to close this chapter of my investigation without at least noting one important point and suggesting a path for pursuing it. The point is this: the Kantian account of the dynamical antinomies and the

Lacanian account of the male antinomies both align themselves with the psychoanalytical description of the superego.

In *The Critique of Judgment*, Kant, speaking of the dynamically sublime,[23] invokes images of threatening rocks, thunderclouds, volcanoes, hurricanes, terrifying images of a mighty and potentially destructive nature, which nevertheless has, he says, 'no dominion over us'.[24] The 'as if' quality that attaches itself to the dynamically sublime has often struck commentators as curious. What does Kant mean by speaking of a fearsome object of which we actually have no fear? He means that from our position in the phenomenal world, we can formulate only the *possibility* of this terrible force and not its *existence*, just as we can formulate only the possibility and not the existence of God, freedom, the soul. This possibility of a realm beyond, unlimited by our phenomenal conditions, is precisely dependent on the foreclosure of the judgment of existence.

This same explanation accounts for the paradoxes of the superego. Here, again, the ferocity of the superego is not exactly to be feared, for this ferocity depends not on the harshness of its prohibitions (in the sense that the superego might be positively imagined as a kind of strict father or that his interdictions might be positively spelled out), but on the conversion of the father into an impossible real; that is, a being on whose existence we cannot pronounce. The prohibition proper to the superego renders something unsayable and undoable, to be sure, but it does not say *what* we should not say or do; it merely imposes a limit which makes everything we do and say seem as naught compared to what we cannot. As Lacan explains, 'the superego . . . [the commandment "Enjoy!"] is the correlative of castration, which is the sign that adorns our admission that the *jouissance* of the Other, the body of the Other, is only promised in infinity'.[25]

Yet once we establish that this logic of the limit, of exception, defines the dynamical antinomies, the male subject and the superego, we have a problem, or so it seems at first blush. For we now appear to lend support to the notorious argument that presents woman as constitutionally indisposed to developing a superego and thus susceptible to an ethical laxity. In response to this, all we can suggest at this point is that the field of ethics has too long been theorized in terms of this particular superegoistic logic of exception or limit. It is now time to devote some thought to developing an ethics of inclusion or of the unlimited, that is, an ethics proper to the woman. Another logic of the superego must now commence.

Summary of the Argument of 'Sex and the Euthanasia of Reason'

Dynamical/Male

Thesis: Causality according to
the laws of nature is not the only
causality operating to originate
the world. A causality of freedom
is also necessary to account fully
for these phenomena.

Mathematical/Female

Thesis: The world has a beginning in time and is also limited in
regard to space.

Antithesis: There is no such
thing as freedom, but everything
in the world happens solely
according to the laws of nature.

Antithesis: The world has no
beginning and no limits in space,
but is, in relation both to time
and space, infinite.

$\exists x \, \bar{\Phi} x$

$\forall x \, \Phi x$

$\bar{\exists} x \, \bar{\Phi} x$

$\bar{\forall} x \, \Phi x$

Notes

1. Immanuel Kant, *Critique of Pure Reason*, trans. J.M.D. Meiklejohn (Buffalo, NY: Prometheus 1990), p. 231; hereafter page references to this work will be given in the text.
2. Judith Butler, *Gender Trouble: Feminism and the Subversion of Identity* (New York and London: Routledge 1990); page references to this work will be given in the text.
3. Sigmund Freud, 'Femininity', *The Standard Edition of the Complete Psychological Works of Sigmund Freud*, trans. James and Alix Strachey (London: Hogarth Press and the Institute of Psycho-Analysis, 1964), p. 114.
4. Quoted by Jacqueline Rose in 'Introduction II', in *Feminine Sexuality: Jacques Lacan and the école freudienne*, ed. Juliet Mitchell and Jacqueline Rose (New York and London: W.W. Norton 1982), p. 47; the quotation is from Lacan's unpublished *Seminar XXI*.
5. Samuel Weber, 'Closure and Exclusion', *Diacritics*, vol. 10, no. 2 (Summer 1980), p. 37.
6. For a further explanation of this psychoanalytic defence of ignorance, see my essay 'The Sartorial Superego', in *October*, 51 (Fall 1989).
7. Étienne Balibar, 'Citizen Subject', in *Who Comes After the Subject?*, ed. Eduardo Cadava, Peter Connor and Jean-Luc Nancy (New York and London: Routledge 1991), p. 49.
8. Sigmund Freud, 'On the History of the Psycho-Analytic Movement' (1914), *SE*, vol. 14, p. 62.
9. This statement need not be taken as dismissive of deconstruction, which would not itself claim that anything other than a signifier is 'deconstructible' or negatable. As a matter of fact, it is only because the other of the signifier does not budge, cannot be negated, that deconstruction is possible in the first place.
10. Jacques Lacan, *Encore* (Paris: Seuil 1975), p. 15.
11. Jacques Lacan, *Television: A Challenge to the Psychoanalytic Establishment*, ed. Joan Copjec, trans. Denis Hollier, Rosalind Krauss and Annette Michelson (New York: W.W. Norton 1990), p. 3.
12. Lacan, *Encore*, pp. 53–4.

13. Ibid., p. 73. This table also appears on page 149 of the translation of this session of the Seminar which is included in Mitchell and Rose, *Feminine Sexuality*.
14. Lacan, *Encore*, p. 94.
15. 'It is not on the side of extension that we must take the not-all' (*Encore*, p. 94).
16. For an excellent discussion of the relation of Kant's notion of indefinite judgment to the conflict of the first two antinomies, see Monique David-Ménard, *La Folie dans la raison pure* (Paris: Vrin 1990), pp. 33ff.
17. Jacques-Alain Miller develops this Lacanian distinction between inconsistency and incompleteness in relation to sexual difference in his unpublished seminar, 'Extimité', 1985–6.
18. Borrowing from Fredric Jameson, Slavoj Žižek adapts the notion of the 'vanishing mediator' for a Lacanian explanation of this disappearance of cause from the field of its effects; see Žižek, *For They Know Not What They Do* (London and New York, Verso 1991), pp. 182–97.
19. Thomas Weiskel, in his notable book, *The Romantic Sublime* (Baltimore, MD: Johns Hopkins University Press 1972), concludes the exact opposite; according to his explanation, the mathematical sublime is associated with 'too little meaning', while the dynamical sublime is characterized by an excess of the signified, or 'too much meaning'.
20. Sigmund Freud, 'Negation' (1925), *SE*, vol. 19, p. 236.
21. Ibid., pp. 237–8.
22. Ibid., p. 238.
23. Jean-François Lyotard, in his *Leçons sur l'analytique du sublime* (Paris: Galilée 1991), argues convincingly that there are not two sublimes, but two modes of considering the sublime.
24. Immanuel Kant, *The Critique of Judgment*, trans. James Creed Meredith (Oxford: Clarendon Press 1988), p. 109.
25. Lacan, *Encore*, p. 13.

3 WHO'S WHO?
Introducing Multiple Personality

MIKKEL BORCH-JACOBSEN

A few years ago, shortly after we moved to the United
States, my wife and I went to a party given by a friend.
Our host introduced us to a young woman named Sharon,
whose speech consisted largely of slang and whose attitude
was extremely aggressive. In particular, she had rather
shocking things to say about raising children, a subject that
seemed to obsess her. A year later we met her again, at the
same friend's house. This time she appeared much more
calm and thoughtful – on the whole, a very agreeable
person. The slang had dropped out of her vocabulary; she
told us she was working as a school teacher, and even
gave us well-considered advice on what school we might
send our eldest daughter to. Obviously, she had changed a
great deal during the year – for the better, so it seemed.
At least that is what we told ourselves as we left the party.
And then we dismissed her from our minds.

It wasn't until a year later that our friend told us that
we had met, not one, but *two* people: the young woman
was actually a patient afflicted with 'Multiple Personality
Disorder' (MPD) and was being treated by a well-known
therapist in town. 'Sharon', the first personality we had
met, was living on the street as a prostitute; 'Mary', whom
we had met on the second occasion, earned her living
from a part-time job in a school – 'part-time' because in
her job she secretly got help from a third personality,
'Cynthia'. There were many other personalities, including
a deaf-mute and a little girl who liked being cuddled by

her therapist. In all, quite a crowd: according to our friend, about twenty different personalities.[1]

I was already interested in the phenomenon of multiple personality (in fact, that was why our friend had finally revealed 'Sharon's' secret to us). I was acquainted with the literature on the subject and had seen numerous videos of patients switching from one personality to another. So, in principle, I should have been prepared for that confrontation with the reality of multiple personality. I remember very well, however, the uncanny feeling that gripped me when I found out the true 'identity', if that is the word for it, of 'Sharon'. And that feeling was not in the least attenuated, but rather strengthened, by the fact that at first I hadn't noticed anything abnormal about 'Sharon' and/or 'Mary'. In fact, if 'they' had originally been introduced as a 'multiple personality', I could have distanced myself from the pathological phenomenon and considered it from the outside, as a pure exhibition. But instead, being dragged unawares *into* the theatre of multiple personality, I had a difficult time re-establishing the difference between play and reality, between mask and face, personage and person. For, in fact, whom had I encountered? Had I really met some*one*? In other words, had I met a single subject who was, consciously or not, affecting two or more different personalities? In that case the 'multiple personality' really was a fake, conscious or otherwise. Or, on the other hand, were 'Sharon' and 'Mary', beyond their bodily identity, really two different people, having distinct histories, memories, behaviours and feelings? In short, *two subjects*, entirely different, two souls in a single body?[2]

I suppose that we all, when confronted with the phenomenon of multiple personality for the first time, must ask ourselves the same questions. Those questions are almost inevitable, and they cause most authors to pose the problem of multiple personality in terms of reality and simulation, authenticity and suggestion. Nevertheless, I am not sure that these are the right questions. In fact, I think their real purpose is merely to help people recover their equilibrium, just as I had, after the shock of not knowing *whom* I had met under the name of 'Sharon'. Indeed, multiple personality does emphasize the question of 'the subject', but not because it offers a choice between a unitary subject, or a double, multiple, fragmented, split or dissociated one. On the contrary, this bizarre phenomenon brings us face to face with a more troubling question: what happens to the subject when there is *no* 'personality', no personal identity, no 'ego' (or 'self'), no memory, no unifying pole of experience? In short, what remains when there is no longer anyone there, when 'I', *Ich, ego*, have disappeared? And what do we call *that, Es, id*? Do we just keep on calling it 'the subject'? Maybe so. But then, *who is that 'subject'?*

Symptomology

'Sharon', 'Mary' and the others faithfully conform to the clinical picture drawn by today's multiple personality specialists in the United States.[3] I say 'conform' for reasons that will become apparent later, but I want to state the principle right off the bat: in this case, clinical reality reflects its description by the psychiatrists as much as the description reflects reality. There is a constant interaction between the two, and it is important to remember that the clinical picture of 'multiple personality' is not a simple notation of reality. In fact, the description is also a prescription, a sort of stage direction which will be played out by the patients with occasional original improvisations (which then become incorporated into the clinical picture, and so on). Remember, then, that the clinical picture is a 'living picture', a *tableau vivant*, an *imitation* of the psychiatrist's clinical picture.

Here is the definition of 'multiple personality' given in 1979 by Bennett Braun, one of the pioneers in its diagnosis. A person affected by 'Multiple Personality Disorder' (MPD) is:

> one human being demonstrating two or more personalities with identifiable, distinctive, and consistently ongoing characteristics, each of which has a relatively separate memory of its life history . . . There must also be a demonstration of the transfer of executive control of the body from one personality to another (switching). However, the total individual is never out of touch with reality. The host personality (the one who has executive control of the body the greatest percentage of the time during a given time) often experiences periods of amnesia, time loss, or blackouts. Other personalities may or may not experience this.[4]

This definition contains nothing really new in comparison with the classical definitions given during the last century by Étienne Azam, Pierre Janet, William James and Morton Prince.[5] In fact, while reading contemporary descriptions, one often gets the feeling they are simply 'remakes' of the great classics, with their typical, caricatural personages: the 'host personality', depressed, agonized, puritan, afflicted with diverse psychosomatic symptoms and memory losses; the seductive personality, coquettish, sexually uninhibited, full of disdain for the host personality, whom the second continually pesters and persecutes; the child personality, cuddly and timid, often remembering the traumas of childhood. Aside from that, however, we note the emergence of new dramatis personae, feverishly inventoried by the specialists: the anaesthetic personality, capable of enduring pain and physical or sexual violence without flinching: the inner persecutor, responsible for the others' 'self'-mutilations and suicide attempts; Ralph Allison's Inner Self

Helper (IHS),[6] a reasonable, genderless personality who collaborates with the therapist; the guardian personality, who protects the others in daily life (which was 'Sharon's' role); the Hidden Observer noted by Ernest Hilgard,[7] who records everything that happens to the other personalities and who can be consulted by the therapist. The list of these new personalities continues to grow and illustrates the increasing complexity of these scenarios in comparison with the classical descriptions. Of the 76 cases noted in 1944 by W. S. Taylor and M. F. Martin,[8] 48 manifested 2 personalities, 12 manifested 3, and only 1 manifested more than 8. This is no longer the case. According to Nicholas Humphrey and Daniel Dennett,[9] the average in 1989 was eleven personalities per patient, and at present a patient's personalities are often numbered by the dozens. And the number is larger still if 'Special Purpose Fragments' are taken into account. These fragments are sub-personalities whose tasks are extremely specialized: 'driving the car on Saturday night', for example, or 'preparing dinner for a guest'. There are also cases of 'polyfragmentation', in which one encounters hundreds of personalities and fragments.

Changes of personality, or 'switches', imply notable transformations in voice, behaviour, accent, vocabulary and handwriting, often quite noticeable and occurring very quickly. Personalities, or 'alters', in the specialist jargon, are often of different age and sex, wear different clothes and have different beliefs and values, sometimes even different sexual orientations. Alters can manifest special somatic symptoms (myopia, allergies, etc.), which do not affect the others.

The relations between different personalities are complex: some personalities are aware of the entire alter system; some have only partial knowledge of it; some believe they alone exist. When two or more personalities know each other, they are said to be 'co-conscious', a term borrowed from the famous case of 'Sally Beauchamp', analysed by Morton Prince. Alters can be related as allies, as mutually indifferent, or as mortal enemies. In the last case, hostilities sometimes escalate to the point of physical aggression or attempted murder, which, seen from outside, are perceived as self-mutilation or attempted suicide. Since multiple personalities literally have no body of their own, they treat their real body with the same disinterest as that of another. This aggression is generally attributed to the 'inner persecutors' mentioned earlier. One of the principal promoters of the diagnosis, Richard Kluft, writes: '[Inner persecutors] may be based on actual abusers or culturally-accepted representations of evil intent. In three recent cases, persecutors were an introjection of an abusive mother, a Nazi concentration camp guard, and the devil.' And he adds, 'The latter resembled a possession state.'[10]

Diagnosis

Specialists base a diagnosis of MPD on the following indications: the presence of memory gaps or periods of 'absence', inappropriate use of 'we', 'he', or 'she', instead of 'I'; persistent migraines; the presence of 'voices' arguing in the patient's head; diverse anomalies like 'finding clothes in the closet that don't belong to you'; and so on. But the decisive criterion in diagnosing MPD is 'switching', the changing of personalities. Whenever MPD is suspected, the therapist, as if speaking to no one in particular, tries asking if there is anyone else in the room who would like to speak. If a different personality manifests itself at that point, there is no longer any doubt: this is definitely a case of MPD. This moment of the diagnosis is truly decisive, even according to the specialists themselves. *Before* the diagnosis, the multiple personalities usually lead a covert life; either they conceal themselves from the outer world, or the host personality conceals its 'own' state from itself. This commonly results in a miserable, chaotic existence, bouncing back and forth between psychiatrists and judges, until the unfortunate person has the luck to run into a therapist who applies the correct diagnosis. *After* the diagnosis, however, the personalities proliferate so quickly that the therapist literally cannot keep track of them. As Richard Kluft explains (or rationalizes):

> In many adult multiple personality disorder cases eager to evade detection, a large number of alters pass as one, forfeiting external signs of difference. In such cases, once the patient realizes that someone has made the correct diagnosis, he or she may relax and show more overt differences with that individual.[11]

Aetiology

American psychotherapists generally agree that MPD is caused by traumatism combined with dissociation. By 'traumatism' they mean an event that provokes a paralysing pain or emotion which prevents the subject from reacting adequately, generally suffered during infancy and inflicted by the parents. 'Dissociation' is the defence mechanism mobilized by the subject who has been disarmed by such a traumatism (especially in the case of babies, those particularly disarmed subjects), in order to survive this invasion of pain or emotion: the subject 'dissociates' as if nothing had happened; or, more exactly, as if the traumatic event had not happened to him, but to *another*, with whom he does not have, nor want to have, any contact, of whom he wants to know nothing, who simply does not exist. Like the lizard, which sheds its tail when threatened with attack, the subject splits itself, multiplies, to avoid being completely annihilated. Dissociation, the authors insist, is a perfectly normal process. Frank Putnam calls it a 'psychophysiological process . . . that produces an alteration in the person's consciousness'.[12] Daydreams or psychical concentration, for example, are forms of dissociation; self-hypnosis is another, simply more marked and less usual. In addition, dissociation is initially a defence mechanism perfectly adapted to the traumatic situation, since it helps the subject to survive. Only later does it take on its properly pathological form, becoming a regular mode of reaction to emotions, to stress or, more generally, to the difficulties of existence. Specialists then speak of 'dissociative disorders', ranging from benign amnesia to the extreme of multiple personality. In the latter case, according to the authors, the trauma is so serious, so unsupportable and so often repeated, that the dissociated parts of the psyche continue their own existence, parallel to that of the so-called 'primary' personality. According to the theory, then, there is a correlation between the seriousness of the trauma and the degree of fragmentation of the personality. Patients struck with MPD are considered, a priori, as true 'survivors', which, in fact, is what they are called in the specialist jargon.

You will undoubtedly have recognized this as a sort of remake of the 'traumatic' theory of hysterical neurosis proposed in the last century by J.M. Charcot and his emulators. In fact, MPD theoreticians often refer to Janet's work on 'dissociation of consciousness'. And, despite their militant anti-Freudianism, they could equally claim descendency from Freud and Breuer's theories in *Studies on Hysteria*. The latter wrote (in reference to hysteria):

> We have become convinced that the splitting of consciousness [*Spaltung des Bewußtseins*] which is so striking in the well-known classical cases under the form of '*double conscience*' is present to a rudimentary degree in every hysteria, and that a tendency to such a dissociation, and with it the emergence of abnormal states of consciousness (which we shall bring together under the term 'hypnoid') is the basic phenomenon of this neurosis.[13]

In fact, the theoretical model used today in the United States to understand MPD is almost identical to Freud's 1896 'aetiology of hysteria': a 'traumatic scene' (usually sexual) that is 'irreconcilable' with the ego, and a 'defence' with the formation of a 'dissociated psychicial group' that is inaccessible to consciousness. In other words, current MPD theoreticians break with Freud at exactly the same point Freud himself broke from his *neurotica* in 1897 when he gave up his 'seduction' theory and replaced it with a theory of desire, fantasy and intra-psychical repression. The trauma, the MPD specialists argue, is not a fantasy *representation*, not a simple 'wish-*thought*' [*Wunschgedanke*] in Freud's sense of the word. On the contrary, it is the unrepresentable itself: first, because it is an irruption into the psyche of an unsupportable reality that literally blows the psyche to bits; and second, because it cannot be thought, imagined, fantasised or remembered, but only repeated, acted and staged, all unconsciously. Nevertheless, you will note that these authors, in their own way, repeat certain interrogations of Sandor Ferenczi's late period; that is, of Freud himself. (See, for instance, chapter 5 of *Beyond the Pleasure Principle*, where Freud, speaking precisely of trauma neuroses, relates the compulsion to repeat to the necessity of 'binding' the quantities of excitation erupting in the psychical apparatus, before any search for pleasure or hallucinatory wish fulfilment).[14]

Therapy

Patients affected by MPD 'suffer from reminiscences', to use Freud and Breuer's formula from *Studies on Hysteria*, and their treatment, therefore, consists of desegregating these 'reminiscences', reintegrating them into the current of psychical associations. Nevertheless, since these memories of the traumatic scene are not simply repressed, but actually *dissociated* from the psyche, the therapists reject the classical method of 'free association' supplemented by interpretation and analysis of the resistances. They say that the trauma has never been represented or 'psychically elaborated'; instead, it has been experienced in an altered state, closely related to the hypnotic state. Therefore, there is no question of remembering or verbalizing an event that, quite literally, never took place for representative or intentional consciousness. The only thing to be done is to repeat the state of dissociation, to reactualize the trauma, to have the patient relive it – in short, to 'abreact' it, as in the era of Breuer and Freud's first 'cathartic cures'.

This is where hypnosis comes in. According to the theory, the original dissociation was already a sort of self-hypnosis, so naturally the therapists use hypnosis to reactivate the trauma. In this light, hypnosis is nothing but a deliberate state of dissociation which artificially reproduces the patients' spontaneous one. In fact, whether the therapist deliberately induces hypnosis or not is of little consequence, since MPD is already a 'hypnotic pathology', as Eugene Bliss says,[15] and the patients have no need of the therapist to go into a trance. In a word, the treatment of MPD *always* takes place under hypnosis, whether 'induced' or 'spontaneous'.

The treatment aims at 'integrating' or 'fusing' the different alters into a single personality. To accomplish this, the therapist communicates with the diverse personalities, either directly or through a 'delegated' personality, to increase their 'co-consciousness'. Part of the therapeutic work consists of establishing 'contracts' between the alters in an attempt to deal with the most pressing symptoms. For example, the therapist might ask a certain 'persecutive personality' not to attack the others during a given time-period, or order another personality not to 'come out' in certain everyday situations, and so on. Another part of the work, the most important part according to the therapists, is the 'abreactive work': the patient is plunged into hypnosis and made to relive one or another aspect of the trauma. Or the therapist might suggest, for example, that the patient retire to a sort of intra-psychic bunker to express his or her rage against another traumatizing character. Or again, the therapist might ask the patient to visualize, as on a cinema screen, one or another scene or scene fragment. Normally, therapists claim not to use direct suggestion, but this does not prevent them relying heavily on indirect suggestion, in keeping with the techniques taught by Milton H. Erickson.[16] Actually, their hypnotic technique is extremely directive or manipulative, and it is difficult to avoid the comparison with modern technology: personalities are 'switched' like television channels; elements of the trauma are decomposed and recomposed as easily as 'processing' words on a computer; and the patient's past is brought back as easily as 'rewinding' a video cassette (in fact, certain therapists speak of 'rewinding the patient').

The treatment is long (six years on average) and taxing ('multiple personalities' demand – and usually obtain – constant attention from their therapist). According to specialist publications, the chance of a cure is very high. But is this really the case? If you speak privately with those same specialists, you will note a certain disenchantment compared to the therapeutic optimism that reigned just a few years ago. Supposedly 'integrated' patients return, sometimes with new personalities, demanding a second 'round', and, in addition to the treatment itself, the patients must often undergo a long supporting psychotherapeutic treatment to help them adapt to their new life as a 'fused' personality. One is inevitably tempted to think of the evolution of psychoanalysis: at first, miraculous 'cathartic cures', then the painstaking analysis of resistances, and finally interminable analysis.

Epidemiology

'Multiple personality' is an epidemic,[17] and psychiatrists are its vectors: such is the enlightening conclusion reached in the work of the anthropologist Sherrill Mulhern, from whom I borrow greatly in what follows.[18]

'Multiple personality', like 'hysteria', has the remarkable property of propogating itself in successive waves. The first wave arose in Europe during the golden age of Charcot, Janet, Binet and Breuer–Freud, and it came to the United States through William James, Morton Prince and other New England psychiatrists, psychologists and philosophers. That first wave quickly died away, supplanted by the new psychoanalytic 'plague', which began around 1909 (when Freud gave his 'Five Lessons' at Clark University).[19] By 1930 'multiple personality' seemed to have virtually disappeared, except for a few isolated cases, such as the famous case of Chris Sizemore, popularized in the film *The Three Faces of Eve*.[20] The diagnosis had a real 'comeback' in 1973, when the psychoanalyst Cornelia Wilbur and the journalist Flora Rheta Schreiber produced *Sibyl*, the therapeutic diary of a serious case of 'multiple personality'.[21] Wilbur, whose articles had been systematically rejected by the scientific journals, claimed to have cured her patient by having her relive the serious physical and sexual cruelties inflicted by her mother, and the book, immediately taken up by Hollywood, struck a chord in the American soul. Psychiatrists such as Ralph Allison, Georges Greeves, Richard Kluft and Bennett Braun once again became interested in multiple personality, which Henri Ellenberger's impressive book *The Discovery of the Unconscious* (1970) had just rehabilitated historically.

According to Humphrey and Dennett, there were two hundred known cases of MPD in the United States before 1980, one thousand in 1984, four thousand in 1989, and the latest estimates are in excess of thirty thousand. After several difficulties in getting the diagnosis of MPD accepted, its pioneers are now in a position of real power. Since the beginning of the 1980s they have had an official association and annual conferences, journals, specialized hospitals, a research laboratory at the National Institute of Mental Health in Washington DC, a powerful network of professional training seminars, which are literally crammed with psychotherapists of every persuasion, and finally an exponentially growing bibliography (a recent listing of scientific books and articles dedicated to the subject contains no less than ninety-four pages).[22] The diagnosis of MPD was officially recognized by the American Psychiatric Association in 1980 and integrated into the *DSM-III*. Another, far from unimportant, vector of the epidemic is the media: there are innumerable newspaper articles, books, radio broadcasts, talk shows and sitcoms dedicated to the subject (certain patients, like Chris Sizemore and Truddi Chase, have even become media stars and multiply, quite literally, on television screens across the United States). The epidemic has recently arrived in Great Britain. Isolated cases have been reported in France and the Netherlands.

There can be no epidemic without predisposing factors. Sherrill Mulhern mentions two in this case: the renewed interest in hypnosis by American psychiatrists after the war, and recognition within American society of the extent of child abuse. Interest in hypnosis in the United States is historically linked to the treatment of 'traumatic war neuroses' (which, at the end of the First World War, had already mobilized Freud's speculation on the 'compulsion to repeat' and 'beyond the pleasure principle'). Indeed, as classical psychotherapeutic techniques (especially 'analytic' ones) became less effective, hypnotic techniques began producing rapid and spectacular effects. This observation by military psychiatrists not only rehabilitated hypnosis as a therapeutic tool, it also opened the way to a reformulation of psychiatric disorders in terms of 'trauma' and 'dissociation'. But this reformulation would probably not have been so well received if, at a given moment, it had not encountered one of the most profound obsessions of modern American society. In this regard, it was no accident that the diagnosis of 'multiple personality' resurfaced in the early 1970s, crystallizing around a theory that viewed it as a result of traumas encountered during infancy. In fact, it was at this time that the notion of child abuse, advanced in the early 1960s by the paediatrician Henry Kempe, began to penetrate popular opinion. The America of baby boomers and gentle Doctor Spock discovered, with horror, that cruelty to children, including sex and incest, was much more widespread than they liked to admit, and that the phenomenon involved all classes of society. That was all it took to call Freud's theories back into question: the feminists accused him of having rejected the reality of incest because of his own 'male' prejudice. The 'trauma' theory of MPD proposed by Cornelia Wilbur and her emulators was obviously inscribed in and owed a great deal of its success to this general movement of controversy. Practically overnight, MPD became *the* disease of child abuse, overthrowing Freud's reactionary 'neurosis' in the camp of psychiatrists and therapists: each memory exhumed by hypnosis from the pit of 'multiple personality' helped confirm the extent and gravity of child abuse in American society; each case of child abuse reported by the media reinforced the probability of the trauma hypothesis. This hypothesis is now so widespread that it is almost impossible to imagine a successful psychotherapy which does not include the unearthing of incest and parental violence.

One last word on the epidemic's most recent developments. Since the early 1980s, the alleged memories of MPD patients have become more and more macabre. People speak of extreme perversities, sadistic tortures and even 'ritual abuse' perpetrated on the infant by a satanic sect, with bloody sacrifices, necrophagy and gang rape. If you believe this satanic rumour, accepted by a growing number of therapists, MPD is not simply a spontaneous 'dissociative disorder', but a deliberate creation of the 'satanists', who use hypnosis against their victims in order to conceal their crimes. Concern for respectability tends to make MPD's principal theoreticians minimize that rumour, but, in fact, they have no way of resisting it: on what grounds can they reject accounts of ritual cruelty, since they have already given credit to accounts of physical and sexual cruelty? In this light, to reject the satanic aetiology would be the same as rejecting the traumatic aetiology itself. It is easy, then, to see why the rumour continues to spread so rapidly. According to the chronology established by Sherrill Mulhern,[23] there were two lectures on satanic aetiology at the 1984 MPD conference; two years later, there were three; in 1987, eleven; in 1989, twenty, plus a full session and a one-day seminar, which included seven speakers. I myself recently participated in a consultation group where the main subject of discussion among therapists was the imminence of the winter solstice, that portentous date in the satanic calendar: the 'persecutive personalities' programmed by the sect were probably about to go into action. One need not be a historian of religion to realize that the propagation of the MPD diagnosis has become a real epidemic of 'demonic possession', comparable to those of Loudun and Morzine in the seventeenth and nineteenth centuries.[24]

Discussion

There is, as I have said, a general consensus among American psychiatrists and therapists concerning the reality of MPD. Some, however, do not hesitate to view it as a pure fabrication of the doctors and media, an 'iatrogenic' mixture of credulity, simulation and suggestion. Paradoxically, this opposition does not come from psychoanalysts, who remain astonishingly silent in a polemic that concerns them in the utmost, but from seasoned specialists in hypnosis such as Martin Orne, Herbert Spiegel and Nicholas Spanos, or anthropologists such as Michael Kenny and Sherrill Mulhern. It should be noted that their critiques, though solidly based, have had absolutely no effect on the propagation of the diagnosis. On the contrary, the MPD theoreticians have very cleverly integrated them into their own discourse in order to increase its scientific credibility. No one needs to tell them that they are dealing with a population of highly suggestible and hypnotizable subjects, or even fakers: the equivalence between dissociative disorders and the hypnotic state is the very foundation of their theory and practice, and the fact that their patients are suggestible, fakes or liars is merely an additional confirmation. This argument is foolproof: the more the patients lie, the more they tell the truth, and the more reason there is to believe their stories.[25] Joined with this is an implicit threat: if you don't believe, you are collaborating with the process of dissociation: you are the accomplice of domestic rapists and tyrants – you are 'one of *them*'.

For anyone familiar with the history of hypnosis and/or hysteria at the end of the nineteenth century, the present debate cannot help but evoke the polemic between Charcot and Bernheim concerning the 'suggestive' nature of the 'grand hysteria' studied at the Salpêtrière. Indeed, MPD theoreticians do not object to the equation of 'multiple personality' and 'hysteria' (they say that both are related forms of dissociative disorder), and, just like Charcot and Freud, they refuse to see it as a pure effect of suggestion. To demonstrate this, Frank Putnam and his collaborators at the Dissociative Disorders Unit of NIMH have even done several sorts of experiments which uncannily recall those of Charcot's assistants on the 'hysterogenous zones' and the 'aesthesio-genic' effects of magnets. Thus they note that important physiological modifications accompany the switching from one personality to another – proof that it really is an objective phenomenon and not an artefact of suggestion: different reactions to medications, changes in cardiac rhythm, respiration, visual acuity, and so on (they even supplement their data with pretty EEGs graphing changes in alpha rhythms).

Confronted with these experiments, the adversaries of MPD emphasize the influence of the observer on the observed phenomena; that is, exactly what Hippolyte Bernheim used to call the 'suggestion' factor. MPD patients, they claim, are usually individuals who manifest what Herbert Spiegel calls the 'Grade Five Syndrome'; that is, a strong hypnotizability accompanied by a nearly limitless capacity to conform to the demands of others.[26] In short, they are highly 'suggestible', as Bernheim said earlier of Charcot's hysterics. Under those conditions, argue the adversaries of MPD, the subjects conform in every way to the doctor's expectations, especially if the experiment or treatment takes place under hypnosis. It is therefore impossible to arrive at any sort of objectivity in this domain. For example, 'calling' on different personalities to manifest themselves, giving them a name, speaking to them, is literally equivalent to *creating* them, to *fabricating* them, to *staging* or *producing* them. As for the somatic phenomena claimed by the MPD theoreticians, they are the same as those that have always belonged to hysterical symptomology, to hypnosis and trance. As astonishing as they are in themselves, they 'prove' the objectivity of MPD no more than the stigmata of those possessed by demons 'proved' the existence of the devil.

The last and most decisive criticism bears on the use of hypnosis to get patients to remember or 'relive' their traumas. The treatment of MPD, just like Breuer and Freud's old 'cathartic cure', puts faith in the 'hypermnesic' capacities of hypnosis. But this faith, which goes back to the 'hyperlucid memories' of Puységur's somnambulists, is completely unfounded, according to experiments conducted by specialists in hypnosis.[27] 'Trance logic', to use

Martin Orne's terminology,[28] knows only one time, the present, which means that subjects under hypnosis are incapable of discriminating between memories, fantasies and external suggestions. For them, everything is equally present and thus equally real, equally certain. Therefore, not only are the supposed 'memories' obtained under hypnosis (or any analogous state) untrustworthy, but even the conviction attached to them by patients is typical of hypnoid states, and there is no reason to believe in them. When therapists support the trauma theory of MPD on their patients' memories, they are simply looking into their own mirror. Janet expressed it well: 'Show me a somnambulist and I can tell you who put him to sleep and what the opinions and beliefs, scientific or otherwise, of his first master are.'[29]

(Provisional) Propositions for a Hypnotic *Cogito*

The dispute between supporters and adversaries of MPD is probably necessary, but does it really get to the heart of the matter? If we hold to the terms of the debate, the adversaries of MPD are probably right: the diagnosis of MPD obviously has no basis in objective reality. I hasten to add that this does not in the least negate the reality of child abuse in general. Unfortunately, child abuse is only too real, and it would be stupid and criminal to deny that it is the basis of all sorts of psychical problems, including those treated by MPD therapists. But MPD is not the 'proof' of child abuse, as those therapists would have us believe, any more than the reality of child abuse 'proves' the reality of MPD. On the contrary, the constant conflating of the two, if we are not careful, may end up discrediting real cases of child abuse, by basing them on accounts extracted under hypnosis. In reality (if that word can be used here), everything leads to the conclusion that 'multiple personality disorder' is a psychical epidemic, exactly like Charcot's 'grand hysteria', Mesmer's 'magnetic crises', Saint-Médard's convulsionaries, the seventeenth century's 'demonic possessions' and all the analogous phenomena. To be perfectly clear: MPD is simply the form adopted by the trance in the given historical and cultural context of the United States in the 1970s, 1980s, and 1990s.

But does this explanation really explain everything that needs to be explained? Does the fact that 'multiple personality' is an artefact necessarily mean that it should be considered as a simple fiction, having nothing to do with the problem of the unity and identity of the subject? Far from it, for, whether it be true or false, that 'fiction' exists, insists, persists. The MPD epidemic is growing, along with its satanic counterpart, and the reason is that people believe in it. Objecting that this belief is merely the effect of hypnosis and suggestibility does nothing to resolve the problem, but only makes it more vexing. For why, in fact, do people believe this or that, in the absence of any 'logical', 'rational' or 'objective' considerations? And who are these 'people'? *Who* is hypnotized? It is not enough to say that they are highly suggestible individuals, responding to the 'Grade Five Syndrome', or that they are 'hysterical personalities', since, as Bernheim made clear once and for all, we are all suggestible in some degree, as is proved, for instance, by the modern Ericksonian techniques of induction. So it is impossible to reduce the problem to a merely morbid or pathological phenomenon: we are all potentially hypnotized, capable of being wrenched from reality to such an extent that we mistake night for day, and ourselves for another. But exactly *who* are we, then? Are we still a 'subject', an 'ego', a 'person'?

It is well known that Freud, in a strictly analogous situation, tried to answer these questions with the notion of 'psychical reality', opposing it to what he called 'material reality': the 'scenes of seduction' reported by his hysterics were false in regard to objective reality, but true in regard to their desire.[30] This elegant solution is equivalent to shortcircuiting any consideration of reality, dealing instead with a pure hermeneutic of the fantasies, thoughts and words of a *subject*. As Lacan excellently restates it at the beginning of his first seminar:

> [The domain of psychoanalysis] is that of the truth of the subject. The quest for truth is not entirely reducible to the objective, and objectifying, quest of ordinary scientific method. What is at stake is the realization of the truth of the subject, like a dimension peculiar to it which must be detached in its distinctiveness in relation to the very notion of reality.[31]

There is no need to emphasize that this 'dimension peculiar to psychoanalysis' is nothing other than the Cartesian *cogito*. It uses the same *epoché* of all realist reference, the same abandon of objective considerations, emphasizing instead the *certitude* of a subject grasping itself in its representations, its *cogitationes*, its *Gedanken*. Maybe my thoughts are false, maybe they are only a dream fomented by a *malin génie* or a 'demonic' unconscious, but they are still *my* thoughts, *my* fantasies, and I am, *ego sum*, as long as I think. The whole meaning of the 'psychoanalytic revolution', as Lacan well understood, is summed up in that reformulation of hysteria (and thus also of hypnosis, and thus also of 'multiple personality') in terms of the subject, of a desiring subjectivity. The fact that this subject is the profoundly decentred and divided subject of the 'unconscious' really makes little difference, since Freud continued to imagine that 'unconscious' as formed of repressed 'representations', of 'representational representatives of the drives'. These *Vorstellungen* may well be inaccessible to the conscious 'ego', but they still belong to a subject. However you look at it, 'someone', some 'X', has to represent those representations to its-*self*. Otherwise it would be impossible even to call them 'representations'. The unconscious is the unconscious of a subject, *its* unconscious. Maybe the hysteric's 'ego' does not know that it wants to be the hero of its fables, but its unconscious *does know*.

Again, this is a very elegant solution, but does it really get us any closer to understanding the question posed by the hypnotic state? I do not think so, for one very simple reason: the hypnotic trance dissolves the subject, plunging it into a pre-representational state, in which it no longer knows *itself*. The hypnotized person has no 'self', no 'ego', not because that subject is divided or absent in relation to itself, but because it is so well enveloped in the 'here and now', so very *present*, that it simply cannot be present *to* itself. There is a profound inability to reflect on itself, think of itself, or represent itself. The hypnotized person has lost the elementary distance from himself which would allow him to be conscious of himself. But is this sufficient reason to speak, as Freud did, of an 'unconscious'? It is true that Freud's famous 'properties' of the unconscious are exactly those of the hypnotic state, so much so that one might ask if both are not cases of one and the same 'trance logic', in which there is no temporality, delay, negation, doubt or 'degrees of certainty', and in which 'external reality' is 'replaced by psychical reality'.[32] But Freud's 'representational' definition of the unconscious prevents us from pushing the comparison any further. Again, a person who is hypnotized does not represent anything, even though we, on the outside, can always say that all sorts of representations 'arrive at' or 'come to' that person. And the 'intemporality' of hypnosis is not, as it is in the Freudian unconscious, that of an 'indestructible' memory. On the contrary, if hypnosis manifests itself primarily in the mode of interruption, 'absence', or amnesia, it is because that state does not retain, remember or stockpile anything, since there *is no time. Zeitlosigkeit*: the hypnotized person has no time to retain anything resembling a 'past-present', no way of 'representing' it to himself, nor does he have the time to anticipate or desire any kind of 'future-present'. In fact, this state, so often described as a loss of consciousness, could equally well be described as *total* consciousness, as a *con-scientia* so closely bound to itself, so *present*, that it literally shortcircuits any self-distancing in which an 'unconscious' could lodge itself.

At this point our question becomes more precise: can we, should we, continue to speak of a 'subject' in this case? Can we still assign a 'subject' 'under' the fable (or fiction, or fantasy) of 'multiple personality'? Obviously, it all depends on what we mean by 'subject'. Traditionally the 'subject' is what is *subjectum*: that is, 'sub-jacent', 'sub-stantial'. In this sense, the subject initially has nothing to do with the 'ego': its essential designation is substance (*hypokeimenon*), its permanence and identity 'under' its accidents. As Heidegger has shown, only when the Cartesian *cogito*'s ego inherits the role of ultimate basis does it become a 'subject' in the modern sense. In other words, the 'subject' is what remains permanent and identical 'under' all the representations in which it poses and thinks *itself: ego cogito, ego sum.* But, as we have just seen, this subject-of-representation is precisely what hypnosis shortcircuits. In the hypnotic state there is no representation in the philosophical sense; there is no *Vor-stellung* in which a subject could 'pose' itself 'before' itself in order to grasp itself as the permanent basis of everything that presents itself to that 'subject', and so on.

But does this mean that *there is no subject whatsoever?* Obviously, the hypnotic state isn't nothing: something 'happens', even though it does not happen in the mode of representation. Nor is 'whatever' or 'whoever' it happens to nothing. In fact, I have just said that it is total presence, total consciousness. Isn't this another way of saying that it is the total subject, the most profound burying of the *subjectum* in its own foundation – in the 'id' that takes the place of its 'ego'? In short, hypnosis reveals what is 'at the bottom' of the subject of representation, before it represents anything whatsoever to itself. Maybe we should even go so far as to say that it is the *cogito* itself, before it has time to reflect on itself and become an 'I think, or represent, *myself*'. In fact, what is it that the hypnotist asks his patient, his 'subject'? Whatever his method of induction, the hypnotist always asks the patient to disregard (or go to sleep in regard to) the world, while remaining awake. In other words, he asks him to use Descartes's 'hyperbolic doubt' or Husserl's 'phenomenological reduction': 'Act as if the world were a dream; put it in brackets; neglect it as a transcendence; become pure immanent consciousness.' What remains after this operation is pure wakefulness or, if you prefer, the degree zero of consciousness, before any 'consciousness of . . . ', any intentionality, any opening on the world. And before any ego: the *cogito* of hypnosis is a *cogito* without ego, an impersonal, anonymous, unqualifiable, and unqualified *cogitare*.

In a certain way, this is what the most rigorous Cartesian tradition already states. In his 'Second Meditation' Descartes insists that the *cogito*'s ego is not the 'man' that 'I originally believed myself to be';[33] that is, the gentleman named René Descartes. Husserl, at the other end of the tradition opened by Descartes, insists on the same point with equal vigour: the life of the immanent consciousness revealed by phenomenological reduction is an anonymous life, since, by definition, it precedes any intraworldly *psyche* and, thus, any empirical biography. The 'transcendental ego', just like the *ego cogitans*, is nameless: 'It is in and for itself indescribable: pure Ego and nothing further.'[34] Nevertheless, Descartes and Husserl both continue to speak of 'ego', of 'self', and this is enough to restore an identity to the *cogito*'s sphere, an essential unity and permanence. For them, as well as their emulators, the ego continually grasps and re-grasps itself as 'the same', even if this 'same' is perfectly empty, neutral and, in the final analysis, ungraspable: 'I am the Same. That is the essential point.'[35]

But hypnosis, precisely because it is not a reflexive operation, pushes the reduction much further, to the point where the *cogito* coincides so well with itself that it can no longer grasp, reflect on or represent itself *as* 'the same'. This is the hypnotic point of the *cogito*, where it becomes the experience of no self, of no ego. I am certain of being, Descartes already affirmed, only 'for as long as I am thinking';[36] that is, only during the *instant* that I think. And nothing allows me to affirm that I, as ego, remain the same through time. Nothing allows it because I have lost time; I have lost memory, and I have already forgotten *who* I am. I cannot even say, 'I am', but only, 'there is something, something is happening, is lived, is life'.

Hypothesis – isn't it precisely this disappearance of the ego that 'multiple personality' stages in its own spectacular and derisive fashion? How, in fact, can an absence of ego be expressed, if not, paradoxically, by multiplying it? Isn't the 'ego inflation' so evident in multiple personality merely the trance subject's response to the therapist's naive and oppressive demand of identity? 'You want to see *who* I am? Well then, watch. I "switch": I am switching. I am in so far as I switch, for as long as I switch. I switch, I am. *Je switche, je suis. Je switche, je suis.*

Translated by Douglas Brick

Notes

1. The names and biographical details have been changed for reasons of confidentiality.
2. See Henry Herbert Goddard, *Two Souls in One Body? A Case of Dual Personality. A Study of a Remarkable Case: Its Significance for Education and for the Mental Hygiene of Childhood* (New York: 1927); and Ian Hacking's excellent commentary, 'Two Souls in One Body', *Critical Inquiry*, no. 17 (Summer 1991).
3. *Tableau clinique* should probably be translated as 'clinical description' (or some more technical term), but since it is later juxtaposed with *tableau vivant*, I have tried to retain something of the literal meaning: Trans.
4. Bennett G. Braun, 'Clinical Aspects of Multiple Personality', communication to the annual congress of the American Society of Clinical Hypnosis (San Francisco: November 1979).
5. Étienne Eugène Azam, *Hypnotisme, double conscience et altération de la personalité*, preface by J.-M. Charcot (Paris: Alcan 1887); Pierre Janet, *L'Automatisme psychologique* (Paris: Alcan 1889); William James, *The Principles of Psychology* (Cambridge, MA: Harvard 1981), pp. 352ff. and *William James on Exceptional Mental States: The 1896 Lowell Lectures*, ed. Eugene Taylor (New York: Scribner 1983); Morton Prince, *The Dissociation of a Personality* (New York: Longmans, Green 1906). On the history of multiple personality in general, see H. F. Ellenberger, *The Discovery of the Unconscious* (New York: Basic Books 1970); Michael G. Kenny, *The Passion of Ansel Bourne: Multiple Personality in American Culture* (Washington:

Smithsonian Institution Press 1986); Jacqueline Carroy, *Hypnose, suggestion et psychologie: L'invention de sujets* (Paris, 1991); Ian Hacking, 'The Invention of Split Personalities', *Human Nature and Knowledge: Boston Studies in the Philosophy of Science*, ed. Alan Donagan, Anthony Terovich and Michael Wedin, 89 (1986); Ian Hacking, 'Multiple Personality Disorder and its Hosts', *History of the Human Sciences*, vol. 5, no. 2 (1992); Ruth Leys, 'The Real Miss Beauchamp: Gender and the Subject of Imitation', *Feminists Theorize the Political*, ed. Joan Scott and Judith Butler (London and New York: Routledge 1992). Contemporary theories of Multiple Personality Disorder are described in Frank Putnam's *Diagnosis and Treatment of Multiple Personality Disorder* (New York: Guilford Press 1989).

6. Ralph B. Allison, *Minds in Many Pieces* (New York: 1980).
7. Ernest Hilgard, *Divided Consciousness: Multiple Controls in Human Thought and Action* (New York: John Wiley 1977).
8. W. S. Taylor and M. F. Martin, 'Multiple Personality', *Journal of Abnormal and Social Psychology*, vol. 39 (1944).
9. Nicholas Humphrey and Daniel C. Dennett, 'Speaking for Ourselves: An Assessment of Multiple Personality Disorder', *Raritan*, no. 9 (Summer 1989).
10. Richard P. Kluft, 'An Introduction to Multiple Personality Disorder', *Psychiatric Annals*, vol. 14, no. 1 (1984), p. 22.
11. Richard P. Kluft, 'The Natural History of Multiple Personality Disorder', *Childhood Antecedents of Multiple Personality*, ed. Richard P. Kluft (Washington, DC: American Psychiatric Press 1985), p. 188.
12. Frank W. Putnam, 'Dissociation as a Response to Extreme Trauma', *Childhood Antecedents of Multiple Personality*, ed. Richard P. Kluft (Washington, DC: American Psychiatric Press 1985).
13. Josef Breuer and Sigmund Freud, 'Preliminary Communications', *The Standard Edition of the Complete Psychological Works of Sigmund Freud*, ed. James Strachey (London: Hogarth Press 1958), vol. 2, p. 12.
14. Freud, *Beyond the Pleasure Principle, SE*, vol. 18, p. 32: 'The fulfilment of wishes is, as we know, brought about in a hallucinatory manner by dreams, and under the dominance of the pleasure principle this has become their function. But it is not in the service of that principle that the dreams of patients suffering from traumatic neuroses lead them back with such regularity to the situation in which the trauma occurred. We may assume, rather, that dreams are here helping to carry out another task, which must be accomplished before the dominance of the pleasure principle can even begin. These dreams are endeavouring to master the stimulus retrospectively, by developing the anxiety whose omission was the cause of the traumatic neurosis. They thus afford us a view of a function of the mental apparatus which, though it does not contradict the pleasure principle, is nevertheless independent of it and seems to be more primitive than the purpose of gaining pleasure and avoiding unpleasure.'
15. Eugene Bliss, 'Multiple Personalities: A Report of 14 Cases with Implications for Schizophrenia and Hysteria', *Archives of General Psychiatry*, vol. 37 (1980).
16. A large number of Ericksonian therapists have recycled themselves into the treatment of MPD and 'dissociative disorders'. (Erickson, on the other hand, was extremely authoritarian towards the alternative personalities that he would accidentally invoke in hypnotherapy: one of his immediate students confided to me that Erickson would simply forbid them to reappear in his presence.)
17. Myron Boor, 'The Multiple Personality Epidemic', *Journal of Nervous and Mental Disease*, vol. 170 (1980).
18. See Sherrill Mulhern, 'De l'hypnose à l'enfer', *La suggestion hypnose, influence, transe*, ed. D. Bougnoux (Paris: 1991); 'Embodied Alternative Identities: Bearing Witness to a World That Might Have Been', *Psychiatric Clinics of North America*, vol. 14, no. 3 (September 1991).
19. See Eugene Taylor, 'James Jackson Putnam's Fateful Meeting with Freud: The Clark University Conference of 1909', *Voices: The Art and Science of Psychotherapy*, vol. 21 (1985);

John Gach, 'Culture and Complex: On the Early History of Psychoanalysis in America', *Essays in the History of Psychiatry*, ed. E. R. Wallace and L. C. Pressley (South Carolina: 1980).

20. Corbett Thipgen and Hervey Cleckley, *The Three Faces of Eve* (New York: 1957).

21. Flora Rheta Schreiber, *Sibyl* (New York: Random House 1973), which appeared on the best-seller list the same year it was published.

22. Carole Goettman, Georges B. Greaves and Philip M. Coons, *Multiple Personality and Dissociation: A Complete Bibliography* (Atlanta, GA: 1991).

23. Sherrill Mulhern, 'Satanism and Psychotherapy: A Rumor in Search of an Inquisition', *The Satanism Scare*, ed. J. T. Richardson, J. Best and D. G. Bromley (New York: A. de Gruyter 1991).

24. To get some idea of the extent of the phenomena, see Lawrence Wright's excellent article 'Remembering Satan', *The New Yorker*, 17 and 24 May 1993. See also Robert Hicks, *In Pursuit of Satan: The Police and the Occult* (Buffalo, CO.: 1991).

25. A good example of this sort of argument is supplied by Jean Goodwin in 'Credibility Problems in MPD Patients and Abused Children', *Childhood Antecedents of Multiple Personality*, vol. 13 (1983).

26. Herbert Spiegel, 'The Grade Five Syndrome: The Highly Hypnotizable Person', *The International Journal of Clinical and Experimental Hypnosis*, vol. 22 (1974); George Ganaway, 'Historical Truth versus Narrative Truth: Clarifying the Role of Exogenous Trauma in the Etiology of Multiple Personality Disorder and its Variants', *Dissociation*, vol. 2. (1989); see also, Mulhern, 'De l'hypnose à l'enfer', pp. 134–6.

27. On this question, see Jean-Roch Laurence and Campbell Perry, *Hypnosis, Will and Memory: A Psycho-Legal History* (New York: Guilford Press 1988).

28. Martin Orne, 'The Nature of Hypnosis: Artifact and Essence', *Journal of Abnormal and Social Psychology*, vol. 58 (1959).

29. Janet, *L'Automatisme psychologique*, pp. 128–9.

30. Cf. the famous letter of 21 September, 1897, in which Freud explains to Fliess his reasons for abandoning his '*neurotica*': 'Thirdly, there was the definite realization that there is no "indication of reality" in the unconscious, so that it is impossible to distinguish between truth and emotionally charged fiction. (This leaves open the possible explanation that sexual phantasy regularly makes use of the theme of the parents.)' *The Origins of Psychoanalysis: Letters to Wilhelm Fliess* (New York: Basic Books 1954), p. 216.

31. *The Seminar of Jacques Lacan: Book I, Freud's Papers on Technique*, trans. John Forrester (New York: W. W. Norton 1988), pp. 20–21.

32. Freud, 'The Unconscious', *SE*, vol. 14, pp. 186–7: 'There are in this system no negation, no doubt, no degrees of certainty . . . To sum up: *exemption from mutual contradiction, primary process* (mobility of cathexes), *timelessness*, and *replacement of external by psychical reality* – these are the characteristics which we may expect to find in processes belonging to the system *Ucs.*'

33. René Descartes, 'Second Meditation', *The Philosophical Writings of Descartes* (Cambridge: Cambridge University Press, 1984) vol. II, p. 17.

34. E. Husserl, *Ideas: General Introduction to Pure Phenomenology*, trans. W. R. Boyce Gibson (New York: Collier 1962), p. 214.

35. 'Je suis le Même, voilà le point capital'; Paul Valéry, *Cahiers* II (Paris: Editions universitaires 1974), p. 304; and p. 281: 'Le moi le plus éternel est le plus impersonnel' [The most eternal self is the most impersonal].

36. Descartes, 'Second Meditation', p. 18.

4 THE PHRENOLOGY OF SPIRIT

MLADEN DOLAR

There is a passage in Hegel's *Phenomenology of Spirit* that has completely baffled interpreters. For almost two centuries now they have been pinching themselves, not believing their own eyes, which tell them that Hegel actually wrote anything thing like it. I am referring to the chapter on phrenology, which constitutes the concluding section of 'Observing Reason', which is itself the first part of the extensive chapter on 'Reason'.[1]

It is strange enough, to start with, that Hegel takes up phrenology at all as an object worthy of philosophical reflection. This science, which had its brief heyday in Hegel's time, has since passed into oblivion and now figures only as a curious chapter in the history of science, a dead branch testifying to the lingering prejudices and deceptive shortcuts in the progress of scientific reason, the infantile errors that this progress has long ago left behind. Its quasi-scientific programme consisted in establishing a necessary relationship between the shape of the skull and the faculties of mind, providing the latter with a material counterpart in the former.[2] Its main proponent was Franz Josef Gall (1758–1828), who happened to be, apart from his phrenological aberrations, one of the major authorities on anatomy at the time. Hegel treats phrenology alongside physiognomy, another forgotten science which tried to do the same thing in relation to facial expressions, and whose main proponent was Johann Kaspar Lavater (1741–1801).

It is stranger still, if Hegel decided (on a momentary

whim?) to use phrenology for his own ends, that he should have chosen for its discussion the particular point of his argument that he did. This point is the concluding moment of something that looks like a classical Hegelian 'triad': observing Reason starts with the observation of outer nature in both its inorganic and organic aspects (here Hegel develops at some length the elements of his theory of natural science); then in the second step, Reason turns to itself and scrutinizes its own inner nature, 'logical and psychological laws', in order finally to proceed to what one would expect to be a 'synthesis' of the two, which bears the title: Observation of self-consciousness in its relation to its immediate actuality. Physiognomy and phrenology'. So after examining outer and inner nature, Reason arrives at a 'higher synthesis' of the two, their 'dialectical integration', which it happens to find in, of all things, phrenology. Is Hegel pulling our leg? Is he parodying his own method? Is he playing a joke at our expense? Does the progress of Reason suddenly regress, ending in catastrophe? For there is no question, in the entire section, of taking phrenology or physiognomy seriously. Hegel does not for a moment consider them as worthy scientific endeavours. He even volunteers a practical piece of advice on how to deal with them: the proper response to the physiognomist is 'a box on the ear': 'This retort is to the point, because it refutes the primary assumption of such a "science" of mere subjective opinion, viz. that the reality of a man is his face.'[3] Accordingly, if one is dealing with a phrenologist, one would have to hit harder: 'The retort here would, strictly speaking, have to go the length of beating on the skull anyone making such a judgment, in order to demonstrate in a manner just as palpable as his wisdom, that for a man, a bone is nothing *in itself*, much less *his* true reality' (p. 205).

Yet, after these humorous rejections of physiognomy and phrenology, and just when we have got used to the unusual sight of Hegel cracking jokes and amusing the audience,[4] things suddenly get serious:

> The crude instinct of self-conscious Reason will reject out of hand such a 'science' of phrenology . . . But the worse the conception, the less sometimes does it occur to one wherein its badness specifically lies and the harder it is to analyse it . . . for only what is wholly bad is implicitly charged with the immediate necessity of changing round into its opposite. . . . Spirit is all the greater, the greater the opposition from which it has returned into itself. (pp. 205–6)

An instinctive and immediate dismissal is not enough: it misses the point that only the worst can hope for the best and that only the basest stupidity can yield the highest wisdom. So there is a moment of speculative wisdom in this banality which we must hold on to; there is an insight overlooked or repressed by those respectable sciences dealt with so far under the heading of 'observing Reason'.

The chapter on Reason started with an equation: Reason is the certainty of consciousness of being all reality, or all truth – Hegel repeats this formula over and over again with slight variations (pp. 138, 139, 141, etc.). Consciousness equals reality in its totality. Objectivity is no longer to be considered as opposed to consciousness, as it was in the beginning, in the domain of 'Consciousness' proper; nor is it to be taken any longer as a purely negative pole, as in the second stage, when consciousness took the self-reflective turn to become self-consciousness; rather, we have now reached the point where consciousness can take the reality opposed to it as its own reality, objectivity and self-consciousness in one. This is the starting point of the position Hegel calls Reason, which is also the basic assumption of Idealism: the identity of thought and being, of self-consciousness and actuality, of the in-itself and the for-itself. Yet this certainty of being the whole truth is not enough: in so far as it is certainty, it is not yet truth – hence the progression of Reason which has gradually to acquire the truth of which it is certain. It has to find itself in its own reality and thus make it its own. But this self-seeking journey through the realms of being is accompanied by failure: observing Reason cannot find itself in the outer reality of nature (since 'organic Nature has no history',[5] it lacks reflexivity, the moment of the for-itself), nor can it grasp itself in its own simple interiority (since both logical and psychological laws fail to establish a mediation between the for-itself and the in-itself, they are stuck either in opposing the two or in a circularity of argument). Thus the third step has to consider the immediate unity of interiority and exteriority, the in-itself and the for-itself – if such a unity could be found, it would be the realization of Reason's endeavour, the attainment of its goal. Reason would have found itself in objectivity and would not have to progress any further. This is precisely what phrenology seems to promise with its basic assumption that 'the *being of Spirit is a bone*' (p. 208). So, is the fundamental equation of Reason with the totality of reality then ultimately to be translated into the equation 'Spirit is a bone'? Is this final equation the solution of the initial one, by its reduction to absurdity, the final answer to the notorious problem of *adaequatio rei et intellectus* which has puzzled the millennia?

There is, as we have seen, a ridiculous part to phrenology, the part represented by its pursuit of meaning through the assignment of spiritual faculties to particular parts of the skull bone. But this immediately dismissable part which necessarily runs into arbitrariness and absurdity only masks what is at stake:

[Consciousness] whitewashes that thought by unthinkingly mixing up with it all sorts of relationships of cause and effect, of sign, organ, etc. which are meaningless here, and it hides the crudity of the proposition [*das Grelle des Satzes*] by distinctions derived from them. (pp. 209–10)

Particular correlations of certain parts of the mind with certain parts of the skull bone divert the attention from the crudity of the equation that underlies them: the Spirit is a bone – the infinity of the spiritual dimension *is* a lifeless piece of materiality. Partial equivalences, by establishing particular relations, obfuscate the radical equivalence between two terms that have no common measure.

This consciousness, in its result, enunciates as a proposition that of which it is the unconscious certainty – the proposition that is implicit in the Notion of Reason. This proposition is the *infinite judgment* that the self is a Thing, a judgment that suspends itself [*sich selbst aufhebt*]. (p. 209)

Since there is no common measure between its terms, the judgment is infinite: it immediately suppresses itself in its own impossibility. There is no common denominator, no *tertium comparationis*, no basis for a relationship that could vouch for the asserted equivalence. What does this suppression mean; how does it function?

Before going any further, let me briefly hint that the mechanism of infinite judgment is, surprisingly enough, also at the basis of Marx's argument at a crucial point in *Capital*. When considering the question of equivalences between different commodities – and the possibility of an equivalence between two different kinds of commodities is what defines the commodity as such – Marx points out that such equivalence requires us to put into brackets, entirely to reduce the positive, palpable properties of the entities compared (that which constitutes their 'use value') in order to take them as equivalent, in addition to putting into brackets their misleading quantitive proportions. '20 yards of linen = 1 jacket', or '1 quarter ton of wheat = x of iron', and so on – these formulas presuppose the basic equation 'linen = jacket', 'wheat = iron'. If such equivalence is to be possible, these entities have to have a common substance which is immaterial and independent of their material properties, the substance of value. How can one pin down this immaterial, 'supersensible' entity? The only way is to read the value equation precisely as an infinite judgment. In '20 yards of linen = 1 jacket', the two sides of the equation are not symmetrical; as Marx points out, the immaterial substance of the first entity (the value) is expressed by the material being of the other: 'The value of the commodity linen is expressed by the body of the commodity jacket, the value of one commodity by the use value of the other.'[6] 'The use value becomes the form of appearance of its opposite, the value.'[7] The 'immaterial' equals the 'material', the 'supersensible' equals the 'sensible', and this is the only way to express it. This is the famous *quid pro quo* which is at stake in every commodity equation and which constitutes the minimal cell of the world of commodities (hence one can deduce from this its higher forms, money as general equivalent, and so on). Of course, there is an obvious difference between this and Hegel's treatment of the infinite judgment: in Marx's equation, the immaterial and supersensible value as such is not directly opposed to the material being as such, the 'spirit' does not directly confront the 'bone', but, to put it in Hegelian terms, the 'spirit' of one bone finds its equivalent in the 'matter' of another bone. The equation can be reversed, the two commodities can shift places, yet this does not affect the mechanism: one cannot hold on to both ends at the same time. All commodities are endowed with a supersensible substance, but this emerges in the equation only if it is read as an infinite judgment.

Let us return to Hegel. Reason tried to find itself in a being, but what it found, with the infinite judgment, is its radical inadequacy, its incommensurability with any being, expressed in the form of a paradoxical equation. This inadequacy found its ultimate formula in a point where all objectivity is reduced to a minimum, not to its concept, but rather to its 'non-concept', its 'anti-concept', the limit of conceptuality, a lifeless thing, a 'bit of the Real' as a leftover of objectivity. 'Reason is all reality' – but only at the price of this object.

The first two parts of *The Phenomenology*, 'Consciousness' and 'Self-consciousness', had as their result the particular form of subjectivity which was able to serve as the subject of Reason, its starting point. One can conceive this process as a gradual emptying of consciousness, its reduction to a minimal point – a subject that was, at the end of 'Self-consciousness' (as the result of the dialectics of 'unhappy consciousness'), the very opposite of an autonomous and self-conscious subject: a subject compelled to give up all its will and possessions to an other and to reduce its own body and pleasure to a vanishing point. But giving up everything and severing all its ties, it turns out, was the only way for the subject to become universal and thus the only possible entry into the standpoint of Reason: it is only this universally reduced subject that can be equal to reality in its totality. The first part of 'Reason', 'Observing reason', has now accomplished an analogous process on the side of objectivity: it has deprived objectivity of its 'flesh and blood' so that what is left is only a bone, its reduced minimum, a positive embodiment of negativity. There is an objectal leftover which serves as the counterpart of the purely negative and reduced form of subjectivity.

The most economic way of expressing this extreme point of reduction is to put it in Lacanian terms: we have, on the one hand, the reduced negative subject as a lack, symbolized as $ in the Lacanian algebra, and, on the other hand, the objectal leftover of reduced objectivity, symbolized as the object *a*. $ was produced by the reduction of its objectal counterpart, that is, of the object in which the subject could recognize itself, which it could appropriate both in thought and in actuality, transform by work, and so forth. By reduction of that counterpart, $ lost its support in objectivity and became a vanishing point of pure negativity. The object *a* which now emerges is that mode of objectivity in which it is impossible to recognize oneself and which cannot be appropriated; it requires the cutting of all ties between subject and object, it is the end of their dialectic relation, the limit of possible mediation between the two.

The self-conscious subject of Reason could not find itself in anything positive, but this bit of the contingent, immediate being represented by the bone demonstrates precisely the fact that the impossibility of finding itself *is* the subject, it is coextensive with it. If it could embody itself as something positive, it would cease to be a subject, it would turn into a lifeless Thing. If the subject is just this impossibility of being anything positive, then the phrenological proposition, 'the Spirit is a bone', is the positive demonstration of this impossibility. Observing Reason does not have to continue its quest into infinity, finding again and again that 'this is not it', and that the subject is that negative force transcending all being. Negativity has found its limit, its positive embodiment, its formula – just as the mathematician can cease to repeat infinitely an operation when its formula has been found. The phrenological proposition is just such a formula. This also implies that, for Hegel, dialectic is a finite process, it comes to an end when it produces a positive formula for the negativity that has been pushing it forward. On a larger scale, looking at *The Phenomenology* as a whole, one could say that 'absolute knowledge', its conclusion, is precisely such a formula. But that is another story.

The two entities, which we have marked as $ and *a*, while being incommensurable and fixed in a radical non-relationship, are nevertheless correlated. Lacan puts them both in a simple, mathematical-looking formula: $ $\lozenge$ *a*. This is, in his theory, the formula of fantasy: fantasy is precisely the establishing of a relation where no relation is possible, and this impossible relationship is the support of any relation to 'reality'. It is only by an essential blinding as to the dimension of the object that our relation to reality can be constituted. In so far as any relationship between subject and object is always underpinned by fantasy, the very notion of cognition is founded on the fantasy of a matching of subject and object, of their complementarity, or *adaequatio* as the traditional formula has it. The fantasy of cognition is the fantasy of a 'successful encounter', ultimately the fantasy of a successful sexual relationship which fills the lack of its absence – hence one of the most famous of Lacan's dictums: 'there is no sexual relation'.[8] Surprisingly enough, Hegel points this out himself in the concluding paragraph of this section, providing it with an astonishing exit line. In the infinite judgment, he says, the greatest stupidity coincides with the greatest wisdom:

> The *depth* which Spirit brings forth from within – but only as far as its picture-thinking consciousness [*vorstellendes Bewußtsein* – representational consciousness] where it lets it remain – and the *ignorance* of this consciousness about what it really is saying, are the same conjunction of the high and the low which, in the living being, Nature naively expresses when it combines the organ of its highest fulfilment, the organ of generation, with the organ of urination [*des Organs der Zeugung, und des Organs des Pissens* – quite literally 'pissing']. – The infinite judgment, *qua* infinite, would be the fulfilment of life that comprehends itself; the consciousness of the infinite judgment that remains at the level of picture-thinking behaves as urination. (p. 210)

As if the rest of the chapter were not enough, this parting shot is really the limit to flabbergast the interpreters. Most of them cautiously decided to pass over it in silence.

The infinite judgment thus allows two opposed readings: the correlation of both sides in representation, which is the cognitive equivalent of the function of urination; and the speculative reading, which would thus be comparable to the other function of the organ in question, that is, precisely the sexual relation – if it were possible. But the radical inadequacy of the two sides, their non-relation, points to its impossibility, and this gives us a clue to Hegel's use of the conditional in the last sentence: the infinite judgment would be (*wäre*) the fulfilment of life and the fulfilment of Concept, but the speculative dimension depends on a non-relation, it is coextensive with the impossibility of correlation. So maybe we can get to the real sense of the metaphor if we read it in reverse: consciousness gets stuck in representation in so far as it relies on the fantasy of correlation, ultimately the fantasy of a sexual relation, while speculative thinking requires a dimension which opens up with the recognition of its impossibility; speculative thinking emerges beyond fantasy. In a certain sense, speculation has to accept 'urination' as its proper site, since by choosing the 'sexual relation' it would either evaporate or get stuck in representation and fantasy. It can exist only in the radical inadequacy. Perhaps a new Hegelian term should be introduced: *speculative pissing*.

Hegel has thus produced a point which seems inherently Lacanian: it brings together, in one and the same place, the subject, $, the object *a*, and the phallus. No wonder we had to wait for the Lacanian conceptual apparatus to make sense of it and no longer discard it as a mere curiosity.

The objection could, of course, be raised that the point has a very limited value since it appears only in one particular spot in Hegel's opus, as a sort of *hapax legomenon*, an interesting symptom perhaps, but from which one should not hasten to draw far-reaching conclusions. But it is not difficult to show that this point is essential for Hegel and that it can be found at many strategic and decisive points of his argument. It reappears later in *The Phenomenology*, in the chapter on Spirit, where the alienating process of *Bildung* at a certain stage arrives at the equation 'the Self is wealth' (cf. pp. 312–15), that is, a mere thing. (And it is no accident that here the objectal equivalent of the Self appears as money.) Of far greater importance is the fact that the entire Hegelian analysis of Christianity as 'revealed religion' is ultimately based on the infinite judgment 'God is a man.' God as the infinite and the beyond is embodied in this particular individual of flesh and blood who has to die. The radical inadequacy of both sides of this equation constitutes the spiritual dimension of Christianity. The same mechanism is also operative in the deduction of the Monarch in the *Philosophy of Right*, which relies on the equation 'the State is the Monarch' – again the state as the sphere of Reason is embodied in this trivial individual chosen by the unreasonable contingency of blood succession and represented merely by his signature. And so on.

If the infinite judgment has, in our view, such a strategic and decisive importance for Hegel, we can venture the hypothesis that it necessarily follows from his basic presuppositions, his fundamental attitude. Hegel himself sums up this standpoint in the 'Preface' to *The Phenomenology*, in the notorious proposition that 'substance is subject' (p. 10). Maybe this statement should be taken as a clue to the infinite judgments which appear in different places throughout his work. *The infinite judgment can be seen as a necessary consequence of the starting point that substance is subject.* Why?

The infinite judgment, in its Lacanian translation '$\$ = a$', can be taken as an inversion of the proposition 'substance is subject'. The subject which appears in the place of the predicate in the latter is relegated to the place of the subject in the former, and what is now predicated to it is precisely a bit of substantiality, its reduced and paradoxical leftover which could not pass into subject, that is, which could not be dissolved in the movement of negativity and mediation. This a is a kernel that resists mediation. Nothing can be predicated to the subject as a pure negative vanishing point – except this remainder of universal mediation that cannot be subjectified. To go even further: the Hegelian subject is subject only in so far as 'all substance' is not subject; a certain non-subjectifiable point is 'the condition of possibility' of the subject. If the subject could get rid of it, dissolve it in the dialectical movement, if it could recognize itself in it or appropriate it, it would cease to be a subject. The infinite judgment denotes this impossibility.

It is no coincidence that on the last page of *The Phenomenology* Hegel comes back to the skull. He describes the entire itinerary of this work as 'the Calvary of absolute Spirit' (p. 493), *die Schädelstätte des absoluten Geistes*, literally the skull-place of absolute Spirit, and thus at the final point confronts Spirit with the *caput mortuum* on which it stumbles.

Before following any further the tribulations of the Hegelian subject, let me make two brief digressions. The first one concerns the status of phrenology. This 'science' was in such vogue for some time that it left several traces in the history of philosophy. Apart from Hegel, it was discussed by Maine de Biran, Schopenhauer, Comte (who was the only one to take it seriously and who included it in his project of 'positive science'), Engels,[9] and others. In spite of its short-lived glory, it quickly passed into oblivion and acquired the reputation of a monster science, a parody of science, a reject of the history of science, an abandoned island of unreason in the progress of reason, its dark spot. Yet, this image is largely misleading, a product of a certain amnesia. This is so not only because Gall was a highly acclaimed scientific authority of his time who made many valid contributions to anatomy; nor because the modern scientific view on the localization of psychic functions (initiated by Broca in the second half of the nineteenth century) relies on certain assumptions not so far from phrenological ones.[10] It is more important to see that if we try to re-establish the original 'horizon of meaning' of the phrenological endeavour (which was impressively accomplished by Lanteri-Laura), we find that it was entirely embedded in the project of Enlightenment. Phrenology tried to provide Spirit with a material basis and to establish a scientific link between psychic functions and their material foundation. It presented an essential link between the materialism of the eighteenth century and the later positivism and scientism (hence Comte's enthusiasm). Gall fell from favour in the period of Restoration – not because of some alleged obscurantism, but because of his adherence to the ideals of Enlightenment and his firm commitment to materialism. He seemed dangerous at the time precisely as an advocate of scientific progress.

I have tried to develop elsewhere[11] the basic paradox that underlies the Enlightenment. It can be pinpointed, in a minimal way, as a discrepancy between the universal subject that the Enlightenment produced (the Lacanian $) and an object that emerged in the same gesture as its counterpart and that eludes this subjectivity and comes to haunt it (the Lacanian object *a*). Phrenology, in the Hegelian reading, embodies this paradox perhaps in its purest form. We could thus propose one final version of the infinite judgment: 'phrenology is science', or in properly Hegelian form, 'science is phrenology'.

My second comment concerns a kind of postscript to Hegel's parting joke. The dialectical wisdom that 'the highest and the lowest coincide' is supposedly anticipated by the 'dialectics of nature'. A poem by Heinrich Heine, 'On Teleology', aims at this point, and since Heine was a connoisseur of Hegel, it seems probable that the poem was inspired by this very passage.[12] The poem is a dialogue between the poet and his beloved, the beautiful Teutelinde. In the first part, the poet presents a number of humorous reasons explaining why God created man with two eyes, ears, hands and feet, but with only one mouth and nose. He tries to demonstrate that this is all for the best, that there is a teleological plan behind it and that God knew what he was doing. But Teutelinde is not convinced. She points to the paramount evidence to the contrary:

> My friend, I have listened to you/ and you have well explained/ how God has most wisely/ created a pair/ of eyes, ears, arms and legs/ while providing man with only a single/ example of mouth and nose./ But now tell me the reason for this:/ why did God, the creator of nature,/ create only one/ scurrilous requisite/ that the man uses/ to reproduce his race/ and at the same time to let his water?/ My dear friend, a duplicate/ would really be necessary here/ in order to represent two functions/ which are so important for the state/ and for the individual,/ in short, for the entire public./ A sensitive maiden/ must be ashamed when she sees/ how her highest ideal/ is so trivially desecrated!/ How the high altar of love/ is converted into a mere pipe!/ Psyche shudders as the little/ god Amor from the dark/ turns by the light/ of her lamp – into a pisser.// Thus spoke Teutelinde/ and I said: Enough!/ Unreasonable as women are,/ you don't understand, dear child,/ the connection of the two functions/ which stand in such a shameful/ and revolting contrast/ that debases humanity./ God's system of utility,/ his problem of economy/ is that both machines/ alternately serve the need in question,/ the profane and the sacred,/ the exciting and the boring – / everything is thus simplified/ and wisely combined:/ in this way he produces his equals./ The same bunch/ plays on the same bagpipe./ The tender hand and the rough paw/ play on the same fiddle./ . . . / thus everybody jumps, sings and yawns,/ and the same omnibus/ takes us all to Tartarus.[13]

The paramount counter-argument thus turns into the best argument for the teleological nature of the universe. It is not enough that each element (and its doubling) has a sufficient reason, its *telos*. Teleology requires something more – at least one element which serves two, maximally opposed, purposes. This element proves the optimal economy of means – the lowest serves the highest, the vulgar the sublime – and at the same time, as a metaphorical condensation in one privileged spot, it makes possible the correlation of all other functions and elements (which is precisely the function of the 'phallic signifier' in psychoanalysis). If nature anticipates dialectics, dialectics must nevertheless make a small step further: not only do the two functions alternate in the same place, but they immediately coincide: the negative *is* the positive, as Hegel never tires of repeating. Psychoanalysis takes this step on the very spot indicated by Hegel and Heine: the paradoxical organ turned into a signifier, the signifier par excellence, the phallic signifier which is the signifier without signified, where the highest 'meaning' coincides with the absence of meaning, plenitude with lack, teleology with contingency, the omnibus of sense with the pit of Tartarus.

The Hegelian and Heinean joke fulfils very well the condition that Freud has posited:

> The pleasure in a joke arising from a 'shortcircuit' like this seems to be the greater the more alien the two circles of ideas that are brought together by the same word – the further apart they are, and thus the greater the economy which the joke's technical method provides in the train of thought. We may notice, too, that here jokes are making use of a method of linking things up which is rejected and studiously avoided by serious thought.[14]

In Freud's examples, the function of the shortcircuit is assumed by a word (e.g. by a pun), while in our case it is the same 'thing' which has opposed purposes; or better still, in psychoanalysis the phallic moment is precisely the privileged shortcircuit between words and things, the place where the signifier gets hold of the body.

Let us now return to Hegel. It seems that with the infinite judgment, the progress of Reason, along with its subject, got stuck. It could not swallow the bone.[15] How is it possible to get beyond this point? Or, indeed, is it necessary to progress any further? Do we not reach some ultimate point here? Yet, a quick glance at the table of contents informs us that we have only reached the end of the first part of 'Reason', 'observing Reason'; the second part bears the title 'B. The actualization of rational self-consciousness through its own activity' (or for quick reference, 'Active Reason'), and there is a third and final part: 'C. Individuality which takes itself to be real in and for itself'. What I am interested in here is just the mechanism of transition between the concluding point of the first part and the beginning of the second part – the question of how and why the progression beyond infinite judgment takes place.

The passage from the one to the other can, on the most obvious level, be seen as a passage from observation to activity. The subject abandons its merely observational 'theoretical' attitude in favour of action. The subject of reason takes its destiny into its own hands instead of contemplating the different regions of being. At the same time, this transition accomplishes a step into the realm of 'self-reflection'. Thus it is largely analogous to the passage from 'consciousness' to 'self-consciousness' which occurred earlier in *The Phenomenology*. There as well consciousness had to cast off its mere contemplation of an objectivity opposed to it. In order to become self-consciousness, it had to act: lord and bondsman had to engage in a struggle of life and death, the subject had to work and thus shape objectivity, unhappy consciousness had to torture its body and soul, and so on. The first point is that the self-conscious subject is for Hegel not a subject of cognition (as observation and contemplation), but it can only reach self-reflection at the price of action. Abandoning the theoretical stance is the condition for self-reflection. Consciousness has to take the risk of a *passage-à-l'acte*.

At the end of 'observing Reason', the subject of Reason 'found itself' in a thing, a piece of senseless materiality, which pinpointed and highlighted the very impossibility of the subject's finding itself, the point that eludes the subject. If the subject could actually be embodied in a thing as its material equivalent, it would cease to be a subject. The passage to action now requires just this: the subject has to make itself a thing ('*das sich zum Dinge machen*', says Hegel literally, p. 213). Action requires that, in a certain sense, the subject lose its status of subjectivity; in action, the subject has to assume its own desubjectivation. This is the starting point of Hegel's curious 'theory of action': the theoretically produced object is not enough, the subject has to experience it by turning itself into that object and thus risking the loss of subjectivity. There is a chance of its becoming 'for-itself' only if it assumes the loss of itself.

If the passage from the 'in-itself' to the 'for-itself' is at the same time the passage from theory to action, this implies the paradox that what is required is not a higher stage of reflection, but quite the contrary, a loss of reflection, not a new insight but a new blindedness. Hegel's process runs counter to all of the theories of self-reflection since Descartes: Hegelian consciousness couldpossess a certain limited knowledge, its problem was posed in terms of knowledge, whereas self-consciousness entails not a higher degree of knowledge, but its loss. Self-consciousness has to lose its head, it presupposes a 'loss of consciousness'.

The structure of Hegelian action is such that action cannot realize its goal. If the subject endeavours to stick to its goal, it can do so only by not acting: action by its very nature perverts the goal, it always realizes something other than what was intended. A pure subjectivity is a non-acting subjectivity; it can only observe the objectivity opposed to it which presents its own limit. By acting, the subject transgresses the limit that constitutes it and thus risks surrendering what makes it a subject. It can realize itself in action only at the price of desubjectivation.

But there is another, more profound ambivalence in this passage to action. We have seen that at the end of 'observing Reason', the subject had reached an extreme and intolerable point: the point where, as a 'theoretical' subject of cognition, it had to confront its pure exteriority. Thought had produced a moment of its own exteriority, its radical heterogeneity, the limit of the categories of Reason which relied on the identity of thought and being; it produced a being beyond thought, a being which is not, and cannot be, conceptually grasped. Thought thus produced an 'unthinkable' being, a point of pure contingency. Such a point, however, cannot be sustained; it can be maintained only through fantasy, which requires precisely a gesture of blinding, an 'unthinking', unreflected support of thought. Hence, the passage to action is in a certain sense also a 'flight into action'. The subject 'escapes' into action in so far as it cannot sustain the extreme, unbearable point of thought – *being unable to think the object, it rather turns itself into an object.* The subject can realize itself only through action, but there is a moment of 'ersatz' involved in acting: an escape from the impossible task of thinking the object, of confronting the Real. By acting, the subject tries to avoid what Lacan calls the 'subjective destitution' which emerges precisely at the point of 'traversing the fundamental fantasy' (one of Lacan's formulas for the final point of analysis). In fleeing from subjective destitution, the subject plunges itself into action, hoping to preserve its status, unaware that this will entail the destitution anyway. Action is thus not only the realization of thought, but a realization that emerges at a point where thought fails, at the point of the unthinkable. But action fails as well, it does not preserve the subjectivity whose 'expression' it is; it brings a loss that will eventually produce the subject of Spirit.

The Hegelian act is thus, like the act in psychoanalysis, by its very nature a failed act, and its failure brings forth the dimension of the subject's truth ('only failed acts are really successful', was one of Lacan's favourite dictums). 'Praxis' always turns out to be 'parapraxis' (to use Strachey's neologism for the Freudian *Fehlleistung*). The act cannot remain 'at the level of its task', or at the level of its concept; it entails a fall from the level of the concept into 'thinghood' (*Dingheit*), the other of the concept. The side of thinghood is that of heterogeneity in relation to the concept, but the concept is a concept only if it can measure up to this heterogeneity. The act is thus not only accompanied by 'false consciousness' (concerning its thwarted intentions), it demands a loss of consciousness, a blind decision that cannot be grounded in a sufficient reason.

Let us now briefly consider the next section, the first part of 'acting Reason', which bears the title 'a. Pleasure and Necessity'. In Lacanian theory, the object *a* is inherently linked with the notion of *jouissance*, with the paradoxical dimension of enjoyment. In fact, in his *Seminar XVII, L'envers de la psychanalyse*,[16] Lacan develops the notion of the object *a* taking as his starting point Hegel's master/slave dialectic. This paradoxical object emerges there as the object of the slave's '*surplus enjoyment*', the objectal remainder beyond the objectivity that the slave can shape and transform by his labour.[17] With the object as the bone in infinite judgment, however, the connection with enjoyment seems to be lacking. The heterogeneity produced by thought, the objectal surplus of theory, does not appear to involve enjoyment (or at least it seems to be completely veiled by the contemplative attitude). But then in the next step, the link with *jouissance* is dramatically reinstated. The passage to action is at the same time a passage to enjoyment. The Thing turns out to be the place where the heterogeneity of enjoyment is inscribed in conceptual cognition.

The 'figure of consciousness' that Hegal introduces here is illustrated, as is well known, by the emblematic figure of Faust. Faust's initial problem is precisely *the turn from theory to enjoyment*. He leaves behind 'the knowledge acquired through observation and theory, as a grey shadow that is in the act of passing out of sight' (p. 217) in order to embrace the living enjoyment of immediate being which is lacking to theory. To do this, he has to leave behind 'the heavenly-seeming Spirit of universality' and to subscribe to 'the Spirit of the earth, for which true actuality is merely that being which is the actuality of the individual consciousness' (p. 217). He has to subscribe to the devil,[18] since only the devil seems to hold the clue to the object of enjoyment.

The Faustian subject is, of course, not striving for some weird Lacanian surplus-enjoyment, but merely for pleasure (*Lust*), as the title of the section indicates. But the pursuit of pleasure beyond 'grey' theory is transformed, in its attainment, into its contrary: necessity. Pleasure vanishes and leaves the subject confronted with cruel fate, the object of pleasure turns out to be

> what is called *necessity*; for necessity, fate, and the like, is just that about which we cannot say *what* it does, absolute pure Notion itself viewed as [mere] *being* [*als Sein angeschaute reine Begriff selbst*], a relation that is simple and empty, but also irresistible and imperturbable, whose work is merely the nothingness of individuality. (p. 219)

The subject striving for pleasure obtains instead necessity and fate, but this empty necessity is ultimately nothing other than the realization of infinite judgment. Necessity is just the Concept transformed into pure and empty being, the Concept turned into thinghood, a reified Concept.

Necessity is, on the one hand, the annihilation of individuality, the destruction of the subject and its hope of finding itself in the individuality of life. The realization of the goal mortifies living individuality and turns it into a lifeless universality. 'The merely single individuality . . . instead of having taken the plunge from dead Theory into Life, has therefore really only plunged into consciousness of its own lifelessness and has as its lot only empty and alien necessity, a *dead* actuality' (p. 220). The subject was striving for pleasure, but along with the dead necessity it got something else: a deadly *jouissance*, a lethal enjoyment that can be attained only at the price of its death – the action is its suicide. 'It experiences the double meaning implicit in what it did, viz. to have *taken* its *life*; it took life, but in doing so it really laid hold of death' (p. 220; translation adapted). It wanted to take hold of its life, but this entailed, literally, taking its life.

This dialectics of action is in a way analogous to that of 'sense certainty'. There, too, consciousness tried immediately to grasp individuality, the living immediacy, but instead it got only a lifeless universality in which all immediacy was lost. But in sense certainty consciousness operated from the standpoint of knowledge, where it discovered that 'in the beginning was the Word'. Here, consciousness turns away from words, which have proved incapable of coping with immediacy, to action: its formula shifts to 'In the beginning was the act', as the famous line in Faust's monologue goes. The act takes the place of the impossible, 'real' Word which is always lacking; yet the act does not succeed any better than the word, and its failure engenders a new dialectic.

This realization of infinite judgment is, on the other hand, the emergence of a relation, *Beziehung*, as Hegel says in the passage above. A relation is set up where no relation was possible. In infinite judgment, we had on the one side Spirit, conceptuality as such, the bearer of universality and necessity, and on the other side the Thing as a point of pure contingency, the positive existence of a purely negative point of individuality. Now in the case of action, the starting point is pure individuality and an attempt to realize it beyond conceptuality by reaching for immediacy, but the product of this realization is precisely the pure universality of the concept turned into being, necessity, fate ('a sheer leap into its antithesis', says Hegel; ibid.). The passage into thinghood required by action is thus at the same time a pure universalization of individuality, its leap into an empty universality. The contingency that pertained to the Thing as an immediate being is transformed by action into the existing concept governed by necessity. The Thing becomes the universal Thing in which contingency and necessity coincide.

Action enacts infinite judgment by reversing it: 'Spirit is a bone' can, on a formal level, be translated as 'universality is individuality' (that is, as the positive existence of the vanishing negative point of pure individuality), while action can be taken as an embodiment of the judgment 'individuality is universality': to make oneself a Thing is to make oneself universal.[19] The intended individuality is taken as the goal that dissipates itself into an empty universality as soon as it acquires a positive existence. By turning itself into a Thing, the subject does not escape the Concept (beyond grey theory, and so on), quite the opposite, it realizes the Concept.

The immediate leap from contingency to necessity indicates the nature of Hegelian necessity. *Necessity is not simply opposed to contingency, it realizes it.* Contingency appears to have vanished when transposed into being; it turned into necessity, but at the price of contaminating necessity: necessity arises as a universalized contingency, 'contingency in general'. In infinite judgment, the pure Concept had no relation with the contingent Thing, there was no common measure, but then through action the two coincided. Thus we have either a non-relation or an immediate coincidence. Hegel maintains, though, that what is at stake here is precisely the emergence of a relation. This relation can perhaps be best understood as what emerges in this reversal: the relation between the non-relation of two incommensurable entities and their coincidence; the relation between the two judgments, infinite judgment and its reversal, which makes it possible to think pure difference – the difference between the Concept and its radical other, the Concept and the Thing, the Concept and what cannot be conceptualized – as a conceptual difference.

The act thus realizes heterogeneity by suppressing it. It accomplishes the step from conceptuality into its other by at the same time realizing the Concept. It realizes the Concept as something radically opposed, as a dead universality, an alien entity in which the subject is lost, but yet as *a heterogeneity pertaining to the Concept and inherent in it.*

The act entailed the death of subjectivity, 'however, self-consciousness has *in itself* survived this loss; for this necessity or pure universality is *its own* essence. This reflection of consciousness into itself, the knowledge that necessity is *itself*, is a new form of consciousness' (p. 221). Consciousness had to perish in its act, it had to die as the 'for-itself' of pure individuality, while 'in-itself' it survived its own death. By this survival, the phenomenological experience can continue, it can pass into a new 'figure of consciousness', a point can be learned through one's own death.

The act failed, but in a double sense. First, it failed by realizing something other than what the subject wanted, it brought death rather than life. Second, it failed in a more fundamental sense; since the subject survived its death, it could include it as a negative moment in its own dialectic: in the alien lifelessness opposed to it, self-consciousness can envisage its own essence. A 'successful' act would coincide with the subject's suicide, the only way for the subject to turn itself effectively into a Thing, but a successful act would also be the end of the dialectic. Suicide, as the Lacanian dictum goes, is the only fully successful act. The operation failed, the patient survived.

So what happens to the subject who had to lose itself in the act by turning itself into a Thing, but nevertheless survived its own death? The act required a certain *suspension of the symbolic order*, which entailed the loss of subjectivity. In the next step (the next section bears the title 'The law of the heart and the frenzy of self-conceit') the subject will actually have to undergo the experience of 'psychosis', which is based precisely on an annihilation of the subject of the symbolic. The subject will have to measure up to insanity, 'frenzy', and what Hegel calls 'self-conceit' is a good clinical description of the states known as megalomania, 'inflation of the Ego', 'loss of reality', paranoia. Nevertheless, the suspension of the symbolic will eventually – after a few more turns – become integrated into the symbolic; what appeared as a limit of the symbolic will itself be symbolized, the symbolic will pose the non-symbolic and the non-symbolizable as its own moment. The subject will, through those experiences, become the subject of community, universal and individual in one, and the Thing will turn into the subject's own thing, 'the thing itself (*die Sache selbst*, rather unfortunately rendered as 'matter at hand' by A. V. Miller), 'the action of *all* and *everyone*' (p. 252), action and being in one. The necessary failure of action will there be seen as yielding a positive result, the production of 'the thing itself'.

So, finally, what about the contingency and heterogeneity that emerged in a pure form in infinite judgment? Are they sustained or suppressed? Or both in one and the same gesture? This is the place of Hegel's ultimate ambiguity, where the ways of interpretation part. Is Hegel in the last instance '*the thinker of the homogeneous*', consummating the reduction of the heterogeneous to the universal self-mediation of the Concept? Or is the only way adequately to get his point to take him as '*the thinker of the heterogeneous*' who draws a limit to conceptual universality, a limit that constitutes the Concept and keeps it inherently open to its Other? Is the *Aufhebung* – the Hegelian gesture par excellence, the gesture of simultaneous retaining and suppression – the locus of the Hegelian fallacy, the disavowal of an internal impossibility, or is it, on the contrary, the inscription of this impossibility into the heart of dialectic, sustaining it as its principle rather than disavowing it? Is this alternative exclusive, an 'either/or' where one has to take sides? Is it exhaustive?

The majority of contemporary and most influential interpreters – particularly in these postmodern times when avoidance of 'grand narratives' and terror of universality reign supreme – are firmly in favour of the first alternative, which they take for the most part as an indisputable and self-evident presupposition. This image is the accepted doxa of virtually all poststructuralist readings of Hegel (and also others, for example, Heidegger's), while Hegel's defenders, on the other hand, have difficulty disentangling themselves from the traditional framework, thus missing the best points in Hegel. Perhaps the simplest answer that I can provisionally propose here is to be sought in the very *irreducibility of this alternative*. An unambiguous solution in favour of 'the heterogeneous' (which can be brought about in a number of different ways) may seem radical and promising, but it has the nasty tendency of quickly sliding into triviality and loses the extreme tension of Hegelian operations. The conceptual formulas that are opposed to Hegel as radical alternatives and final exits from the Hegelian labyrinth tend to get rapidly entangled in very Hegelian paradoxes and end up in a 'homogenization' much more trivial than the one they tried to avoid. Sticking to the unsuppressable alternative and to the inherent ambiguity of the Hegelian enterprise may be the best way to 'salvage' heterogeneity. Focusing on heterogeneity, making it into a slogan, runs the risk of losing it; perhaps the only way to maintain it is to produce it 'laterally', as it were, in an oblique way, as a necessary by-product, by insisting on universal conceptuality rather than giving it up as a superseded blunder. The attempt to fix it as a 'concept' or a general slogan (Derrida's *la différance* and Lyotard's *le différend* are two possible ways of doing this) ends up dissipating it, necessarily running, by a roundabout way and against the best intentions of its proponents, into the Hegelian puzzles of conceptual determination. The solution loses what it was supposed to rescue. Maybe the irreducibility of Hegel's ambivalence gets much closer to the heterogeneous, which, in its 'lateral' emergence, keeps dissolving in the conceptual progression, but that progression nevertheless maintains it as its inner limit, an ambiguous condition that founds it. By dissipating the ambiguity, one loses both.

Notes

1. One of the very few readers who did not need to pinch himself was Slavoj Žižek, who maintained, rather, that nothing less could be expected of Hegel. See *The Sublime Object of Ideology* (London and New York: Verso 1989), pp. 207–12 and *For They Know Not What They Do* (London and New York: Verso 1991), pp. 90, 119. My reading here is very much indebted to his; but while he highlights just one point in Hegel, I try to situate this point in a larger perspective and I draw slightly different conclusions.
2. The best and most extensive account of phrenology, its goals and methods, its rise and fall, its background and influence, is to be found in Georges Lanteri-Laura, *Histoire de la phrenologie* (Paris: PUF 1970). Lanteri-Laura was a pupil of both Canguilhem and Hyppolite, so he was well aware of the theoretical dimensions of the matter and well acquainted with Hegel's treatment of it.

3. Georg Wilhelm Friedrich Hegel, *The Phenomenology of Spirit*, trans. A. V. Miller (Oxford: Oxford University Press 1977), p. 193. All further references will be to this translation and will be made in the body of the text.

4. Hegel, for example, even suggests a possible extension of phrenology: 'From this aspect phrenology is capable of still greater expansion; for in the first instance it seems to confine itself to connecting a bump [in the skull] with a property in the *same individual*, that is, the individual possesses both. But natural or everyday phrenology . . . already goes beyond this restriction. It not only declares that a cheating fellow has a bump as big as your fist behind his ear, but also asserts that, not the unfaithful wife herself, but the other conjugal party, has a bump on the forehead' (p. 203).

5. 'But organic Nature has no history; it falls from its universal, from life, directly into the singleness of existence, and the moments of simple determinateness, and the single organic life united in this actuality, produce the process of Becoming merely as a contingent movement . . . ' (pp. 178–9).

6. Karl Marx and Friedrich Engels, *Werke* (Berlin: Dietz Verlag 1956–69), vol. 23: p. 66.

7. Marx and Engels, *Werke*, vol. 23: p. 70.

8. 'Until then [the advent of modern science], no knowledge was conceived that would not participate in the fantasy of an inscription of the sexual link . . . Let us only consider, e.g., the terms active and passive which dominate everything that was thought about the relation between form and matter, a fundamental relation to which every step of Plato and then of Aristotle concerning the nature of things refers. It is visible, palpable, that these statements are supported only by the fantasy by which they have tried to supplement what can in no way be said, namely, the sexual relation' (Jacques Lacan, *Encore*, text established by Jacques-Alain Miller [Paris: Seuil 1975], p. 76).

9. See Marx and Engels, *Werke*, vol. 20: pp. 338–9.

10. On this issue, see Alasdair MacIntyre, 'Hegel on Faces and Skulls', in *Hegel: A Collection of Critical Essays*, ed. A. MacIntyre (Notre Dame: Notre Dame University Press 1972), pp. 219–36.

11. See my 'The Legacy of the Enlightenment: Foucault and Lacan', *New Formations*, 14 (Summer 1991), pp. 43–56 and 'I Shall Be with You on Your Wedding Night', *October*, 58 (Fall 1991), pp. 5–23.

12. The poem, which was not published during Heine's lifetime, was probably written in the 1830s. The rough translation is mine.

13. Heinrich Heine, *Werke* (Wiesbaden: R. Lowit n.d.), vol. II: pp. 466–7.

14. Sigmund Freud, *The Pelican Freud Library*, ed. Angela Richards (London: Harmondsworth), vol. 6: pp. 168–9.

15. . . . 'the object that cannot be swallowed, as it were, which remains stuck in the gullet of the signifier' (Jacques Lacan, *The Four Fundamental Concepts of Psychoanalysis*, trans. Alan Sheridan, text established by Jacques-Alain Miller [London: Hogarth Press and the Institute of Psycho-Analysis 1977], p. 270). It is no coincidence that Lacan uses the same metaphor of the bone for the object *a*. The subject of Reason, as $, is of course the subject of the signifier.

16. Jacques Lacan, *L'Envers de la psychanalyse*, text established by Jacques-Alain Miller (Paris: Seuil 1991).

17. For a more detailed account, see my 'Lord and Bondsman on the Couch', *American Journal of Semiotics*, vol. 9, nos 2–3 (1993), pp. 69–90.

18. Hegel here commits one of his famous misquotes, recalling from memory a few lines from *Faust*: 'It despises intellect and science/ the supreme gifts of man/ it has given itself to the devil/ and must perish' (p. 218). Leaving aside the fact that Hegel mixes up *Vernunft* (Reason) in the original with *Verstand* (intellect) in the very chapter on Reason, we are more astonished to find that the second part of the quotation says exactly the opposite of what Hegel says: '*Und hätt' er sich auch nicht dem Teufel übergeben/Er müßte doch zugrunde gehn!*' (And even if he had not given himself to the devil/ he would nevertheless have to perish!) Faust is doomed even before Mephisto appears. The spirit that pushed him beyond theory, from words to action, from knowledge to enjoyment, only found its

materialization in Mephisto. Goethe's original turns out to be more Hegelian than Hegel's version of it: the fall has already occurred, the Devil arrives too late; he has only to realize what was 'in-itself' already accomplished.

19. There are several instances where Hegel accomplishes the passage from one 'figure of consciousness' to another by the reversal of a judgment. Most memorably, the passage from the Greek aesthetic religion into Christianity as the revealed religion (in the chapter on 'Religion') hinges on such a reversal. The judgment 'the self is absolute Being' is the ultimate point of Antiquity, the point reached in the Greek comedy and its 'levity' (p. 453); the gesture of Christianity is to reverse this judgment: 'the Absolute is the Self' – the revealed religion is based on the subjectivation of the absolute beyond, its embodiment in a mortal individual. One could say: 'the birth of Christianity from the spirit of comedy.'

5 IS THERE A CAUSE OF THE SUBJECT?

SLAVOJ ŽIŽEK

In order to enliven our awareness of the full extent of the Freudian revolution, it is worthwhile, from time to time, to return to the basics, that is, to the most 'naive', elementary questions. How, for example, does psychoanalysis stand with regard to the traditional couple *Naturwissenschaften* and *Geisteswissenschaften*, that is, causal determinism and hermeneutics? Is psychoanalysis simply the most radical version of psychic determinism; is Freud a 'biologist of the mind', does he denounce mind itself as the plaything of unconscious determinism and, consequently, its freedom as an illusion? Or, on the contrary, is psychoanalysis an 'in-depth hermeneutics', which opens up a new domain for the analysis of meaning by demonstrating how, even in the case of (what appears as) purely physiological, corporeal disturbances, we are still dealing with a dialectic of meaning, with the subject's distorted communication with himself and his Other? The first thing to be noted here is that this duality is reflected in the very Freudian theoretical edifice, in the guise of the duality of the metapsychological *theory of drives* (oral, anal, phallic stages, and so on), which relies on the physicalist-biologist metaphorics of 'mechanisms', 'energy' and 'stages', and *interpretations* (of dreams, jokes, the psychopathology of everyday life, symptoms . . .), which remain thoroughly within the domain of meaning.

Does this duality prove that Freud did not resolve the antagonism of causality and sense? Is it possible to bring both sides into a 'unified theory of the Freudian field', to evoke the suitable Einsteinian formulation of J.-A. Miller? Clearly, no solution is to be found in the pseudo-dialectical 'synthesis' of both sides or in offering one side as the key to the other. We can no more conceive the notion of a causal determinism of the psyche as the paradigmatic case of objectivist 'reification', of a positivist misrecognition of the proper subjective dialectic of meaning, than we can reduce the domain of meaning to an illusory self-experience regulated by hidden causal mechanisms. What if, however, the full extent of the Freudian revolution is to be sought in the way it undermines the very opposition between hermeneutics and explanation, sense and causality? Up to now, the explicit conception of psychoanalysis as a science that puts these oppositions into question has come from only two sources: the Frankfurt School and Jacques Lacan.

Contradiction as the Index of Theoretical Truth

The Frankfurt School undermines the opposition between hermeneutics and causal determinism by way of bringing to light the historical 'mediation' of what Freud conceived of as 'nature', as biological or at least philogenetical heritage. Psychic 'nature' is the result of a historical process which because of the alienated character of history, assumes the 'reified', 'naturalized' form of its opposite, of a pre-historical, given state of things:

> The 'sub-individual and pre-individual factors' that define the individual belong to the realm of the archaic and biological; but it is not a question of pure nature. Rather it is *second nature*: history that has hardened into nature. The distinction between nature and second nature if unfamiliar to most social thought is vital to critical theory. What is second nature to the individual is accumulated and sedimented history. It is history so long unliberated – history so long monotonously oppressive – that it congeals. Second nature is not simply nature or history, but frozen history that surfaces as nature.[1]

Such 'historicizing' of the Freudian theoretical edifice has nothing in common with focusing on socio-cultural problems, or on the ego's moral and emotional conflicts: rather it stands squarely against the ego-psycho-logical gesture of 'domesticating' the unconscious, that is, of attenuating the fundamental and irresolvable tension between the ego, which is structured according to social norms, and unconscious drives, which are opposed to the ego – the very tension that confers on Freud's theory its critical potential. In an alienated society, the domain of 'culture' is founded on the violent exclusion ('repression') of man's libidinal kernel which then assumes the form of a quasi-'nature'. This 'second nature' is the petrified evidence of the price paid for 'cultural progress', the barbarity inherent to 'culture' itself.

Although one finds in Freud some places which point towards a historical 'mediation' of the dynamic of the drives, his theoretical position none the less implies a notion of the drives as objective determinations of psychic life. According to Adorno, this 'naturalistic' notion introduces into the Freudian edifice an irresolvable contradiction: on the one hand, the entire development of civilization is condemned, at least implicitly, for repressing drive potentials in the service of social relations of domination and exploitation; on the other hand, repression as the renunciation of the satisfaction of drives is conceived as the necessary and insurmountable condition of the emergence of 'higher' human activities, that is to say, of culture. One intra-theoretical consequence of this contradiction is the impossibility of distinguishing in a theoretically relevant way between the *repression* of a drive and its *sublimation*: every attempt to draw a clear line of demarcation between these two concepts functions as an inapposite auxiliary construction. This theoretical failure points towards a social reality in which every sublimation (every psychic act that does not aim at the immediate satisfaction of a drive) is necessarily affected by the stigma of pathological or at least pathogenic repression. There is thus a radical and constitutive *indecision* which pertains to the fundamental intention of psycho-analytical theory and practice: it is split between the 'liberating' gesture of setting free repressed libidinal potential and the 'resigned conservatism' of accepting repression as the necessary price for the progress of civilization.

The same impasse repeats itself at the level of treatment: in its beginnings, psychoanalysis, inspired by the passion of radical Enlightenment, demanded the demolition of every agency of authoritarian control over the unconscious. However, with the topical differentiation between id, ego and superego, analytical treatment increasingly aimed not to demolish the superego, but to establish the 'harmony' of the three agencies; analysts introduced the auxiliary distinction between the 'neurotic, compulsive' superego and the 'sane', salutary superego – pure theoretical nonsense, since the superego is defined by its 'compulsive' nature. In Freud himself, the superego already emerges as an auxiliary construction whose function is to resolve the contradictory roles of the ego. The ego stands for the agency of consciousness and rational control which mediates between intrapsychic forces and external reality: it restrains the drives in the name of reality. However, this 'reality' – alienated social actuality – forces upon individuals renunciations which they cannot accept in a rational, conscious way. The ego, as the representative of reality, thus paradoxically operates in support of unconscious, irrational prohibitions. In short, we necessarily become stuck in a contradiction according to which 'the ego – inasmuch as it stands for consciousness – must be the opposite of repression, yet simultaneously – inasmuch as it is itself unconscious – it must be the agency of repression'.[2] For this reason, all the postulates about the 'strong ego' embraced by the revisionists remain deeply ambiguous: the two operations of the ego (consciousness and repression) entwine inextricably, so that the 'cathartic' method of early psychoanalysis, prompted by the demand to tear down all barriers of repression, inevitably winds up tearing down the ego itself, that is to say disintegrating the 'defense mechanisms at work in resistances, without which it would be impossible to sustain the identity of the ego as the opposition to the multiple urges of the drives';[3] on the other hand, any demand to 'strengthen the ego' entails an even stronger repression. Psychoanalysis escapes this deadlock by way of a compromise-formation, a 'practico-therapeutical absurdity according to which defense mechanisms must be in turn demolished and strengthened':[4] in the case of neuroses, where the superego is too strong and the ego not strong enough to provide the minimal satisfaction of drives, the resistance of the superego must be broken, whereas in the case of psychoses where the superego, the agency of social normality, is too weak, it must be reinforced. The goal of psychoanalysis and its contradictory character thereby reproduce a fundamental social antagonism: the tension between the individual's urges and the demands of society.

At this point, we must be careful not to miss the epistemological and practical wagers at stake in Adorno: in no way does he aim at 'resolving' or 'abolishing' this contradiction by way of some conceptual 'clarification', but, on the contrary, he aims at *conceiving of this contradiction as an immediate index of the 'contradiction', that is, the antagonism, that pertains to social reality itself*, in which every development of 'superior' ('spiritual') capacities is paid for by the 'repression' of drives in the service of social domination, in which the underside of every 'sublimation' (redirection of libidinal energy towards 'higher', non-sexual goals) is an indelibly 'barbaric', violent oppression. What first appears as Freud's 'theoretical insufficiency' or 'conceptual imprecision', possesses an inherent cognitive value, since it marks the very point at which his theory touches the truth. And it is precisely this unbearable 'contradiction' that the various psychoanalytical 'revisionisms' try to avoid, to soften its sting in the name of a 'culturalism' that advocates the possibility of a non-repressive 'sublimation', of a 'development of human creative potentials' not paid for by the mute suffering articulated in the formations of the unconscious. One thus constructs a consistent and homogeneous theoretical edifice, but what gets lost is simply the truth of the Freudian discovery. Critical theory, on the contrary,

values Freud as a non-ideological thinker and theoretician of contradictions –
contradictions which his successors sought to escape and mask. In this he was a
'classic' bourgeois thinker, while the revisionists were 'classic' ideologues. 'The
greatness of Freud,' wrote Adorno, 'consists in that, like all great bourgeois thinkers,
he left standing undissolved such contradictions and disdained the assertion of
pretended harmony where the thing itself is contradictory. He revealed the
antagonistic character of the social reality.'[5]

Those who align the Frankfurt School with 'Freudo-Marxism' encounter
here their first surprise: from the outset, Adorno denounces the failure and
the inherent theoretical falsity of 'Freudo-Marxist' attempts to provide a
common language for historical materialism and psychoanalysis, i.e. a bridge
between objective social relations and the concrete suffering of the individual.
This failure cannot be 'thought away' by the immanent theoretical procedure
of 'surmounting' the 'partial' character of both psychoanalysis and historical
materialism through some kind of 'larger synthesis', since it registers the
'actual conflict between the Particular and Universal',[6] between the individual's
self-experience and the objective social totality.

The theoretical 'regression' of revisionism emerges most clearly in the
relationship posited between theory and therapy. By putting theory at the
service of therapy, revisionism obliterates their dialectical tension: in an
alienated society, therapy is ultimately destined to fail, and the reasons for this
failure are provided by theory itself. Therapeutical 'success' amounts to the
'normalization' of the patient, his adaptation to the 'normal' functioning of
existing society, whereas the crucial achievement of psychoanalytical theory is
precisely its explanation of how 'mental illness' results from the very structure
of the existing social order; that is to say, individual 'madness' is based on a
certain 'discontent' endemic to civilization as such. The subordination of
theory to therapy thus requires the loss of the critical dimension of
psychoanalysis:

> Psychoanalysis as individual therapy necessarily participates *within* the realm of social
> unfreedom, while psychoanalysis as theory is free to transcend and criticize this same
> realm. To take up only the first moment, psychoanalysis as therapy, is to blunt
> psychoanalysis as a critique of civilization, turning it into an instrument of individual
> adjustment and resignation. . . . *Psychoanalysis is a theory of an unfree society that
> necessitates psychoanalysis as a therapy.*[7]

We thus obtain what amounts to a social-critical version of Freud's thesis on
psychoanalysis as an 'impossible profession': therapy can only succeed in a
society that has no need of it, that is, one that does not produce 'mental
alienation' – or, to quote Freud: 'Psychoanalysis meets the optimum of

favorable conditions where its practice is not needed, i.e., among the healthy.'[8] Here we have a special type of 'failed encounter': psychoanalytic therapy is necessary where it is not possible and is only possible where it is no longer necessary.

'Repressive desublimation'

The logic of this 'failed encounter' bears witness to the Frankfurt School's conception of psychoanalysis as a 'negative' theory: a theory of self-alienated, divided individuals, which implies as its inherent practical goal the achievement of a 'disalienated' condition in which individuals are undivided, no longer dominated by the alienated psychic substance (the 'unconscious'), a condition thereby rendering psychoanalysis itself superfluous. Freud himself, however, continued to conceive of his own theory as 'positive', as describing the unalterable condition of civilization. Because of this limitation, that is to say, because he comprehended 'repressive sublimation' (traumatic repression *qua* the underside of sublimation) as an anthropological constant, Freud could not foresee the unexpected, paradoxical condition actualized in our century: that of 'repressive desublimation', characteristic of 'post-liberal' societies in which 'the triumphant archaic urges, the victory of the Id over the Ego, live in harmony with the triumph of the society over the individual'.[9]

The ego's relative autonomy was based on its role as the mediator between the id (the non-sublimated life-substance of the drives) and the superego (the agency of social 'repression', the representative of the demands of society). 'Repressive desublimation' succeeds in getting rid of this autonomous, mediating agency of 'synthesis' which is the ego: through such a 'desublimation', the ego loses its relative autonomy and regresses towards the unconscious. However, this 'regressive', compulsive, blind, 'automatic' behaviour, which bears all the signs of the id, far from liberating us from the pressures of the existing social order, adheres perfectly to the demands of the superego and is therefore already enlisted in the service of the social order. As a consequence, the forces of social 'repression' exert a direct control over the drives. The bourgeois liberal subject represses his unconscious urges by means of internalized prohibitions and, as a result, his self-control enables him to get hold of his libidinal 'spontaneity'. In post-liberal societies, however, the agency of social repression no longer acts in the guise of an internalized law or prohibition which requires renunciation and self-control; instead, it assumes the form of a hypnotic agency which imposes the attitude of 'yielding to temptation', that is, its injunction amounts to a command: 'Enjoy yourself!' An idiotic enjoyment is dictated by the social environs which includes the

Anglo-American psychoanalyst, whose main goal is to render the patient capable of 'normal', 'healthy' pleasures. Society requires us to *fall asleep* into a hypnotic trance, usually under the guise of just the opposite command: 'The Nazi battle cry of "Germany awake" hides its very opposite.'[10] Adorno interprets the formation of the 'masses' in terms of this 'regression' of the ego towards an automatic and compulsive behaviour:

> To be sure, this process has a psychological dimension, but it also indicates a growing tendency towards the abolition of psychological motivation in the old, liberalistic sense. Such motivation is systematically controlled and absorbed by social mechanisms which are directed from above. When the leaders become conscious of mass psychology and take it into their own hands, it ceases to exist in a certain sense. This potentiality is contained in the basic construct of psychoanalysis inasmuch as for Freud the concept of psychology is essentially a negative one. He defines the realm of psychology by the supremacy of the unconscious and postulates that what is id should become ego.[11] The emancipation of man from the heteronomous rule of his unconscious would be tantamount to the abolition of his 'psychology'. Fascism furthers this abolition in the opposite sense through the perpetuation of dependence instead of the realization of potential freedom, through expropriation of the unconscious by social control instead of making the subjects conscious of their unconscious. For, while psychology always denotes some bondage of the individual, it also presupposes freedom in the sense of a certain self-sufficiency and autonomy of the individual. It is not accidental that the nineteenth century was the great era of psychological thought. In a thoroughly reified society, in which there are virtually no direct relationships between men, and in which each person has been reduced to a social atom, to a mere function of collectivity, the psychological processes, though they still persist in each individual, have ceased to appear as the determining forces of the social process. Thus, the psychology of the individual has lost what Hegel would have called substance. It is perhaps the greatest merit of Freud's book [*Group Psychology and the Analysis of the Ego*] that though he restricted himself to the field of individual psychology and wisely abstained from introducing sociological factors from outside, he nevertheless reached the turning point where psychology abdicates. The psychological 'impoverishment' of the subject that 'surrendered itself to the object' which 'it has substituted for its most important constituent', that is, the superego, anticipates almost with clairvoyance the post-psychological de-individualized social atoms which form the fascist collectivities. In these social atoms the psychological dynamics of group formation have overreached themselves and are no longer a reality. The category of 'phoniness' applies to the leaders as well as to the act of identification on the part of the masses and their supposed frenzy and hysteria. Just as little as people believe in the depth of their hearts that the Jews are the devil, do they completely believe in their leader. They do not really identify themselves with him but act this identification, perform their own enthusiasm, and thus participate in their leader's performance. It is through this performance that they strike a balance between their continuously mobilized instinctual urges

and the historical stage of enlightenment they have reached, and which cannot be revoked arbitrarily. It is probably the suspicion of this fictitiousness and their own 'group psychology' which makes fascist crowds so merciless and unapproachable. If they would stop to reason for a second, the whole performance would go to pieces, and they would be left to panic.[12]

This long passage offers a condensed version of the entire critical appropriation of psychoanalysis by the Frankfurt School. The notion of psychology at work in psychoanalysis is ultimately a negative one: the domain of the 'psychological' comprises all those factors which dominate the individual's 'inner life' behind his back, in the guise of an 'irrational', heteronomous force eluding his conscious control. Consequently, the aim of the psychoanalytical process is to make plain that 'what is id should become ego', that is, 'man should be emancipated from the heteronomous rule of his unconscious'. Such a free, autonomous subject would be *stricto sensu* a *subject without psychology* – in other words, psychoanalysis aims to 'depsychologize' the subject. It is against this background that we should measure the impact of 'repressive desublimation': in it, psychology is also surpassed, since subjects are deprived of a 'psychological' dimension in the sense of a wealth of 'natural needs', of spontaneous libidinal motivations. Psychology is not, however, surpassed here through a liberating reflection that enables the subject to appropriate his repressed content, but 'in the opposite sense': it is surpassed through a direct 'socialization' of the unconscious brought about by the 'shortcircuit' between the id and the superego at the expense of the ego. The psychological dimension, i.e. the libidinal life-substance, is thereby 'sublated' [*aufgehoben*] in the strict Hegelian sense: it is maintained, but deprived of its immediate character and thoroughly 'mediated', manipulated by the mechanisms of social domination. As an example, let us take again the formation of the 'masses': in a first approach, we encounter here an exemplary case of the 'regression' of the autonomous ego, which is suddenly seized by some force beyond its control and yields to its heteronomous, hypnotic power. However, this appearance of 'spontaneity', of the explosion of a primordial irrational force that can be grasped only via a psychological analysis, should in no way obfuscate the crucial fact that the contemporary 'masses' are already an artificial formation, the result of an 'administered', directed process – in short, they are a 'post-psychological' phenomenon. The 'spontaneity', the 'fanaticism', the 'mass hysteria' are all ultimately fake. The general conclusion to be drawn from this account is that the 'object of psychoanalysis', its central topic, is a historically delimited entity, the 'monadological, relatively autonomous, individual, as the stage of the conflict between the drives and their prohibition'[13] – in short, the liberal bourgeois subject. The pre-bourgeois universe, in which the individual is plunged into the social substance, does not yet know this conflict; the contemporary, wholly socialized 'administered world' does not know it anymore:

> The contemporary types are those in whom any Ego is absent; consequently, they do not act unconsciously in the proper meaning of this term, but simply mirror objective features. Together, they participate in this senseless ritual, following the compulsive rhythm of repetition, and grow poor affectively: the demolition of the Ego strengthens narcissism and its collective derivations.[14]

The last great act to be accomplished by psychoanalysis is therefore to 'uncover the destructive forces which, in the midst of the destructive Universal, are at work in the Particular itself'.[15] Psychoanalysis must discern those subjective mechanisms (collective narcissism, and so on) which, in accordance with social coercion, work to demolish the 'monadological, relatively autonomous individual' as the proper object of psychoanalysis. In other words, the last act of psychoanalytical theory is to articulate the conditions of its own obsolescence.

Something is amiss in this otherwise ingenious conception of 'repressive desublimation'. Adorno is compelled again and again to reduce totalitarian 'depsychologization' to an attitude of conscious, or at least preconscious, 'selfish calculation' (manipulation, conformist adaptation), which is allegedly concealed beneath the façade of irrational seizure. This reduction has radical consequences for his approach to fascist ideology: Adorno refused to treat fascism as an ideology in the proper sense of the term, that is, as 'rational legitimization of the existing order'. The so-called 'fascist ideology' no longer possesses the coherence of a rational construct that calls for conceptual analysis and ideologico-critical refutation. Thus, 'fascist ideology' is not taken seriously even by its promoters; its status is purely instrumental and ultimately relies on external coercion. Fascism no longer functions as a 'lie necessarily experienced as truth' – as a true ideology is.[16] But is the reduction of 'fascist ideology' to conscious manipulation or conformist adaptation the only way to comprehend the depsychologization at work in totalitarian ideological edifices? Lacan opens up the possibility of a different approach when, apropos of G. G. de Clérambault's description of the phenomenon of psychosis, he insists that we must always bear in mind its

> *ideationally neutral* nature, which in [Clérambault's] language means that it's in total discord with the subject's mental state, that no mechanism of the affects adequately explains it, and which in ours means that it's structural . . . [T]he nucleus of psychosis

has to be linked to a relationship between the subject and the signifier in its most formal dimension, in its dimension as a pure signifier and . . . everything constructed around this consists only of affective reactions to the primary phenomenon, the relationship to the signifier.[17]

In this perspective, 'depsychologization' means that the subject is confronted with an 'inert' signifying chain, one that does not seize him performatively, does not affect his subjective position of enunciation: towards this chain, the subject maintains a 'relation of exteriority'.[18] It is this very exteriority which, according to Lacan, defines the status of the superego: the superego is a law that is not integrated into the subject's symbolic universe, in so far as it functions as an incomprehensible, nonsensical, traumatic injunction, incommensurable with the psychological wealth of the subject's affective attitudes, and bears witness to a kind of 'malevolent neutrality' directed at the subject, indifferent to his empathies and fears. At this precise point, as the subject confronts the 'agency of the letter' in its original and radical *exteriority*, the signifier's nonsense in its purest, he encounters the superegotistic command 'Enjoy!' which addresses the most *intimate* kernel of his being. Suffice it to recall the unfortunate Schreber, who was constantly bombarded by divine 'voices' ordering him to enjoy (that is to change into a woman and copulate with God): the crucial feature of Schreber's God is that he is *totally unable to understand us, living humans*, or, to quote Schreber himself: '*in accordance with the Order of Things, God really knew nothing about living men* and did not need to know'.[19] This radical incommensurability between the psychotic God and man's inner life (in contrast to the 'normal' God who understands us better than we understand ourselves, that is, the God for whom 'our heart holds no secrets') is strictly correlative to his status as an agency that imposes enjoyment. In the domain of literature, the supreme example of this *shortcircuit between Law and enjoyment* is the obscene agency of the Law in Kafka's great novels (which for that very reason announces the arrival of the totalitarian libidinal economy).[20] Therein consists the key to 'repressive desublimation', to this 'perverse reconciliation of the id and the superego at the expense of the ego': '*repressive desublimation' is a way – the only way open within the horizon of the Frankfurt School – to say that in 'totalitarianism' social Law assumes the features of a superegoic injunction.*

It is precisely the lack of an explicit concept of the superego which underlies Adorno's continuous reduction of the 'depsychologization' of the fascist crowd to an effect of conscious manipulation. This insufficiency originates with Adorno's starting point, with his conception of psychoanalysis as a 'psychological' theory, that is, a theory whose object is the psychological individual. As soon as one accepts this notion, one cannot avoid concluding that the only thing psychoanalysis can do when faced with the passage from the 'psycho-logical' individual of liberal bourgeois society to the 'post-psychological' individual of 'totalitarian' society is to discern the contours of the process that leads to the demolition of its own object. Here, however, Lacan's 'return to Freud' based on the key role of the 'agency of the letter in the unconscious' – in other words, on the strictly *non-psychological* character of the unconscious – inverts the entire perspective: at the point where, according to Adorno, psychoanalysis reaches its limit and witnesses the demolition of its 'object' (the psychological individual), *at this very point the 'agency of the letter' emerges as such in 'historical reality' itself,* in the guise of the superego imperative at work in 'totalitarian' discourse.

This Lacanian inversion of Adorno's approach enables us to account for the fascist 'aestheticization of the political': the foregrounded 'theatricality' of fascist ideological rituals reveals how fascism 'feigns', 'stages' the performative power of political discourse, transposing it into the modality of as-if. All the emphasis on the 'leader' and his 'escort', on 'mission' and the 'spirit of sacrifice', should not deceive us – such exhaltations ultimately amount to a theatrical *simulation* of the pre-bourgeois discourse of the Master. Adorno is quite justified in highlighting this moment of 'simulation'. His error lies elsewhere: in perceiving this simulation as an effect of external coercion and/or the pursuit of material gains (*'cui bono?'*) – as if the mask of the 'totalitarian' ideological discourse conceals a 'normal', 'commonsensical' individual, that is, the good old 'utilitarian', 'egoistic' subject of bourgeois individualism who simply feigns being carried away by 'totalitarian' ideology out of fear or hope of material profit. On the contrary, one must insist on the thoroughly 'serious' character of this feigning: it involves the 'non-integration of the subject into the register of the signifier', the 'external imitation' of the signifying game akin to the so-called *as if* phenomena characteristic of proto-psychotic states.[21] More to the point, this 'inner distance' which separates the subject from the 'totalitarian' discourse does not enable the subject to 'elude the madness' of the 'totalitarian' ideological spectacle, but is the very factor which renders the subject 'mad'. Now and then, Adorno himself has a presentiment of this, as, for example, when he implies that the subject 'beneath the mask' who 'feigns' his captivation must already be 'mad', 'hollow'. It is in order to escape this void that the subject is condemned to take refuge in the ceaseless ideological spectacle – if the 'show' were to stop for a moment, his entire universe would disintegrate.[22] In other words, 'madness' does not turn on effectively believing in the Jewish plot, in the charisma of the leader, and so on – such beliefs (in so far as they are repressed, i.e. the unacknowledged fantasy-support of our universe of signification) form a constituent part of our ideological 'normality'.

'Madness' emerges rather, in the *absence* of such engaging beliefs, in the fact that 'in the depth of their hearts, people *do not* believe that the Jews are the devil'. In short: madness emerges through the subject's 'simulation' and 'external imitation' of such beliefs; it thrives in that 'inner distance' which the subject maintains towards the ideological discourse that constitutes his social-symbolic network.

Habermas: Psychoanalysis as Self-reflection

'Repressive desublimation' thus plays the role of the 'symptomatic' element, that which makes it possible for us to discern the fundamental antinomy in the Frankfurt School's appropriation of psychoanalysis. On the one hand, the notion of 'repressive desublimation' distils the critical attitude of the Frank-furt School towards Freud by highlighting what had to remain 'unthinkable' for Freud, namely the uncanny 'reconciliation' of the id and the superego in 'totalitarian' societies. On the other hand, the self-cancelling, structurally ambiguous nature of this notion betrays the extent to which 'repressive desublimation' is a 'pseudo-concept', which signals the need to re-articulate the entire theoretical field. How was this extreme tension resolved in further developments of the Frankfurt School? It was Jürgen Habermas who carried out the radical break in the relationship between the Frankfurt School and psychoanalysis. He begins by asking: 'What goes on in the psychoanalytical process?' That is to say, he rehabilitates the cure as the cornerstone of psychoanalysis's theoretical edifice, in clear contrast to Adorno and Marcuse. This shift of accent hints at a more fundamental break: Adorno and Marcuse accept psychoanalytical theory as it is, since, in the dialectical antagonism between theory and therapy, the truth for them resides on the side of the theory. But according to Habermas, Freud's theory lagged behind psychoana-lytical practice, mainly because Freud misrecognized the crucial dimension of psychoanalytical treatment: the self-reflective power of language. Con-sequently, Habermas accomplishes his own 'return to Freud' by reinterpreting Freud's entire theoretical framework from the perspective of language. His starting point is Dilthey's division of the 'elementary forms of comprehension' into linguistic elements, action patterns and expressions:

> In the normal case, these three categories of expressions are complementary, so that linguistic expressions 'fit' interactions and both language and action 'fit' experiential expressions; of course, their integration is imperfect, which makes possible the latitude necessary for indirect communications. In the limiting case, however, a language game can disintegrate to the point where the three categories of

expressions no longer agree. Then actions and non-verbal expressions belie what is expressly stated . . . The acting subject himself cannot observe the discrepancy; or, if he observes it, he cannot understand it, because he both expresses and misunderstands himself in this discrepancy. His self-understanding must keep to what is consciously intended, to linguistic expression – or at least to what can be verbalized.[23]

If, by means of an ironic tone or grimace, we let it be known that we do not take seriously what we are asserting, the gap between the content of our utterance and our true intention is still 'normal'; if, however, the refutation of what we are saying intervenes 'behind our back', in the guise of a 'spontaneous', unintended slip of the tongue, then we encounter a pathological case. The criterion of 'normality' thus resides in the unity of (conscious) intentions-of-signification that governs all three forms of expression. More precisely, since our conscious intention coincides with what can be expressed in language, 'normality' resides in the traductibility of all our motives into intentions that can be expressed in public, intersubjectively recognized language. What causes pathological discrepancies is repressed desire: excluded from public communication, it finds an outlet in compulsive gestures and acts, as well as in distorted, 'private' usages of language. Starting from these discrepancies, Habermas ultimately arrives at the ideological falsity of every hermeneutics that limits itself to the (conscious) intention-of-signification, abandoning errors and deformations of the interpreted text to philology. What hermeneutics cannot admit is that it is not sufficient to repair the mutilations and restore the 'original' text to its integrity, since 'mutilations have meaning as *such*': 'The omissions and distortions that it [psychoanalytic interpretation] rectifies have a systematic role and function. For the symbolic structures that psychoanalysis seeks to comprehend are corrupted by the impact of *internal conditions*.'[24]

The standard hermeneutical attitude thus seems radically subverted: the true position of the speaking subject emerges precisely in the gaps of his self-comprehension, in the apparently 'meaningless' distortions of his text. But the reach of this subversion is strictly limited: Dilthey's standard model of the unity of language, action patterns and expressions retains its validity – not as a description of the *actual* functioning of communicative activities, but as a *practical-critical paradigm*, the norm by which we measure the 'pathology' of our actual communication. Dilthey's error was to use as his model for describing actual structures of signification that model which could be used only under conditions of a 'non-repressive' society, thus deafening himself to what is repressed by the actual discourse:

In the methodically rigorous sense, 'wrong' behaviour means *every deviation from the model of the language game of communicative action*, in which motives of action and linguistically expressed intentions coincide. In this model, split-off symbols and the need dispositions connected with them are not allowed. It is assumed either that they do not exist or, if they do, that they are without consequences on the level of public communication, habitual interaction, and observable expression. This model, however, could be generally applicable only under the conditions of a non-repressive society. Therefore deviations from it are the normal case under all known social conditions.[25]

This passage already suggests the link established by Habermas between psychoanalysis and the critique of ideology. What Freud baptized the superego emerges as the intra-psychic prolongation of social authority, that is, the pattern of knowing and desiring, of object-choices, and so on, sanctioned by society. In so far as this pattern is 'internalized' by the subject, the motives which come into conflict with it are 'repressed'. Excommunicated from the domain of public communication, they assume a 'reified' existence in the guise of the id, of an alien power in which the subject does not recognize himself. This defence of the subject against his own illicit motivations does not have the character of conscious self-control but is itself unconscious; on that account, the superego resembles the id, since the symbols of the superego are 'sacralized', exempted from argumentative, rational communication. This conception involves an entire 'pedagogy', a logic of the ego's development up to its 'maturity'. In the (ontogenetically as well as philogenetically) inferior stages of its development, the ego is not capable of controlling its drives in a rational, conscious way, so only an 'irrational'/'traumatic' agency of prohibition can induce it to renounce unrealizable surplus. With the gradual development of productive forces and of forms of symbolic communication, the rational approach to renunciation becomes possible, that is, the subject can consciously undertake the necessary sacrifices.

Habermas's principal reproach to Freud is not that he set the barrier of repression 'too low', making it into a kind of anthropological constant instead of historicizing it; Habermas's reproach concerns instead the epistemological status of Freud's theory: the conceptual framework by means of which Freud endeavours to reflect his practice falls short of this practice. Psycho-analytical theory confers on the ego the function of accommodating intel-ligently to reality and of regulating the drives. What is missing here is the specific act whose negative is the mechanism of defence: *self-reflection*. Psycho-analysis is neither a *comprehension* of the hidden meaning of symptoms nor an *explanation* of the causal chain which brought about the symptom: the act of self-reflection dialectically transcends this very duality of comprehension and causal explanation. How? When libidinal motivations are prevented from emerging as conscious intentions, they assume the features of pseudo-natural causes, i.e. of the id *qua* blind force dominating the subject behind his back. The id penetrates the texture of everyday language by distorting grammar and confounding the proper use of public language through false semantic identifications: in symptoms, the subject speaks a kind of 'private language' incomprehensible to his conscious ego. In other words, symptoms are fragments of the public text chained to the symbols of illicit desires which have been excluded from public communication:

> At the level of the public text, the suppressed symbol is objectively understandable through rules *resulting* from contingent circumstances of the individual's life history, but not connected with it according to intersubjectively *recognized* rules. That is why the symptomatic concealment of meaning and corresponding disturbance of interaction cannot at first be understood either by others or by the subject himself.[26]

Psychoanalytic interpretation unearths the idiosyncratic link between the fragments of public text and the symbols of illicit libidinal motivations; it retranslates these motivations into the language of intersubjective communication. The final stage of the psychoanalytic cure is reached when the subject recognizes himself, his own motivations, in the censured chapters of his self-expression and is able to narrate the totality of his life-history. In a first approach, psychoanalysis thus proceeds along the path of causal explanation: it brings to light the causal chain which, unbeknown to the subject, produced the symptom. However – and herein resides the proper notion of self-reflection – *this very explanation of the causal chain cancels its efficacy.* An adequate interpretation does not only lead to 'true knowledge' of the symptom; it simultaneously involves the symptom's dissolution and thereby the 'reconciliation' of the subject with himself – the act of knowing is in itself an act of liberation from unconscious coercion. Consequently, Habermas can conceive of the unconscious according to the Hegelian model of self-alienation: in the unconscious, the communication of the subject with himself is interrupted, and the psychoanalytic cure amounts to a reconciliation of the subject with the id, his alienated substance, his misrecognized self-objectivization; that is, the cure amounts to the subject's deciphering of the symptom as an expression of his own unacknowledged motivations: 'For the insight to which analysis is to lead is indeed only this: that the I of the patient recognize itself in its other, represented by its illness, as in *its own* alienated *self* and identify with it.'[27]

One must avoid yielding too readily, however, to this apparent 'Hegelianism': already at work behind it is a kind of 'return to Kant'. The coincidence of true motivations with expressed meaning and the concomitant translation of all motivations into the language of public communication play the part of the Kantian regulative Idea approached in an asymptotic movement. The repression of the symbols of illicit desires, the subject's interrupted communication with himself, the falsity of the ideological universal which conceals a particular interest – all these occur because of *empirical* reasons which act *from outside* on the framework of language. To put it in Hegelian terms, the necessity of distortion is not inscribed in the very concept of communication but is due to the actual contingent circumstances of labour and domination that prevent the realization of the ideal – the relations of power and violence are not inherent to language.[28]

By obliterating the 'material weight' of the historical real, by reducing it to a contingent force which from outside affects the neutral transcendental grid of language and prevents its 'normal' functioning, Habermas disfigures the psychoanalytical interpretive process. What gets lost as a result is Freud's distinction between the latent dream-thought and unconscious desire, that is, his insistence on the fact that 'a normal train of thought' – normal and as such expressible in the language of public communication – 'is only submitted to the abnormal psychical treatment of the sort we have been describing' – to the dream-work – 'if an unconscious wish, derived from infancy and in a state of repression, has been transferred onto it'.[29] Habermas reduces the work of interpretation to retranslating the 'latent dream-thought' into the intersubjectively recognized language of public communication, without accounting for the fact that this thought is 'pulled' into the unconscious only if some already unconscious wish finds an echo in it by means of a kind of transferential 'shortcircuit'. And, as Freud put it, this already unconscious wish is 'primordially repressed': it constitutes a 'traumatic kernel' which does not have an 'original' in the language of intersubjective communication and, for that very reason, *forever, constitutively, resists symbolization, that is (re)translation into the language of intersubjective communication.* Here we confront the incommensurability between hermeneutics (as 'deep' as it may be) and psychoanalytic interpretation: Habermas can assert that distortions have meaning as such – what remains unthinkable for him is that *meaning as such results from a certain distortion*, that is, that the emergence of meaning is based on a disavowal of some 'primordially repressed' traumatic kernel.

This traumatic kernel, this remainder which resists subjectivization-symbolization, is *stricto sensu* the *cause* of the subject. And it is with regard to this kernel that the unbridgeable gap separating Habermas from Adorno appears at its clearest: Habermas resuscitates the pseudo-Hegelian model of the subject's appropriation of the alienated-reified substantial content, whereas Adorno's late motif of the 'preponderance of the object' calls into question this very model by evoking a 'decentring' which, far from bearing witness to the subject's alienation, outlines the dimension of possible 'reconciliation'. True, Habermas does resolve the tension detectable in late Adorno; however, he does so not by 'bringing to the concept' the 'unthought' of Adorno, but by changing the entire problematic so as simply to render invisible, flatten out, the tension at work in Adorno's thinking. How, then, does *Lacan* manage to accomplish what Habermas failed to do, expose the unthought of Adorno's conceptualization (since, if we are to throw our cards on the table, Lacan's achievement in this regard has been the underlying premise of our reading of Adorno)?

The Lacanian Solution: *Objet a* as Cause

Lacan began his work with an unconditional espousal of hermeneutics: as early as his doctoral thesis of 1933, and especially in the 'Rome Discourse', he opposes determinism in favour of a hermeneutical approach: 'All analytic experience is an experience of signification.'[30] This originates the great Lacanian motif of the *futur antérieur* of symbolization: a fact counts not as *factum brutum*, but only as it is always already historicized. (What is at stake in the anal stage, for example, is not excretion as such, but how the child makes sense of it: as a submission to the Other's – the parent's – demand, as a triumph of his control, and so on.) This Lacan can be easily translated into the later problematic of anti-psychiatry or existential psychoanalysis: Freudian clinical designations (hysteria, obsessional neurosis, perversion, and so forth) are not 'objective' classifications stigmatizing the patient; instead, they aim at subjective attitudes, 'existential projects', which have grown out of the subject's concrete intersubjective situation and for which the subject, in his freedom, is ultimately responsible.

But by the mid-1950s, this hermeneutical attitude was undermined by a worm of doubt. If nothing else it insists on the fact that Freud unambiguously resisted reducing psychoanalysis to hermeneutics: his interpretation of dreams took shape through his break with the traditional inquiry into the meaning of dreams. This resistance of Freud, his persistent quest for a cause (in the traumatic event), cannot be dismissed as a naturalist-determinist prejudice. Likewise, Lacan's similar shift away from hermeneutics involves no regression to naturalism, but rather renders visible the 'extimate', inherent decentring of the field of signification, i.e. the cause at work in the midst of this very field. This shift occurs in two steps. First, Lacan embraces structuralism: the decentred cause of signification is identified as the signifying structure. What is at stake in this first shift from hermeneutics to structuralism is thus precisely the question of cause. As we move *from signification to its cause*, signification is conceived of as the *effect*-of-sense: it is the imaginary experience-of-meaning whose inherent constituent is the misrecognition of its determining *cause*, the formal mechanism of the signifying structure itself.

This shift from signification to the signifying cause (correlative to the notion of signification as an effect) does not reduce signification to a product of positive determinism, that is to say, this is not a step from hermeneutics to natural sciences. What forestalls this reduction is the gap that separates the symbolic from the real. Thus, Lacan's next step involves precisely the insight into *how this gap between the real and the symbolic affects the symbolic order itself*: it functions as the *inherent* limitation of this order. The symbolic order is 'barred', the signifying chain is inherently inconsistent, 'not-all', structured around a hole. This inherent non-symbolizable reef maintains the gap between the symbolic and the real, that is, it prevents the symbolic from 'falling into' the real – and, again, what is ultimately at stake is this decentring of the real with regard to the symbolic is the cause: the real is the absent cause of the symbolic. The Freudian and Lacanian name for this cause, is, of course, *trauma*. In this sense, Lacan's theoretical enterprise already lies 'beyond hermeneutics and structuralism' (the subtitle of Dreyfuss and Rabinow's book on Foucault).

The relationship between cause and the law – the law of causality, of symbolic determination – is therefore an antagonistic one: 'Cause is to be distinguished from that which is determinate in a chain, in other words the *law* . . . there is cause only in something that doesn't work.'[31] The cause *qua* real intervenes where symbolic determination stumbles, misfires, that is, where a signifier falls out. For that reason, cause *qua* the real can never effectuate its causal power in a direct way, as such, but must always operate intermediately, under the guise of disturbances within the symbolic order. Suffice it to recall slips of the tongue when the automaton of the signifying chain is, for a brief moment, derailed by the intervention of some traumatic memory. The fact that the real operates and is accessible only through the symbolic does not authorize us, however, to conceive of it as a factor immanent to the symbolic: the real is precisely that which resists and eludes the grasp of the symbolic and, consequently, that which is only detectable within the symbolic under the guise of its disturbances. In short, the real is the absent cause which perturbs the causality of symbolic law. On that account, the structure of overdetermination is irreducible: cause exercises its influence only as redoubled, through a certain discrepancy or time-lag, that is, if the 'original' trauma of the real is to become effective, it must hook onto, find an echo in, some present deadlock. Recall Freud's crucial statement about how 'a normal train of thought' –

expressing a present deadlock – 'is only submitted to the abnormal psychical treatment of the sort we have been describing' – to the dream-work – 'if an unconscious wish, derived from infancy and in a state of repression' – that is, a desire concomitant to the 'original' trauma – 'has been transferred onto it'.[32] Overdetermination means that this statement must also be read in the opposite direction: 'An unconscious wish, derived from infancy and in a state of repression, can only exert its influence if it is transferred onto a normal train of thought.'

Consequently, a certain radical ambiguity pertains to cause: cause is real, the presupposed reef which resists symbolization and disturbs the course of its automaton, yet cause is simultaneously the retroactive product of its own effects. In the case of the Wolf Man, one of Freud's most famous patients, the cause, of course, was the traumatic scene of the parental *coitus a tergo* – this scene was the non-symbolizable kernel around which all successive symbolizations whirled. This cause, however, not only exerted its efficiency after a certain time-lag, it literally *became* trauma, that is, cause, through delay: when the Wolf Man, at the age of two, witnessed the *coitus a tergo*, it was not yet traumatic; the scene acquired its traumatic features only in retrospect, with the later development of the child's infantile sexual theories, when it became impossible to integrate the scene within the newly emerged horizon of narrativization–historicization–symbolization. Herein lies the vicious circle of the trauma: it is the cause that perturbs the smooth engine of symbolization and throws it off balance, it gives rise to an indelible inconsistency in the symbolic, but for all that, the trauma has no existence of its own prior to symbolization; it remains an anamorphotic entity, which gains its consistency only in retrospect, viewed from within the symbolic horizon – it acquires its consistency from the structural necessity of the inconsistency of the symbolic field. As soon as we obliterate this retrospective character of the trauma and 'substantialize' it into a positive entity, one that can be isolated as a cause preceding its symbolic effects, we regress to common linear determinism.

This paradox of trauma *qua* cause, which does not pre-exist its effects but is itself retroactively 'posited' by them, involves a kind of temporal loop: *it is through its 'repetition', through its echoes within the signifying structure, that cause retroactively becomes what it always already was.* In other words, a direct approach necessarily fails: if we try to grasp the trauma directly, irrespective of its later effects, we are left with a meaningless *factum brutum* – in the case of the Wolf Man, with the fact of the parental *coitus a tergo*, which is not a cause at all since it involves no direct psychic efficiency. It is only through its echoes within the symbolic structure that the *factum brutum* of the parental *coitus a tergo* retroactively acquires its traumatic character and becomes the traumatic cause.

This is what Lacan has in mind when he speaks of the signifier's *synchrony* as opposed to a simple atemporal simultaneity: synchrony designates such a paradoxical synchronization, coincidence, of present and past, that is, such a temporal loop where, by progressing forwards, we return to where we always already were. Herein resides the sense of Lacan's obsession with topological models of 'curved' space in the 1960s and 1970s (the Möbius strip, Klein bottle, inner eight, and so on): what all these models have in common is the fact that they cannot be seized 'at a glance', 'in one view' – they all involve a kind of logical temporality, that is, we must first let ourselves be caught in a trap, become the victim of an optical illusion, in order to reach the turning point at which, all of a sudden, the entire perspective shifts and we discover that we already are 'on the other side', on another surface. In the case of the Möbius strip, for example, 'synchrony' occurs when, after passing through the whole circle, we find ourselves at the same point, yet on the opposite surface. It is impossible to miss the Hegelian overtones of this paradox: this repetition of the same, this return to the same, which brings about the change of the surface, does it not offer a perfect illustration of Hegel's thesis that identity is absolute contradiction? Moreover, does not Hegel himself assert that, through the dialectical process, the thing *becomes what it is*?

Such a 'curved' surface-structure is the structure of the subject: what we call 'subject' can only emerge within the structure of overdetermination, that is, in this vicious circle where the cause itself is (presup)posed by its effects. The subject is strictly correlative to this real *qua* cause: $\$-a$. In order to grasp the constitutive paradox of the subject, we must therefore move beyond the standard opposition between 'subjective' and 'objective', between the order of 'appearances' (of what is 'for the subject') and the 'in-itself'. Likewise, we must reject the concomitant notion of the subject as the agency that 'subjectivizes', moulds and makes sense of the inert – senseless in-itself. The *objet a* as cause is an in-itself, which resists subjectivization–symbolization; yet far from being 'independent of the subject', it is *stricto sensu* the subject's shadow among the objects, a kind of stand-in for the subject, a pure semblance lacking any consistency of its own. In other words, if the subject is to emerge, he is to set himself against a paradoxical object that is real, that cannot be subjectivized. Such an object remains an 'absolute non-subject' whose very presence involves *aphanisis*, the erasure of the subject; yet this presence is as such the subject himself in his oppositional determination, the negative of the subject, a piece of flesh that the subject has to lose if he is to emerge as the void of the distance towards every objectivity. This uncanny object is the subject itself in the mode of objectivity, an object which is the subject's absolute otherness precisely in so far as it is closer to the subject than anything that the subject can set against itself in the domain of objectivity.[33] This is what the Kojevean, quasi-Hegelian, negative ontology of the subject *qua* negativity, nothing, a hole in the positivity of the real, and so on, fails to see: this void of subjectivity is strictly correlative to the emergence, in the real itself, of a stain which 'is' the subject.[34]

We can see, now, how Lacanian theory surmounts the antagonism between explanation and comprehension, between signification and determinism: the traumatic real is *stricto sensu* the cause of the subject – not the initial impetus in the linear chain of causes that brings about the subject, but, on the contrary, the missing link in the chain, that is, the cause as remainder, as 'the object that cannot be swallowed, as it were, which remains stuck in the gullet of the signifier'.[35] As such, it is correlative to the subject *qua* break in the chain of the signifying causality, *qua* hole in the signifying network: 'the subject sees himself caused as a lack by *a*'.[36] This Lacanian concept of the subject as $, correlative to *a*, also elucidates Adorno's prefiguring of a subject that is paradoxically concomitant with a 'preponderance of the object'. This object can only be the *objet petit a*.

Notes

1. Russell Jacoby, *Social Amnesia: A Critique of Conformist Psychology from Adler to Laing*, (Hassocks: Harvester Press 1977), p. 31.
2. Theodor W. Adorno, 'Zum Verhältnis von Soziologie und Psychologie', in *Gesellschafts-theorie und Kulturkritik* (Frankfurt: Suhrkamp 1975), p. 122.
3. Adorno, ibid., p. 131.
4. Adorno, ibid., p. 132.
5. Jacoby, *Social Amnesia*, pp. 27–8.
6. Adorno, 'Zum Verhältnis von Soziologie und Psychologie', p. 97.
7. Jacoby, *Social Amnesia*, pp. 120, 122.
8. Jacoby, *Social Amnesia*, p. 125.
9. Adorno, 'Zum Verhältnis von Soziologie und Psychologie', p. 133.
10. Theodor W. Adorno, 'Freudian Theory and the Pattern of Fascist Propaganda', in *The Culture Industry: Selected Essays on Mass Culture* (London: Routledge 1991), p. 132.
11. '. . . *dass, was Es war, Ich werden soll*': Adorno changes in a crucial way Freud's *wo es war, soll ich werden* in which there is no mention of *quidditas*, of 'what id is', but only of a *place*, of 'where it was' – I must arrive at the place where it was.
12. Adorno, 'Freudian Theory', p. 130–31.
13. Adorno, 'Zum Verhältnis von Soziologie und Psychologie', p. 134.
14. Adorno, ibid., p. 133.
15. Adorno, ibid.
16. See Theodor W. Adorno, 'Beitrag zur Ideologienlehre', in *Gesammelte Schriften: Ideologie* (Frankfurt: Suhrkamp 1972).
17. Jacques Lacan, *The Seminar of Jacques Lacan. Book III: The Psychoses (1955–1956)* (New York: Norton 1993), p. 251.
18. Lacan, ibid.
19. Sigmund Freud, 'Psychoanalytic Notes on an Autobiographical Account of a Case of Paranoia (Schreber)', in *Case Histories II* (Harmondsworth: Penguin Books 1979), p. 156.
20. As to this notion of the superego in its connection with Kafka's universe, see Slavoj Žižek, *For They Know Not What They Do* (London: Verso 1991), pp. 236–41.

21. Lacan, *Seminar*, p. 251.
22. In the case of Schreber, the corresponding phenomenon is his constant need for God's speech: he 'no longer has the customary significant security, except through the accompaniment of a constant commentary on his gestures and acts' (Lacan, *Seminar*, p. 307). Some interpreters of Freud and critics of Lacan perceive Freud's text on Schreber as a patriarchal-reactionary dissimulation of the unbearable truth of Schreber's text: Schreber's desire to become 'a woman full of spirit' [*geistreiches Weib*] must be taken as a prefiguration of a non-patriarchal society; only a patriarchal perspective can reduce this desire to the expression of a 'repressed homosexuality' or of 'failed paternity'. In opposition to such readings, it is worth recalling the fundamental structural homology between Schreber's 'visions' and Hitler's 'world-view' (the universal plot, the general cataclysm followed by a rebirth, etc.): in different circumstances, one can well imagine Schreber becoming a Hitler-like politician.
23. Jürgen Habermas, *Knowledge and Human Interest* (London: Heinemann 1972), pp. 217–18.
24. Habermas, ibid., p. 217.
25. Habermas, ibid., p. 226.
26. Habermas, ibid., p. 257.
27. Habermas, ibid., p. 235–6.
28. The same goes also for sexuality, in contrast to Lacan for whom sexual difference is the non-symbolizable real that hollows out the symbolic order from within. For this reason, the Lacanian subject of the signifier is always 'sexed', never neutral-asexual.
29. Sigmund Freud, *The Interpretation of Dreams* (Harmondsworth: Penguin Books 1977), p. 757.
30. Jacques Lacan, *The Seminar of Jacques Lacan, Book II; The Ego in Freud's Theory and in the Technique of Psychoanalysis (1954–55)* (New York: Norton 1991), p. 325.
31. Jacques Lacan, *The Four Fundamental Concepts of Psycho-Analysis* (London: The Hogarth Press 1977), p. 22.
32. Freud, *The Interpretation of Dreams*, p. 757.
33. The paradox of this object – of *objet petit a* – is that, although imaginary, it occupies the place of the real, i.e. it is a non-specularizable object, an object that has no specular image, and which as such precludes any relationship of empathy, of sympathetic recognition. In the course of psychoanalysis, the analysand has to reach the point at which he experiences his impossible identity with this absolute otherness – 'Thou art that!'
34. In the domain of philosophy, perhaps the only concept that corresponds to this uncanny object is Kant's transcendental object: the noumenal 'in-itself', an absolute presupposition, yet simultaneously pure positedness, i.e. the only object thoroughly posited by the subject and not – as is the case with ordinary phenomenal objects – some transcendentally moulded stuff in whose guise the in-itself affects the passive subject.
35. Lacan, *The Four Fundamental Concepts*, p. 270.
36. Lacan, ibid.

6 THINGS TO COME
A Hysteric's Guide to the Future Female Subject

JULIET FLOWER MACCANNELL

What does a woman want? – Freud

Tell me why your daughter does not speak. – Lacan

Jacques Lacan wanted us to understand that discourse is
what makes a man a man: 'Man, the male, the virile, such
as we know it, is a creation of discourse.'[1] But what is it
that makes a woman a woman? Before Lacan, the answer
to this question was nature, society or the particular fate of
her relation to men.[2] For post-Freudian psychoanalysis
and its rebellious feminist daughters, the hysteric's silent
speech – her body's language – has provided a crucial
alternative to 'virile discourse', a primary challenge to
'male' domination of discursive forms.[3] Here I want to
question if an adoption of hysteric discourse can support
and suffice for – or even offer the best opening towards –
a concept of the female subject.[4] It may prove necessary to
enlarge the concept somewhat before this work can be
done. The presence of the hysteric, whose radical question
is 'Am I a man or a woman?', accrues special interest at
this moment in our cultural history, practically as well as
theoretically, since it indexes the way in which sexual
difference presents itself as a persistent problem even
under the global, 'universal' regime of neighbourly or
brotherly love.

Castration, the Superego and Feminine Desire

If the *subject* in psychoanalytical terms is what is 'castrated'
or divided by language and mobilized into a universe of

desire, the presumption that the form of this desire is universal, i.e. phallic, renders woman essentially speechless. Her silence as daughter, her wifely echoing of her man, her professionally 'masculine' adoption of male language would seem to be the only channels open to her as she closes off and drowns out her mother's voice. These two options – speechlessness or fully male speech – structure the whole story of woman's speech, of her relation to the signifier. If woman does not accept castration because she is wholly invested in the logic of exception to the logic of the phallic signifier, a specifically female subject would seem to be moot, and her perpetual silence assured. But if, as Lacan presented the argument, she has a *differently* nuanced way of relating to this signifier, then 'feminizing the subject' becomes an open possibility. Woman's speech (her way of desire) would be at the heart of the issue. A female subject – not object – of desire has not been posed in quite these terms either by feminism or by psychoanalysis,[5] unless we were to count seriously Freud's querulous 'What does a woman *want?*' as a formulation of the question of woman's *desire*, of woman as *subject*. The two questions, 'Am I a man or a woman?' and 'What does a woman want?' are linked at a deeper level as one and the same question from two different sides.

Answering them demands, though, that we remain hard and fast in our conviction that the 'bedrock' of castration is the firm foundation underlying theories of sexual difference. Castration succeeds our 'failed' faith in the 'universal' solution of the Oedipus complex, which manages only the male's problematic relation to the enjoyment of the mother. The hopeful side of the successor to the oedipal father, the superego, is that it presumes a 'unisex' Other, a transcendental coupler that ought to treat the sexes equally. (Freud explains, in 'The Passing of the Oedipus Complex', that the superego includes *both* mother and father in its structural foundations.) These hopes are dimmed somewhat, however, by the fact that, unfortunately, the gift of the signifier seems prone to be bestowed exclusively on the male.

The internalization of the superego – which enables discourse and desire – still 'works' almost exclusively for the male, despite its 'unisex' character. Perhaps any model identified as 'oneness' or selfsameness (Lacan will call it '*le je identique à lui-même*') is inclined to shadow and represent itself as double of the singular male organ. Physically absent and spiritually present, the penis gives the phallus its imaginary figure.

The tenacious linkage of the signifier-as-phallus to the representation of the male is historical and institutional. As such, it is subject to change. Each sex's distinctiveness in relation to the phallus, a matter raised repeatedly by Lacan,[6] should be confronted, not because it is an irrational leftover from less enlightened times, but because it indicates the tenacity of sex, of sexual difference in the composition of the human subject. Lacan correctly perceived that the transcendental modality of love – neighbourly love – was intended to dispense with sexual difference.

If a feminine counterpart to the superego did exist, it would be another matter. At the very least we might imagine the superego less as 'unisex' than as constructed doubly, like the hysteric, through a heteronomy, an irreducible contradiction in its sexual make-up. After all, Freud's initial question was how a woman became a woman out of an originally 'bisexual disposition'.[7] The hysteric demands that attention be paid to sexual difference as the contradiction that inhabits her, body and soul. This alternation in her means that she has to reverse continually from being an object (a mystery inside a riddle wrapped up in an enigma: a complete, if anaesthetized, anaesthetic posture) to being a subject (empty, devastated, desiring).

The Feminine Superego?

What woman becomes under the unisex superego can now begin to be reformulated. Freud denies the superego to woman, saying that it is impossibly 'weak' in her because her 'organ' is absent at the origin; yet Freud also says that woman rejects castration less for herself than for others. The sexually empowered organ is physically absent but fantasmically a constant presence for her – in others. She feels her own particular (and quite 'real') castration is not a universal necessity, but only accidental; surely, she tells herself, some women (and all men) escape it. Because she feels no need to acknowledge the universality of castration, speech is not a necessity for her identity: she does not personally need to undergo the metaphorization of her organ-body for the speech mantle to descend upon her. This is because, for her, someone exists – some father or mother – whose castration can be denied, an Other for whom *jouissance* persists unabated, uncastrated. Even when it is taken into herself, this *jouissant* Other remains a foreign object, alien, extimate, a Thing, not an internalized limit, as it is said to be for the male.

For Freud, once the 'bedrock' is laid down for woman, she is humbled in many ways, unable to access the higher climes of universal signification, bearing the awful stigmatizing *jouissant* organ[8] within or demanding repeatedly that it be given to her by those who have it. Her posture is unattractive or more precisely unappealing, it lacks lack, it lacks 'desire'. The 'presencing' of the full phallus within her can supposedly take many forms, including uterine centring, attributing speech to the lips of the vagina, offering lovingly sacrificial support for 'great men'. These positions, which are thought to vary among 'types' of women, ultimately all bespeak the same refusal of castration:

the same denial of lack of phallic power; the same forfeiture of desire; the same preservation of *jouissance* elsewhere. Woman as such is reduced to the level of demand – demand that the phallus exist really, somewhere, in some ideal man.

Woman's impaired access to speech, fully determined by the default of castration in her, by the positive 'presencing' of the phallus within her, would thus be irredeemable. Moreover, her structural speech impediment would align her with the 'metaphysics of presence' tracked down by Jacques Derrida[9] (but not linked by him to the psychic set-up of the woman as such). This is so, however, only if there *is* no, only if there *can be* no specifically *feminine* castration, no 'lady's way' of accepting the signifier that would grant her a special deal with regard to the unbearable, uncastrated *jouissance* within her, her horror, her Thing. Once we have accepted the 'bedrock' of castration (as indeed we must), and once psychoanalytic feminists concede (as we must) that the maternal superego is a horrifying Thing, we must set to work (or to war). We must strategize, and ferret out ways to uncover whatever special *savoir* (knowledge), as well as whatever *know-how* women may have and have devised for fending off this Thing. We need to know how woman finds a recognizably *female* relation to *her jouissance*. These will not be the time-honoured male strategies, but they could lead the way to feminine speech, feminine desire: to the feminine subject.

This brings us back, then, to hysteria, but from the other side, to that question, 'Am I a man or a woman?' Though it is enabled by the formal unisexuality of the superego, the fact that it takes the form of a question should, according to Lacan, not be taken lightly: it grants the hysteric a form of speech. The feminist celebration of hysteria's brilliance at communicating, silently but expressively, a woman's desire (from Bertha's birth fantasies to Dora's punctuation of her speech by fiddling with her purse; from Monique David-Ménard's reading of hysteria to Millot's sophisticated text), has still failed to provide a *model* for feminine desire (acceptance of castration *in her own way*) that would enable her speech, permitting her a *woman's* way of relating to her *jouissance*, beyond 'fiddling with her purse'.

Analysts who have addressed Freud's castration-construction of woman do not often nuance the possible feminine forms of her relation to the castration complex. Lacan, however, made a kind of opening. He implied that, for all the difficulties woman had with speech and the signifier, mistrusting its promises because they *de facto* fail the woman, a certain freedom of play was available to her: if man is a creature of discourse, it is also the case that, for Lacan, 'Women are less enclosed than their partners in the cycle of discourse.'

Now, Lacan uses a word here, *discours*, which is neither *la parole* nor *le langage*, nor any of the terms for speaking he ordinarily uses when he discusses speech as desire. *Discours* is reserved for the complex of speech and act, 'discursive practices' – even acting – whose significance arises from their conjunction, disjunction and sequencing in a complex 'hyper-signifier'. *Discours* takes a certain *cours*, or course of feeling, thought, event, presentation into account; it implies a longer term, a tracing, tracking, even backtracking over time. *Discourse* means, then, a certain history, even a destiny.

A specifically sexual split *within* the field of the signifier is contained in Lacan's first elaboration of the *discourse of hysteria*. I want first to work this particular conjoining of woman's *desire* (her relation to the signifier) to the discursive practice of hysteria. We can then raise seriously the possibility of a feminine ego-ideal,[10] an internalizable feminine superego, which would be opposed to the 'maternal' superego located outside, keeping us on a leash, or at least under voice command, or erupting full-blown as an alien within.

Hysteria has a special privilege in relation to the concept of the subject, not because it offers an allegorical, indirect representation of what 'male' discourse leaves out, but because, I have already suggested, it vehicles a demand that *jouissance persists uncastrated, unabated* in and for man: man as an Ideal Other, a Master. But it pushes this demand to such a crisis point that it verges on making that ideal collapse. Through its devotion to the Master signifier, its dispossession before this signifier's pure phallic power, hysteria 'preserves' the feminine subject from falling into the 'psychotic' world of pure rejection of the signifier. By reserving the phallus to the ideal Man, however, hysteria shows the limits of that assignment of mastery to the male, limits that indicate where we must go to formulate the ethical structure of feminine desire.

Hysteria and the Feminine Subject: *The Handmaid's Tale*

A testing of the limits of the claim that there is not yet a *female subject* because there is not yet a female *desire* (a specifiable *ethical* mandate for the woman through *speech*) shows up in an unlikely place: a recent popular novel, made into a less successful film, Margaret Atwood's *The Handmaid's Tale*. This tale bears reading as other than a fiction, for in it Atwood raises the stakes of the two questions posed by hysteria ('What does a woman want?' 'Am I a man or a woman?) by doubling each, shadowing the first with the underlying question, 'Does a man want?' and the second with, 'Am I a man's woman or a woman's woman?' And, in the event that I am one and/or the other, 'What do I, a woman, want?'

For those who have not read it, Atwood's *The Handmaid's Tale* is a dystopic vision of a breakaway, semi-fundamentalist totalitarian state, somewhere in North America (the scene is set in the north-east; I recognize it as Cambridge, Mass.). Called the Republic of Gilead, it is ruled by Masterful Males (the Commanders) and watched over by their 'Eyes', 'Guardians' and 'Angels'. The Commanders hold women in positions of absolute submission to their reproductive and supportive roles (there are 'Wives', who run complex bourgeois-type households; 'Handmaids', who are breeders, Mistresses; 'Aunts', who indoctrinate other women, or teachers; and 'Marthas' – these are what they were for Victorians, cleaning ladies. In addition, there are the 'Econowives', who combine all four functions). The narrator is never called by her own true name, but by the genitive and generous 'Offred': she is of Fred; she is offered.

Atwood's *Tale* is to be read, I believe, as an anatomy of hysteria in every conceivable sense. It is also ultimately a damning of the undamming of the concept by a contemporary feminism that has failed to consider hysteria's absolute passion.[11] Atwood forces hysteria's 'unconscious' process directly into what the blurb for the novel calls the 'history of the near future'. It is 'hysterical' in the mundane sense in that it is an accusatory woman's (author's or narrator's – who can tell the difference when a fictional 'I' is at stake?) projection of a worst-case scenario for the future, extrapolated from a negative judgment on the contemporary 'white male domination of the social and symbolic order'. It is a book that not so modestly proposes, as it were, a final solution to the Woman Question (as the Victorians used to call it), one that could even be taken as a satire *on* feminism.

The *Tale* is also thematically hysterical, a pastiche of tabloid issues – abortion, biological clocks, toxic pollution, televangelism, lesbianism, *Playboy*, overpopulation, white heterosexual male domination, militarization, central-ized control of media and technology – which fill the media today. It was precisely because I had heard these were the novel's concerns that I was averse to reading it. It turns out to be however, neither a grim satire nor a monological extrapolation of a single feature of the present, as one might find in a Philip K. Dick novel, for example. Instead, the book poses these burning 'issues' in a way that questions how issues become 'burning', how they are 'issued'. (From whose mouth do these mutually contradictory imperatives emerge?) Why, it makes us wonder, do 'burning issues' so consistently crystallize, in Gilead as on Capitol Hill, around the evidently hidden *jouissance* of a woman? Offred is so devoid of *jouissance* that its very absence should be read as revealing its 'presence' in her, but it must also be read as a mode of accommodation of that presence and, thus, an opening onto female desire.

On the best-seller lists in 1986 despite its narrator's passive voice, despite the fact that she is apathetic, disembodied and devoid of any image but the red nun-like uniform the Commanders have her wear (she is no one with whom we would reflexively identify), the *Tale* struck an immediate chord with the public (as *Fatal Attraction* did in a different way). The reasons for its popularity exceeded its genre as satire or fable or, one might say, that it hit (its) genre right on the mark. I want to pose the question of the hysterization of the female subject on a more fundamental level by attending to the logical structure of the novel's style, its language and voice.

The style is one of complete familiarity skewed by a strangely mild exaggeration, in which the logic of 'normal' everyday life in the present is simply extended. When asked about himself, Offred's Commander claims, 'I'm just an ordinary kind of guy',[12] and he is believable. There are no extraordinary devices, technologies run wild, unheard-of aliens or small subgroups (fascists or robots, mutants or schizos) taking over from the normal. It is the normal that has taken over, that's all. We are told 'there wasn't even an enemy you could put your finger on' (*HT*, p. 225). This state just 'happened' to happen. But for that very reason, there can be no doubt that it responds to some imperative, some will to *jouissance*.

Interestingly, the book is supposed to be a woman's speech-act: it is a future transcription of oral tape-recordings made by Offred as she attempts a belated flight from Gilead. Her deadpan voice, presented as extraordinarily calm, passive, decorous, rejects all autobiographical devices (there are no tricks to evoke sympathy or disgust in the listener/reader), refuses any desiring dimensionality. Even less is Offred speaking as a 'camera', a mere record-keeper of events; her reporting is detailed, factual-seeming, uncoloured by emotionality; but this flatness is not particularly objective, it is not the product of a will to a truth or to a science of its object. It is flat because the fact of the matter is that there are no *real* events in her Gilead. Quotidian incidents, present and past alike, surface in the same undifferentiated detail, with Offred making only the most minimal efforts to connect them. Nor is she subjective: she does judge some events, but in the most impersonal way, without reference to her own feelings of enjoyment or disgust. Neither fictionalized nor story-like, her narrative is so devoid of obvious motivations (emotional or truth-seeking) that, ultimately, the book stirs us strangely, for Offred reveals that she has unexpectedly responded to, and continues to respond with an inexplicably total passivity to, the Will that has taken over the polity.

Offred is under no explicit threat; yet she is not only perfectly obedient, she neither expresses nor experiences any desires, no wants or needs beyond what she is permitted to have, at least initially. Later, she offers herself some small indulgences – butter for her skin, a certain degree of enjoyment in bathing. Even her memories of the Time Before the takeover of Gilead are apathetic, distanced from her personally, and provide virtually no entrée into her specific *desire*. One has the impression that she has responded to the will of the Commanders because their imperatives are so pure, so unself-interested. She bends not to the desire of the Commanders, but to their lack of desire, their total *jouissance*. For the Commanders are not just men, but over-men, ideals (negative as they may be) of Man-as-such, of Man as absolute possessor of All. 'Men' are those subjects whose 'I' is whole, perfect, strictly identical-to-itself.

Less obvious, perhaps, is the fact that the 'will' to which Offred responds so passively is also at least as much that of women as of 'men'. Although he is blaming the victim, challenging the feminists with a world the way 'they wanted it', it is also true that the Commander's ideality as Man is linked to the demands expressed by the wives. (These Wives, who cannot themselves bear children, have their husbands reproduce through Handmaids. Set up in households with servants, they cannot command, though they do demand, despairingly, their husbands' love.) Atwood's choice is to include the unvoiced voice of the Wife (the wife of Offred's Commander is named Serena Joy) as well as the feminists' historic demands as integral parts of the Command he carries out. The Commander explains that Gilead has been constructed in part to meet the demands of feminists and sympathetic males to mitigate the offences of sexual harassment and women's treatment as sex objects in the Time Before the Republic. Atwood's *Tale* is, in part, a sociology of the fundamentalisms of both the religious Right and of feminism; but it is more than that. It is also structurally astute. By making the 'will' which the Handmaids serve ambigendered, Atwood's text outlines the superego along Lacanian lines, conjuring it up as an Other who is neither maternal/female nor paternal/male but moral, fake and, above all, imperative in character.

In point of fact, the topical issues framed by the novel are posed as neither 'soluble' nor 'insoluble': they are not actually laid at the feet of a dominant interest group, however much this may seem to be the case (this is no simple indictment of white male domination as being *responsible for* x, y or z). Rather, Atwood shows these subjectless issues forming to cover up a central weakness or fault in ideal gender identification, especially where sexuality and *jouissance* are at stake, for male and female alike. The Commander asks Offred where 'they' went wrong in trying to please women as totally as possible, in caring for women the way they seemed to want. And he readily admits that the troubles that led to the New Order were not only with the women but with the men as well: there was 'nothing for men anymore', the Commander complains, somewhat plaintively adding, 'there was nothing for them to do with women' (*HT*, p. 272).

So far in the novel, we see woman as defined by her non-relation to the *logos*, the phallus, unable to take up the signifier. This incapacity for speech is not resolved by either of the novel's feminists (Moira and Offred's mother). Nor is it resolved by the fundamentalist/essentialist womanism of the Wives, Aunts and Marthas. The 'bedrock' of the castration complex as laid out by Freud leaves little to choose between the one and the other, no absolute distinction to be made between these two versions of woman: both are woman as ideally and really 'uncastrated', each bearing a full organic *jouissance* within, or making her absolute dispossession of *jouissance* the support for its existence elsewhere. Atwood illustrates this dilemma concretely: despite liberations and conquests of 'public discourse', women were never quite able, before Gilead, to articulate their gender-ideals differently from those posed by male discourse. They had to become the phallus in order to figure and shape their *jouissance*. *They had to imagine themselves the way they imagined the sexual male was imagining them.* Offred reflects:

> I used to think of my body as an instrument of pleasure, or a means of transportation, or an implement for the accomplishment of my will. I could use it to run, push buttons of one sort or another, make things happen. There were limits, but my body was nevertheless lithe, single, solid, one with me.
>
> Now the flesh arranges itself differently. I'm a cloud congealed around a central object, the shape of a pear, which is harder and more real than I am and glows red within its translucent wrapping. Inside it is a space huge as the sky at night and dark and curved like that, though black-red, rather than black. (*HT*, p. 95)

The uterus is positioned here as if it were the ultimate real, but the work it is doing is, of course, imaginary: it gives circular consistency to Offred. And women, including this woman, pictured thus, are passive receivers of ideas in the most literal way: their 'inmost' sense of their history, their most 'intimate memories' are what is 'extimate'. Offred's 'personal history' is from the start no more than a pastiche of stereotypes she has taken to heart. The book opens, for example, with her nostalgic reminiscences of high school and the 'old sex' which, along with the basketball games, used to fill gymnasiums of the sort she and the other women are being detained in, for purposes of re-educating them to be Handmaids:

> I thought I could smell, faintly like an afterimage, the pungent scent of sweat, shot through with the sweet taint of chewing gum and perfume from the watching girls, felt-skirted as I knew from pictures, later in miniskirts, then pants, then in one earring, spiky green-streaked hair. Dances would have been held there: the music

lingered, a palimpsest of unheard sound, style upon style, an undercurrent of drums, a forlorn wail, garlands made of tissue-paper flowers, cardboard devils, a revolving ball of mirrors, powdering the dance with a snow of light. There was old sex in the room and loneliness, and expectation. (*HT*, p. 3)

It takes a second thought to realize that a 33-year-old woman with 'viable ovaries' in her time-period could hardly have been a personal witness to this procession of epochs in romance (1950s to 1980s). But these are normal, historically verifiable memories, are they not? Are they?

That the novel is framed, finally, as an alternative set of fantasy scenes seems to be indubitable. (Late in the text Offred begins to acknowledge that her recordings are 'reconstructions': 'When I get out of here, if I'm ever able to set this down, in any form, even in the form of the voice of another, it will be a reconstruction', *HT*, p.173.) Less obvious though is the specifically hysterical nature of these scenes, because they are set not towards the personal memory of a forbidden enjoyment from a remote past, but towards a proximal future, a fleshing out of a renunciation of enjoyment.

The central fantasy is that of the State of Gilead as a totalizing master discourse wherein the contradictions between a gendered female 'I' and the female subject of *jouissance* are finally abolished. Not necessarily to the benefit of the phallic, of male desire, but to the end of foreclosing the Thing, the threatening internal 'tidal wave' of maternal (oro-vaginal-anal) *jouissance*.[13] Note that the actual commandments to which Offred responds are those that were once reserved for making girls into 'ladies', that is, for inducing feminine behaviour. Her transgressions are often framed as violations of decorum, her potential laughter, for example, is seen as 'a fart in church', (*HT*, p.117.) The hysteric demands, as Danielle Bergeron puts it, that the 'pervert set the limit' (see also Aunt Lydia's remark, 'freedom from; don't underrate it'; *HT*, p. 33). In other words, the Aunt Lydias act as the moral form of the externalized superego which, by urging decorum, permits the persistence within of the Thing through the simple device of barring it from woman's conscious experience and overt expression.

The Ideal Unisex Ego and the Bisexed I: The Truth of the Subject and the Freudian Thing

The signifier of the unisex superego/Other is the 'I' (the Eyes). The mere enunciation of 'I' grants this purely formal 'shifter' status as bearer of the voice of truth. Atwood's novel (perhaps not unknowingly) reproduces Lacan's analysis of the relation of the Discourse of the Master (of the 'I' not as male or female but as truth-bearing, truth-speaking Other) to the Discourse of

Hysteria. It so happens that the Offred tapes in Margaret Atwood's novel are suspended precisely where Lacan suspended hysteria – between the two 'collective' discourses, that of the Master and that of the University. In the world of the Masters of Gilead, Offred is reduced to her reproductive role, to being nothing more than the fruit her flesh might bear. In the world of the University she fares no better: her tale is entirely disconnected from her own narrative which, at the hands of her future historians, is reduced, sniggeringly, to being a Handmaid's 'tail' as in 'a piece of . . . '. In the fantasy world of the hysteric, however, Offred falls between these two stools, these two discourses presumed to bear a special relation to 'truth'.

Lacan saw the 'sororal' position of truth in relation to *jouissance* as enunciated differently in the discourse of hysteria.[14] Truth is borne in the discourse of the 'I' (the Discourse of the Master, the Commander's 'I') as much as it is in the discourse of the manipulator of the signifier (the Discourse of the University; the academic historian who 'reads' Offred's tapes at the 25 June 2195 conference devoted to them). But it is the hysteric, Lacan tells us in the 'Rome Discourse' who witnesses the birth of truth in speech: '[Hysterical revelation] presents us with the birth of truth in speech' (*EE* p. 47). If woman is only a body bearing full *jouissance* both for the Master and for the University and is therefore speechless, as Hysteric she does have a privileged relation to their speech – if only as the one who has been cast aside from it.

Lacan therefore taught, during the turbulent days of May 1968, that 'When woman takes on discourse, she becomes an eminent guide: this is what defines the hysteric, and therefore why I put her in the centre' (that is, between University and Master). Woman stands to benefit from a certain culture defined by discourse, but we have to strive to maintain *her* speech within it. Otherwise, we will remain locked into male discourse, or will risk the 'women's culture' (Aunt Lydia's term) of Gilead's female economy, devoid of all feminine discourse (women's reading, writing and speaking to each other are proscribed, except under certain strictly limited conditions).

I wish to reapproach the discourse of the hysteric now from the inside out, to try to see how hysteria could serve to set out some preliminary guidelines for female desire. I want to look at hysteria differently, not only from the perspective of the collective discourses, Mastery and Universitarian, where its content is intriguing but irrelevant to the epic march of the symbolic. I want to move onto the ground of the subject itself, the female subject, where the hysteric takes on discourse, inhabits the same fantasy universe of desire, as potentially more than its 'silent partner'.

Freud, Again

Though hysteria in Freud's discourse is always characterized by an engagement in fantasies (psychicial façades constructed to bar the way to memories of primal scenes of premature sexual enjoyment), it remains by and large indefinite, at best doubly registered. Hysterical fantasies combine things that have been experienced *and also* perceived through inference. So, in the beginning, as so often in Freud, were the word and the deed intertwined; as Lacan later put it, we are all creatures of the *plus-de jouir* language leaves us: 'We have logical needs because we are creatures born from the *plus-de-jouir* resulting from the use of language' (*Seminar XVII*, p. 74).

While Freud found the somatic *origin* of the hysterical symptom lay in 'premature' stimulation of infantile genitals, he also noted a second origin: 'Things heard by children and only understood later.' When Freud found he was unable to make an absolute diagnostic distinction between hysteria and obsessional neurosis, he moved further and further back in time to 'the first period of childhood' – $1\frac{1}{2}$ years old (in the 1894 letter on the mechanism of the neuroses; by letter 59, in 1897, he had pushed this back even further, to 'six or seven months').

On one point, though, Freud seems invariant: he says that no hysterical symptom can arise from real experience alone, but in every case, memory (at least 'reminiscence') of an earlier experience plays a part in causing *symptoms* – or the peculiar alteration of 'premature' (pre-oedipal) sexual excitation named the hysterical 'conversion of affect'. (See the 1896 'Aetiology of Hysteria'.) According to Freud, this doubling or equivocation is true at all levels, from the somatic to that of group psychology.

Thus, while we complained that it was difficult to segregate hysteria *per se* from 'normal human misery', Freud embarked on a quest for its specificity; but, since the question involved *memory*, he focused his research consistently on hysteria's history: its origin, or first truth. That this was to remain a frustrated quest, is, I think, the result of his having given an unwitting gender slant to his earliest conceptual architecture of hysteria. His 1896 paper on 'Neuropsychoses' sought, for example, to differentiate hysteria from obsessional neurosis by envisaging two different primal scenes of sexual enjoyment: the hysteric is someone who experienced premature sexual pleasure as a passive participant; the obsessional took an active role. This 'passivization' effectively feminized hysteria, marvellously aligning word and organ. Freud thus imaginatively reconstructs a primal scene in which, characteristically, the maternal part(s) are granted the role of 'organic origination' through quiescence and passive receptivity. The *hyster-uterine matrix*, like the mother, is conceived by him as playing no active role in constructing the master narrative or dominant history of human sexuality. Feminine speech is thus quieted, woman's desire denied by this hysterical destiny, slated from the origin. At best, she becomes a passive subject desiring only in so far as she is divided from *her* (maternal) *jouissance* by the hand of another, not, as the obsessional male, by verbal negations.

Lacan, Again

Lacan's 'Function and Field of Speech and Language in Psychoanalysis' (the 'Rome Discourse') opened a different perspective on hysteria, oriented away from origins and attentive to something else entirely.[15] As with Freud, word and deed for Lacan are imbricated in hysteria, but this is the case for any 'historical' act, understood in the primary sense of the term, the recounting of past events in language.

Lacan nuances the narration of the past by pondering whether the 'subject' – read 'patient' – analysed by behaviourist psychology is ever actually called on to remember 'anything whatever from the past' (*EE*, p. 46). Has he ('he' is, as you will see, intentional) not, Lacan asks, always only 'simply recounted the event' by making

> it pass into the *verbe*, or, more precisely, into the *epos* by which he brings back into present time the origins of his own person . . . [H]e does this in a language that allows his discourse to be understood by his contemporaries, and which furthermore presupposes their present discourse. (*EE*, p. 46)

The past[16] has been reduced, in the behaviourist *Aufhebung* of Freud's technique, to being a modality of the *present*. Contemporary psychoanalysis refuses to recognize that something social and synthetic, histrionic, clings to the patient's discourse. His 'historical' form of recounting marks it as indelibly 'male': valorized as the hero of his own life, his traits become objects of a *genealogical* rather than a *genetic* quest by a subject who seeks 'the origins of his own person' (we know these will be noble, and so he won't find Mother or her *jouissance* there):

> [T]he recitation of the *epos* may include a discourse of earlier days in its own archaic, even foreign language, so may even pursue its course in present time with all the animation of the actor; but it is like an indirect discourse, isolated in quotation marks within the thread of the narration, and, if the discourse is played out, it is on a stage implying the presence not only of the chorus, but of spectators. (*EE*, pp. 46–7)

The speech of the 'hero' is 'empty'. Assuming its rightful genealogical 'place' in speech, especially the narrative mode, the masculine subject glides easily from fiction to fact as equally honourable modes of avoiding the horrors of *jouissance* and the whole feminine Thing.

Lacan contrasts this hypnotic-histrionic, though charmingly literary, discourse in 'quotation marks' with another kind of historical recollection, which he calls the ambiguous 'hysterical revelation of the past'. Both modes are 'speech-acts', as it were, though 'speech' dominates the 'acting' in the first; and 'acts', of course, classically stand in for the hysteric's speech. But the hysteric's mode is obviously seen by Lacan as truer, if only because it is more honestly and more overtly *ambiguous*. Its fantastic conflations are not due to 'the vacillation of its content between the imaginary and the real' (*EE*, p. 47), for from the first it is 'situated in both' – nor to its being 'made up of lies'. Instead, hysterical fantasy is a unique way of revealing history. Whereas the masculine subject's 'histrionic' speech is indirect discourse rooted in a nonabsolute, heroicized, epic past (open to revision for political reasons), hysteria evokes an absolute, not provisional, future:

> [Hysterical revelation] presents us with the birth of truth in speech, and thereby brings us up against the reality of what is neither true nor false . . . for it is present speech that bears witness to the truth of this revelation in present reality, and which grounds it in the name of that reality. Yet in that reality, only speech bears witness to that portion of the powers of the past that has been thrust aside at each crossroads where the event has made its choice. (*EE*, p. 47)

This is not to say that what *is said* in the fantasy is a truth dredged *from the past*, for it may indeed speak falsely. Rather, its birthing of truth arises from *the* peculiar 'witnessing' granted by its linguistic form of expression: the witnessing of what has been left out of 'present reality'.

Hysterical fantasy constitutes the 'history' of that half of the subject that has been 'saved' from a devastating relation to *jouissance*.[17] But it also constitutes 'present reality' as the effect of a series of strong foreclosures: a woman's hysterical body attests more profoundly than aesthetic trimmings ('quotation marks') to *the radical cutting off of the body of the past as the place where 'truth' lies* (in both meanings of the term). The hysterical fantasy tilts instead towards the future: it 'witnesses the birth of truth *in* speech', becoming less a mode of revelation of the past than a regathering of revolutionary potentiality. At least this is the sense we get from the 'Rome Discourse' of 1953, when Lacan's position as witness to radical cuts is exceptional, having just been himself expelled from the International Psychoanalytic Association.

In 1968, in *Séminaire XVII: L'Envers de la psychanalyse* ('underside, seamy side, dirty side, back side'), he articulates his position in different terms. Here he speaks of his first picture book, 'L'Histoire d'une moitié d'un poulet' and muses on his perennial concern with such 'Stories about half of a subject,' (*Seminar XVII*, p. 63). His future biographers, he is convinced, are bound to read his first picture book as significant for his subsequent intellectual development, and, indeed, he has always searched for the 'cut-off side'. But he has done so more in the sense of the road not taken, the foreclosed or repressed (the two are not the same), and less in the sense of the *content* of what was lost in the cut-off part of the chicken. What counts is what is being *affirmed* by the cut: the truth, the truth of the book, was *not in* this 'other, cut off side', but only in *what was said in the book*. Its expressive form – the book – wholly contained whatever link to truth there was, its 'truth' being intrinsic to its mode of proposition.

Now, philosophically, analytical accounts[18] of 'truth' posit it as not being *internal to the proposition* (*Seminar XVII*, p. 68). The subject of the enunciation is assumed to be motivated by some external prompting for him to trouble marking his proposition as 'the truth' *per se*. To state a 'truth' without making explicit reference either to the speaking subject or to 'the truth' of the statement capitalizes on the way the rhetorical tradition has always dealt with the truth of the subject. The subject is implicitly granted an ethos, and this, in turn, becomes correlative and corroboration of the 'indirect discourse' of the histrionic patient. What is missing is the strictly 'ethical' relation in the psychoanalytical sense, of 'not ceding one's desire'. For it is the explicit character of desire-as-speech that is hidden within the rhetorical form, the imputed 'truth' of the speaker. The subject automatically speaks *Truth* as 'I'; 'I' am 'authentic'.

The 'histrionic' as opposed to 'hysterical' subject thus capitalizes on the classic ethos as well as the tried-and-true forms of the *epos* ('unwritten, heroic song') to avert the truth of the Thing. I say 'capitalizes' because, however ironic it may be, it is the very ability to avoid the Thing that becomes the 'glory' of the epic hero as subject; a true heir of the artificial patriarchy, the master of the signifier becomes the person in whom *Truth itself* speaks as 'I', having gracefully avoided, through verbal wit and rhetorical form, having to bear witness to the horror of *jouissance*.

For Lacan, this assumption of truth-speaking in person is a political matter, the grounds for the elaboration of a veritable '*Je-cratie*'/'I'-ocracy (*Seminar, XVII*, p. 71). Positing truth exclusively as ethos, as an effect of the authenticity of the speaker, makes the S, a '*je de maître*'. Any 'I' identified tacitly or implicitly with truth is 'identical' with itself: this 'I', identical-to-itself, speaks in the mode of the pure imperative.

Fantasy – the privileged mode of the hysteric – is politically so charged because, on the one hand, as the handmaid or passive partner to the speech-act couple here, it is the absolute support for the master's evasion of *jouissance*; while on the other, it is organized entirely around and by *jouissance*. Fantasy ($ ◊ a) has an infinite degree of power with respect to truth – it is capable of birthing it, of producing it as a Thing. If hysterical fantasy bars access to remembered *jouissance*, by a second alienation of the subject, it turns around again and supports this 'presence' within the terms of the fantasy itself, that is, in a mode that is completely inaccessible neither to language nor to memory. Fantasy organizes drive around the 'substance' – object or bit of *jouissance* – so as to reveal rather than conceal the way the epic liar claims his or her primary relation to enjoyment to be intrinsically alienated. Enjoyment returns to the subject, but in the guise of its being the *jouissance* of an/the Other.[19]

This creates a dilemma for feminism: on the one hand, hysterical 'discourse' suddenly accrues value as a formal means of woman's expression, requiring skilled and sympathetic interpretation; but on the other, its consequences for the possible construction of a feminine ethic, an ethic of woman's desire, are devastating, since she becomes doubly subject to the signifier she can only in fantasy displace by her possession of the Real Thing.

Lacan II/Atwood I/Freud 0

Hysteria, indeed, at the simplest, non-technical level abounds, as we have said, in Atwood's book. Serena Joy, Wife of the narrator's Commander, is a thinly disguised version of Tammy Faye Bakker, a former evangelist with 'her sprayed hair and her hysteria', who wept on demand for her weekly television show (*HT*, p. 61; 'How furious she must be now that she's been taken at her word'). Offred's submission of her identity to her uterus has already been mentioned; she repeats this organic submission as her understanding of the sexual contract: for the men of Gilead 'we are for breeding purposes . . . two-legged wombs, that's all, sacred vessels, ambulatory chalices' (*HT*, p. 176). There are also mass hysterias in the novel, such as the Salvagings (*HT*, pp. 353–5), where women who have gone astray are reclaimed; and Particicutions, where men convicted of 'sex crimes' are torn apart by the furious collected Handmaids. When a Handmaid actually gives birth, the Wife of her Commander simulates her childbirth postures and actions (*HT*, p. 149), but the group of Handmaids must go further. They are compelled to witness the birth and are told by the Aunts to 'identify with your body' (*HT*, p. 159).

Offred tells us, 'Already I can feel slight pains, in my belly, and my breasts are heavy.' There is even direct reference to Galen's 'wandering womb' (*HT*, p. 189).

More important thematically, Serena Joy is structurally placed by Atwood in the position of Freud's 'witty butcher's wife' – the classic analysis of hysterical identification with a sexual rival. Recall the butcher's wife's desire to keep all desire at bay, choosing as her imaginary rival a thin woman whom she knows cannot be desired by her husband, since he is known always to prefer a woman with a 'good slice of backside' on her. Significantly, she herself desires at some level not to be desired by her husband either, for she has already determined to 'give up caviar', in order to keep herself thin.[20] Thus the wife's renunciation, her 'giving up' the food she loves, actually speaks, Lacan decided at length, to a hysteric's demand for a limit to be placed by a mastering subject on the other *jouissance* which threatens her from within. By preventing her husband from desiring, she formally insists that he retain the fullness of that *jouissance* for himself (something which he, a mere man, can never, of course, do).[21]

Serena must hold the Handmaid on her belly while the Commander makes love to Offred during the Ceremony, so that she can identify in the flesh with this competitor who is being 'had' by her husband, but whom she knows, because of the conditions of the sexual encounter, he must always *enjoy* and can never desire.

It is also the case that Atwood's *Tale* could not be faulted even as a technical definition of *hysteria*. It crystallizes nearly every aspect of traditional and modern versions of hysteria around Offred – including, for example, the awe and respect she feels for flowers. (Freud's 1897 'L' draft on the 'Architecture of Hysteria' tells of a girl who was afraid to pick a flower, or even pull up a mushroom, because it was against the command of God, who did not wish living seeds to be destroyed.) Offred longs for a dandelion (*HT*, p. 275), and is horrified by her Commander's Wife who 'mutilates the genitals of flowers'. Her first intensity of tone appears when she describes Serena Joy in the garden

> snipping off the seedpods with a pair of shears . . . she was aiming, positioning the blades of the shears, then cutting with a convulsive jerk of the hands. Was it the arthritis, creeping up? or some blitzkrieg, some kamikaze committed on the swelling genitalia of the flower: The fruiting body. To cut off the seedpods is supposed to make the bulb store energy. (*HT*, p. 195)

What the cutting does, of course, is allow the flowers to continue to bloom, to grow lush: they are specifically *not* sacrificed directly to reproduction, although Offred strains to that conclusion. In fact, the resultant luxurious flowering appears to Offred as 'subversive' (*HT*, p. 196), too purely a pleasure for the senses, without higher, later or ultimate purpose.

So total, I propose, is this hystericized definition of Woman in the novel, that no woman escapes it: certainly not the narrator's women's lib mother (who burned *Playboy* because of its representation of women as sex objects and who chose to bear a child without a husband – 'What use are [men] except for ten seconds' worth of half babies. A man is just a woman's strategy for making another woman'; *HT*, p. 155). Nor the 'rebel' Moira (Gaelic: 'hope'), the tough, wisecracking, 'loose woman' (*HT*, p. 172), lesbian roommate (she's the one who, in the Time Before, used to fix her own car, and managed to escape from Gilead's Red Center). Moira ends up, however, like the Greek rather than the Gaelic meaning of her name, as an embodiment of Fate.[22] Her anatomy, too, turns out to be her destiny, and she is last seen as a whore plying her trade in a faded *Playboy* bunny suit (*HT*, p. 312) at *Jezebel's*, the Commanders' mocked-up brothel, throwing into reverse Gloria Steinem's own infamous career shift.

The setting-up of Offred as 'hysteric' is more than a play on words, for she is also set up as the product of the most enlightened 'education of women' currently available in modern times.[23] One might be tempted to conclude that her utter passivity and submission offer a conservative critique by Atwood of visionary, untried revolutionary ideas about changing the arrangements between the sexes, Atwood's judgment of the feminist woman as the 'beautiful soul' who assists in the construction of the reality she accuses. But I don't think so. For if we 'diagnose' Offred as a hysteric – and I think we must – we have to understand that her projection, her fantasy, assembled out of mnemonic fragments, reminiscences, partially remembered scenes, past images, is not the *repetition of a past enjoyment but only of past passivity*, which serves to preclude her enjoyment in the present.

That Gilead is *her* fantasy is not to be doubted. Her Commander in Gilead is clearly no more (nor less) than one exaggerated aspect of Luke,[24] her husband in the Time Before, the husband who said he would 'always take care of her' (*HT*, p. 232). Like the Commander, Luke was unsatisfactorily married when they met. In fact, the parallels are nearly absolute: she was, then as now, the girlfriend 'on the side' of a married man, meeting her lover in hotel rooms – which never really seemed to offer enjoyment for her, not even with Luke, for they took place when he 'was in flight from his wife, when I was still imaginary for him. Before we were married and I solidified' (*HT*, p. 67). When the Commander takes her to a hotel to have sex without Serena for the first time, Offred hears herself screaming over his threatened impotence: 'Fake it!' (*HT*, p. 331) She must keep her man from being less than omnipotent, overmastering, whole. (But *for* whom: for him or for her? Does she not want him to set the limits on her *jouissance*?)

Offred goes rigid when Nick (the nicked, the cut man), the chauffeur, tries to make an opening: 'Nice walk?' he says,

> I nod, but do not answer with my voice. He isn't supposed to speak to me. Of course some of them try, said Aunt Lydia. All flesh is weak. All flesh is grass, I corrected her in my head. They can't help it, she said, God made them that way but He did not make you that way. He made you different. It's up to you to set the boundaries. Later you will be thanked. (*HT*, p. 60)

Earlier she has seen the bodies of doctors who once performed abortions in the past hanging on hooks against The Wall (*HT*, p. 42); later, she is sent to buy meat for the Commander's household at a butcher shop called 'All Flesh', whose sign, a picture, not words, is a cut of meat. The cut, the weak, the person who lacks, is here pictured as the man, not the woman. What Offred refuses intercourse with is a man who might *want*, who may desire. At the same time, this fear of the less-than-Total-Man can be traced to her memory of detecting an inadequacy in her own 'man', her husband, Luke. Her daughter was nearly abducted by a fanatical fundamentalist (who felt the Lord had given her the baby) when she and her daughter had been out grocery shopping with Luke. Offred had her back turned, while Luke had been

> over at the side of the store, out of sight, at the meat counter. He liked to choose what kind of meat we were going to eat during the week. He said men needed more meat than women did, and that it wasn't a superstition and he wasn't being a jerk, studies had been done. There are some differences, he said . . . mostly he said it when my mother was there. He liked to tease her. (*HT*, p. 83)

The memory does double work in producing the fantasy: in it Luke appears to be a commanding figure, but he is not up to the job of protecting the family; the figures hung like meat carcasses on the wall are a reproach to him for his inadequacy – he needs meat, he is meat, he's a pig, he's dead meat. But as the little bit of reality at the base of Offred's fantasy, the incident precipitates whole chains of images which, like everything else in her Gilead, Offred has to reduce down to their root in a natural understanding of sexual difference – in order to distance herself from the possibility of her own *jouissance*.

All the more so in that each of the rules, or commands, she claims and believes are absolute, is broken by virtually everyone else in the novel from the Commander to the cook. The Commander, who sees Offred 'on the side' and sins with her (they play *Scrabble* together; he gives her old forbidden magazines to read; they drink and smoke together in private, though they do not, until later, have sex outside of The Ceremony). Lame Serena Joy 'fixes Offred up' with Nick, the chauffeur, to help her get pregnant, yes, but isn't she offering her bliss, too? Serena also promises to help Offred get her daughter back (*HT*, p. 266). Nick at night transgresses these absolute rules: he lets her in when she knocks, full of desire, at his door ('He didn't have to,' she tells us; *HT*, p. 344). If it is anyone's, Gilead is Offred's 'hysterical' fantasy, her self-offering to a master discourse into which she would be fitted, and to which her own weak flesh ('*Chair:* leader of a meeting; mode of execution, first syllable in charity, French word for flesh'; *HT*, p. 140), divided from any *jouissance* or enjoyment of its own, would be sacrificed – to her total Man, her Commander.

Which is not to say that male discourse is blameless, just because we've called its critic a 'hysteric'. On the contrary, the hysteric has here simply birthed, in her fantasy, the 'truth' of the tacit, subjectless, arrogation of the truth by the 'I': if there ever was one, Gilead is the '*Je-cratie*' (the 'I'-ocracy) of indirect discourse, history at its most epic, truth in quotation marks.

So we must now try to account for the sympathy we feel for Offred and her projection of an omnipresence of commanders and commandments, mastering males, and universally joyless, hysterical women. To do so, we must first look at the Discourse of the Master, and then at how the hysteric woman rewrites her 'history' as a relation to a maternal *jouissance*, the *jouissance* of the non-barred Other.

The Commander is, just like Luke, in every sense of the term, believable, like the spoken truth. Yet looked at very closely, he is composed of nothing more, for himself as well as Offred, than a series of stereotyped pictures of the Man, conceived on the model of the totemic father ('he looks us over as if taking inventory'; *HT*, p. 112):

> The Commander has on his black uniform, in which he looks like a museum guard. A semi-retired man, genial but wary, killing time. But only at first glance. After that he looks like a midwestern bank president, with his straight neatly brushed silver hair, his sober posture, shoulders a little stooped. And after that there is his mustache, silver also, and after that his chin, which really you can't miss. When you get down as far as the chin he looks like a vodka ad, in a glossy magazine, of time gone by . . . now he looks like a shoemaker in an old fairy-tale book. Is there no end to his disguises, of benevolence? We watch him, every inch, every flicker. (*HT*, pp. 111–12)

When Offred tries, as they say in film studies, to reciprocate and 'return the gaze', she quickly reaches a limit that is no less than the limit of the constructability of perfect male identity in any ideal/imaginary discourse:

> To be a man, watched by women. It must be entirely strange . . . sizing him up . . . to have them thinking. He can't do it, he won't do . . . to have them putting him on,

trying him on, trying him out, while he himself puts them on, like a sock over a foot, onto the stub of himself. (*HT*, p. 113)

Man's desire is quickly glossed over here, and turned into his failure, his castration in the most abject, literal sense. How soon 'her' discourse becomes 'his' turns, for Offred, around his penis, which from being seen, evaluated and estimated, transforms from a phallus into the very promise of a power of seeing her own inner 'truth'. At first she calls the penis which will enter her an 'extra, sensitive thumb', then a 'tentacle', then a 'stalked slug's eye, traveling forward as if along a leaf, into them, avid for vision . . . sharp eyed' (*HT*, p. 113). Defeated in her not very real demand for equal participatory access to vision, Offred hurls a silent defiance: 'But watch out Commander: I tell him in my head. I've got my eye on you. One false move and I'm dead' (*HT*, p. 113). (Again, note the ambiguity: if you falter as master subject, I do not exist.)

Thus, even if these are stereotypical advertising images of the successful Man, we cannot dismiss them as merely that: if they meet a particular need to construct an ideal gender, the total Man, it is by now clear that either of them, Offred or he, could have framed that image out of the elements of discourse; it is Offred, though, who alone can push it to the extreme of totalization where her own 'kernel of the real' can again become a question for her.

Of course, in so far as she lifts the bar, even just a little bit, on her discourse's structured disavowal of *jouissance*, and in so far as she does so not in spite of, but through her 'reconstructions' (her fantasies), Offred offers us, as Lacan said, a different 'guide', to the history not of the past, but of the future. In each situation where Offred discovers, minimal as it may be, *jouissance in* her hysteria, a little fragment of the discourse of the Master falls away. This *jouissance* plays doubly:

(1) *As jouissance through hysterical fantasy*: with Nick the imperative to 'Fake it!' lifts off, and she admits – after how many hesitations? – that she went back, night after night, and that she did so not for him, nor to save her life (for she risked it by doing this), but for herself alone, for her *jouissance*: 'I went back to Nick. Time after time, on my own, without Serena knowing. It wasn't called for, there was no excuse. I did not do it for him, but for myself entirely. I did not even think of it as giving myself to him, because what did I have to give?' (*HT*, p. 344). In other words, Nick is not acting as the instrument of Serena's *jouissance* except in the most roundabout, indirect way: Serena wants the baby, but less for its own sake than for the status it would permit her husband to retain. Thus Nick only partially participates in the sadistic structure of Gilead: he shows his power or potency to be something in addition to the instrument of 'divine *jouissance*', to use Lacan's term (*Seminar XVII*, p. 75).

But Nick is acting even less on his own behalf as a site of the absolute *jouissance* the hysteric structurally demands from him. Less than Command-ing, Nick is ambiguous (Offred is never certain whether he will let her in or turn her in). A 'man made of darkness' (*HT*, p. 338), without a face for her, Nick is obviously 'less' than The Man. He declines, from the start, participation in the 'I'-ocracy of spoken truth: he is an 'eye' that cuts his gaze by winking at her (*HT*, p. 24). He is a mode of transportation, an instrument of pleasure; yes, just what Offred had imagined herself to be in the Time Before, But he is also a joking partner, someone who wears his hat askew, a comforter, one who allows her to make those indecorous 'sounds, which I am ashamed of making' (*HT*, p. 340). Of course, he is no different from other stereotypes of romantic, if hard-boiled, leading men. (Isn't he a private eye? A tough, but virile T-shirted bachelor, the loner who takes women as they come, without complica-tions?) But Atwood/Offred does not attempt to depict him as a Total Man, the summation of 'All': he is just enigmatically partial enough that she has to keep on her toes, and though her life really depends on him, she no longer links that life-dependency to the set of phallic curtailments of her *jouissance* Gilead is for her. (Nick's gestures never become for her the kind of moves the Commander makes, the ones that cause her to flinch; she even tells Nick her real name (*HT*, p. 345.)

(2) *Hysterical jouissance as radical resistance*: at one point Offred spontaneously resists the imposition of an epic history that has cut off *jouissance* in a certain way. Alone in her room, another of her pre-digested, pre-figured narratives surfaces in her mind, but this time with a media-frame around it. Offred tells us she remembers having seen an interview once, on television, with the dying mistress of a concer tration camp commander (*HT*, p. 189): in it the woman had spoken of the gentleness of her man, of whose dirty work she had known nothing except that he performed it as a pure duty and not with enjoyment or relish. And he was so kind to the dog. 'How easy it is to invent a humanity, for anyone at all. What an available temptation,' Offred reflexively thinks, almost verging on a judgment, though the diction seems alien to her (*HT*, p. 189). And then suddenly,

> I've broken, something has cracked, that must be it. Noise is coming up, coming out, of the broken place, in my face. Without warning . . . If I let the noise get out into the air it will be laughter, too loud, too much of it, someone is bound to hear, and then there will be hurrying footsteps and commands and who knows? judgment: emotion inappropriate to the occasion. The wandering womb, they used to think. Hysteria. And then a needle, a pill. It could be fatal. (*HT*, p. 189)

Why *this* hysteria, at this moment? this rising gorge, this wandering womb, which surely is not the Bakhtinian laughter of carnival? Offred is laughing *in the face of* the sheer absurdity of the mistress's narrative, her epic depiction of *her* Commander as a hero of ordinariness, a real regular guy and forgivable any crime as long as he remains a Total Man. Given that Offred has been experiencing her Gileadic existence as that of the concentration camp inmate, the real one for whom laughter was really forbidden, the one who was really barred from all *jouissance*, Offred is laughing at the mistress's Myth of Man – and at her own. Such fairy-tales of the 'truth' in writing are important to desecrate. At the same time, it is crucial that Offred *be* hysterical in the other sense, 'out of control', in order to make this, her 'unconscious', yet all the more accurate critique, of the Biggest of Lies link up with the active voice of the 'truth' as such.

How, then, do Offred's hysteria and the history of the near future of Gilead intersect? Starting with a fragmented or dissociated sensibility, someone whose very sense of her own body is so remote that taking a bath ('My nakedness is strange to me already'; *HT*, p. 82) and rubbing purloined butter on her skin are monuments of self-awareness, she gropes sidelong towards a recounting of her 'own' history, her time for understanding: it will never, of course, be in time, in her time, or her discourse. But it will be in her reconstructed voice.

So what emerges in her apathetic, affectless assemblage of memory fragments is a kind of 'birth of truth in speech', in which reality is what is neither one nor the other – Gilead and all its institutions, laws, rules, regulations, everyday routines centrally commanded and organized around a single purpose (supposedly the reproduction of fathering, but really the demand to sacrifice totally her *jouissance* to the *jouissance* of the Other, to obviate her desire). What that 'truth' is, I have argued, is that of hysteria itself, its being paired with woman, and its intrusion into history, a special voicing that allows the return of *jouissance*. And what has surfaced in Offred's hysterical laughter is an avowable enjoyment, another relation beyond sacrifice and foreclosure, to the insistence of the *jouissance* within.

Notes

Acknowledgement

I wish to thank University of California Irvine for the Irvine Faculty Fellowship, which supported the writing of this chapter, the ORI in Women and the Image, and the Marin Headlands Center for the Arts where I was an artist-in-residence. Special thanks to Jennifer Dowley, Holly Blake, Ann Chamberlain, Fritizie Brown, and the staff of Headlands, as well as fellow residents Mardith Louisell, Bernie Lubell, Victor Zabala, Flo Wong and Elizabeth Young for their stimulating discussions.

1. Jacques Lacan, *Le Séminaire XVII: L'Envers de la psychanalyse*, ed. J.-A. Miller (Paris: Seuil 1991), p. 62.

2. See my entry 'Freud' in *The Oxford Companion to Women's Writing in the United States* (forthcoming):

> Femininity can now be seen as the direct result of a contradiction or double-bind in woman's relation to her own *jouissance*, created by her structural relation to the Mother; but it is potentially productive in effectively liberating her from the narrow band of choices granted her by an absence of 'identification' (with the rival father). Woman's 'choice' and consent remained narrow for Freud – she could basically choose her father or her brother. Nevertheless, structurally, Freud freed up the pleasurable rather than the purely reproductive aspects of her sexuality.
>
> For Freud, 'by thirty' woman's 'libido' appears to have 'taken up final positions and seems incapable of exchanging them for others.' ('Femininity', p. 119) On this 'unfriendly', not to say sour note, Freud tried to close the book on femininity, keeping it a mystery inside a riddle wrapped up in an enigma: a completely anesthetized, anesthetic posture. Yet, by his own account in the essay, the rigidified version of 'femininity' produced in women 'by age thirty' is already the product of a 'masculine' libido which has blunted the potential for development of an *aesthetics of femininity* resulting from the potential breadth of her range of choices for pleasurable objects beyond familial limits.

3. Catherine Millot's work summarizes best the central impasse: woman is denied identification with any woman/ego-ideal so long as that ideal must include the factor of phallic power. She is stuck with a Father with whom she cannot identify; a Mother who, if phallic, remains mythic, since no real woman could fulfil this requirement. In *Nobodaddy: L'hystérie dans le siècle* (Cahors: Point Hors Ligne 1988), pp. 54–7, Millot argues that for the girl the Oedipus complex is a refuge from rather than an acceptance of castration. Freud and Lacan see the castration complex as deepening the girl's demand for the phallus, but directing it away from the mother (who cannot meet it) towards the father (or the brother). This accounts for woman's 'weak' superego: she never renounces her demand for the father's penis in the form of a child from him; yet she never develops the *identification* with the father (ego-ideal) necessary for her to acquire a cultural superego.

   Consequently, as Millot explicates this logic, the woman has only an 'external' superego, and her 'love object' is never anything but a 'real' Other from whom she continually demands the phallus. She often becomes echo-logical, miming, seconding and identifying with her man-become-superego-for-her. Neither Klein's pre-oedipal superego nor the phallic mother have the power to reconfigure this limit. Woman is structured either by a persistent waiting for the penis or an insistent denial that she lacks it.

4. In *The Regime of the Brother: After the Patriarchy* (London: Routledge 1991), p. 25, I commented this way:

> The girl under patriarchy is faced with an inhuman choice: to do without an identity, or to identify with what she is not (it amounts to the same thing). She can accept that she has no symbol, no way of expressing her special needs, and thereby identify with what is 'only an absence', as Lacan puts it (p. 198). Or, she can identify with what she is *not*: her father, a man. Under Oedipus her 'identity' is either absent or the reverse of her reality – and her 'desire' is always a misstatement: her *lack* is seen as a quite literally unsatisfiable *desire*.
>
> Now, a 'missing' body part is a terrible model for her 'identity': the woman is set up from the start as one who cannot have one.

5. A recent issue of *Topoi*, no. 12 (1993), includes essays by Lucie Cantin, Willy Apollon and Danielle Bergeron, which provide some pointers; beyond these, few if any have attempted to describe a model of feminine *desire*.

6. See the remarkable paper by Joan Copjec on the formulas of sexuation in this volume, chapter 2.

7. Freud stated that 'Psycho-analysis does not try to describe what a woman is – that would be a task it could scarcely perform – but sets about enquiring how she comes into being, how a woman develops out of a child with a bisexual disposition' – 'Femininity', *The Standard Edition of the Complete Psychological Works of Sigmund Freud*, trans. James and Alix Strachey (London: The Hogarth Press and the Institute of Psycho-Analysis 1964), 22: p. 103.

8. Millot's analysis of *jouissance* gives the definite impression that she sees it as a kind of original sin, an inherent human failing. In her reading, Lacan would have pitted Spinoza's optimistic universalization of desire against Kant's universalizing of *jouissance*.

9. Interestingly, Derrida's general reading of 'woman' is as a function of the phallus, though he never makes this explicit. His grammatological assault on 'speech' is not as nuanced as are Lacan's subtle yet all-important distinctions among 'discourse', 'speech' and 'voice' as object *a*, as part-object part-organ.

10. This is the crux of the matter, as Millot has correctly seen, but her resignation before this absence ought perhaps to fire our imaginations rather than frustrate any further discussion.

11. Hélène Cixous, in her *Portrait de Dora*, has emphasized the revolutionary potential of hysteria over a more compliant attitude that acquiesces to hysteria's silence.

12. Margaret Atwood, *The Handmaid's Tale* [*HT*] (New York: Fawcett Crest 1985), p. 239.

13. For an exceptional essay which relates 'femininity' to the defence against the Other's *jouissance*, see Danielle Bergeron, 'Femininity', *The American Journal of Semiotics*, vol. 8, no. 4 (1991).

    Remarking that Freud saw the girl as striving to find man's organ as a bodily limit that would enable her to endure her lack, Bergeron counters that none of Freud's resolutions ('phallic phase', 'Oedipus complex', 'penisneid') of this lack are anything but imaginary. Yet the signifier cannot resolve this lack either, since it is too 'unreliable'. Instead, Bergeron writes, 'the Father's word of love, manifesting his love for his girl in the absence of sexual lust', is what 'situates her as subject in the order of language and manages the libidinous writing of the body' (p. 13). Thus the Father's word of love is seen as 'putting a limit to the Other's *jouissance* that is insisting in the girl-child's body'. In this way, the girl is placed 'in the register of the desiring subject . . . It follows that a failing in the father may result in psychosis or hysteria.'

    Offred's lack of any Father in the book makes her 'normality' in pre-Gilead America a concern.

14. Jacques Lacan, 'Vérité, soeur de la jouissance', chapter 4 of *Seminar XVII*.

15. Jacques Lacan, 'Function and Field of Speech and Language', *Ecrits* [*EE*] (New York: W. W. Norton 1977), pp. 30–113.

16. As in Bakhtin's anatomy of epic as pseudo-patriarchal discourse. See 'Epic and Novel', in M. M. Bakhtin, *The Dialogic Imagination* (Austin: University of Texas Press 1982).

17. This internal hypnotic drama functions for wide-awake consciousness like the theatre in antiquity:

    in which the original myths of the City State are produced before its assembled citizens stands in relation to a history that may well be made up of materials, but in which a nation today learns to read the symbols of a destiny on the march. In Heideggerian language one could say that both types of recollection constitute the subject as *gewesend* – that is to say, as being the one who thus has been.

    Lacan objects, of course, to how this picture distorts, decrying the extent to which alternative outcomes have been cast aside in this destinal marching: 'other encounters being assumed to have taken place since any one of these moments having been, there would have issued from it another existent that would cause him to have been quite otherwise' (*EE*, p. 47). It is this 'other side' that Lacan tracks via *hysterical revelation*.

18. This is because, according to Wittgenstein, only *facts* are articulated. (Prop. 6.51, 2, 3, 4); hence, any affirmation of truth beyond annunciation would be an 'added value'. To articulate 'Truth' is to take on what Kant would call a 'synthetic' status. It is something added, *d'en plus* – a supplement or surplus over what is in the subject of the phrase. To

rephrase Wittgenstein à la Kant, then, truth retains the character of being outside discourse, in some other world, even if its mode is fiction, fantasy, superfluity.

Lacan argues, by contrast, that the *sentence* as synthetic (i.e. not an analytic judgment and not concerned with the object) supports only the signifier. Wittgenstein's willingness to impute 'truth' to the signifier is simply wrong: it depends on his having made grammatical structure the truth of the whole world, turning any assertion whatsoever into a tacit, unspoken annunciation of 'truth' (*Seminar XVII*, pp. 66–7). For Lacan, however, the discourse of synthesis is the very Discourse of the Master. In '*Le Champ Lacanien*', chapter 5 of *Seminar XVII*, p. 79, Lacan (quoting his anonymous 'best friend' – Merleau-Ponty, perhaps) defines the discourse of consciousness as the 'discourse of synthesis'). What synthetic discourse tries to master is the 'referent' – the object of discourse.

19. Lacan used Freud's analysis of 'A Child is Being Beaten' for his first formulations here. Later, in logical formulations, Lacan depicted the discourse of the hysteric as:

$$\begin{array}{ccc} \$ & \longrightarrow & S_1 \\ \uparrow & & \downarrow \\ a & // & S_2 \end{array}$$

This matheme implies that the hysteric's way of existing as a split subject consciously and conscientiously relates directly to the 'first' or master subject, subject of mastery, and unconsciously represses the object a of her fantasy.

20. Moreover, she even puts herself in the place of her husband, who has expressed a desire to be thinner.

21. Freud asks why the butcher's wife stands 'in need of an unfulfilled wish'. Her husband had praised a thin lady friend of hers, who had subsequently expressed the wish to grow stouter, and requested an invitation to dinner from the wife. At this point, the butcher's wife's dream of having virtually nothing in the house (only 'a little smoked salmon') and thus of being forced 'to abandon my wish to give a supper-party' must be understood as her *identifying* with the imagined rival, with the extended implicit demand that this rival *give up* her desire and its subsequent *jouissance*. ('It is just as though . . . you said to yourself: "A likely thing! I'm to ask you to come and eat in my house so that you may get stout and attract my husband still more! I'd rather never give another supper party." ' Freud, *The Interpretation of Dreams, SE*, vol. 4: p. 182.

The demand entails a further interpretation, however, which Freud does not miss. At another level, the woman in the dream is the *rival*, not the wife, who 'had put herself in her friend's place . . . "identified" with her' (p. 182) at the level where, outside the dream, the wife had attempted a renunciation (of her beloved caviar). Freud located the *hysteria* of the dream at this second interpretative level; the level which requires us to ask: 'Who enjoys?' The point is that the butcher's wife does not want her husband to *desire* but to *enjoy*: we must not be permitted to be seen as lacking. In Lacan's terms, the husband, the full subject or S_1, must appear the most powerful in order to set the limits on the Thing, or the non-phallic 'other' *jouissance* which drives the wife. Her renounced *jouissance* circulates around the salmon/caviar which functions as an object *a*.

22. The Fates (Clotho, Atropos and Lacassis) all – phallically – deal with the threads of narrative or textual life: web, length, cut. The Latin word *fatum* is, moreover, the perfect passive participle of the verb *to say*.

23. Yet her 'cultural memory' is pre-set for her, in pre-digested renditions. Once she is within the space of pre-conditioned 'memories' of her past, she sounds like a perfectly normal, modern, educated woman, of independent mind and critical judgment. Yet Atwood is careful to ensure that the context, the precise situation in which Offred's memory is allowed to return to her, is shown to be part of an overall phallic discourse, male 'history'. Then *and* now.

Offred, for example, marvels at how free women used to feel before Gilead; but she only remembers that freedom when her own Commander, breaking the rules, dangles a forbidden copy of *Vogue* magazine before her 'like fish bait, I wanted it' (*HT*, pp. 200–201).

I wanted it with a force that made the ends of my fingers ache. At the same time, I saw this longing of mine as trivial and absurd, because I'd taken such magazines lightly enough once. I'd read them in dentists' offices, and sometimes on planes; I'd bought them to take to hotel rooms, a device to fill in empty time while I was waiting for Luke. After I'd leafed through them I would throw them away . . . and a day or two later I wouldn't be able to remember what had been in them. Though I remembered now. What was in them was promise. They dealt in transformations; they suggested an endless series of possibilities, extending life like the reflections in two mirrors set facing one another, stretching on, replica after replica, to the vanishing point.
They suggested one adventure after another, one wardrobe after another. They suggested rejuvenation, pain overcome and transcended, endless love. The real promise in them was immortality . . . I took the magazine from him and turned it the right way round. They were there again, the images of my childhood: bold, striding, confident, their arms flung out as if to claim space, their legs apart, feet planted squarely on the earth. There was something Renaissance about the pose, but it was princes I thought of, not coiffed and ringleted maidens. Those candid eyes, shadowed with makeup, yes, but like the eyes of cats, fixed for the pounce . . . Pirates, these women, with their ladylike briefcases for the loot and their horsy acquisitive teeth. (*HT*, p. 201)

24. Offred/Atwood taps the resources of the Gospel according to Luke for crucial imagery. In Luke 1 (King James version, New York: New American Library 1974), Luke declares himself an 'eyewitness', writing because he has 'had perfect understanding of all things from the very first' (Luke 1:3, 50). Mary submits to the Archangel of the Annunciation with the words, 'Behold the handmaid of the Lord; be it unto me according to thy word' (Luke 1:38, 51). Luke also deals with the 'sisterhood' of birthing, as Mary's elderly, barren cousin Elisabeth 'quickens' as a result of Mary's linkage to annunciation (Luke 1:41, 51: 'When Elisabeth heard the salutation of Mary, the babe leaped in her womb and Elisabeth was filled with the Holy Ghost'). 'Blessed is the fruit of thy womb' is first enunciated in Luke 1:42, and the parable of the barren fig tree appears in Luke 13:7–9, 68. The tree must be cut down if it fails to bear fruit for the third season. It relates to Offred's memory of being told to 'pretend you're a tree' in childhood dance classes, as well as to her general identification with plant life. Finally, Jesus tells us that 'life is more than meat' (Luke 12:23, 67). My argument that Offred is a *hysteric* requires that none of these Biblical references exists at a *conscious* level for Offred (the novel cites only Genesis 30: 1–3 and the story of Rachel and Leah as its Biblical 'source'). It is also crucial that they not be *unconscious* either. They are *pre-conscious*. As such they surface repeatedly in fragments. The repressed *unconscious wish* of hysteria has to take the 'path' of a *pre-conscious* memory, a 'mnemonic fragment', from which it *draws an inference* and extends it (*SE*, vol. 4: p. 183). The hysteric's speech and gestures are not an *imitation* but an '*assimilation* on the basis of a similar aetiological pretension' (*SE*, vol. 4: p. 183)
Thanks to Jonathan Cohen and Tracy McNulty for pointing out the Luke connection to me.

7 EXPERIMENTAL DESIRE
Rethinking Queer Subjectivity

ELIZABETH GROSZ

> To me, queer transcends any gender, any sexual persuasion and philosophy. Queerness is a state of being. It is also a lifestyle. It's something that's eternally the alternative. To both the gay and lesbian mainstream. What's queer now may not be queer in five years' time. If transgender queer was accepted by both communities, then there would be no queer. It's a reflection of the times you live in.
>
> (Jasper Laybutt, 'male lesbian', female-to-male transsexual who edits the Australian edition of *Wicked Women* in *Capital Q*, 9 October 1992, p. 9)

This is the final paper in a trilogy on queer sexuality and queer theory which I have written over the last few years.[1] The three papers have little in common other than a positive desire to utilize, to stretch (perhaps beyond the limits of its tolerance) and maybe, if necessary, to subvert and undermine, to experiment with and explore, the usefulness or otherwise of those forms of contemporary French theory that have come to earn themselves the somewhat dubious label 'postmodern', in the context of a rethinking of sexual politics.[2] They also share a negative concern to avoid the kinds of narrow-minded, dogmatic moralism and assurances of political correctness, that is, to avoid the *ressentiment* and reactiveness which, perhaps understandably, characterize so much of the literature on notions of oppression, whether class, race, sexual or religious.

These essays have sought to remove the constraints preventing a reinterrogation of presumptions, proclamations, methods of generalization, criteria and goals governing feminist and queer theory, whether these constraints are imposed from the straight world of academic values and scholarship, or from within the political terrain of feminist and queer theory itself; and, by clearing such an intellectual free space, to refuse to repeat the axioms and dogma of traditional understandings of queerness, exploring improbable discourses and theoretical models in the hope of thinking something new. Such an ambition always involves the risk of incoherence, obscurity and ridicule, but it is a risk we must face if we are to develop a way out of the impasses imposed on us by heterocentric, patriarchal cultures and knowledges.

I want to look at a set of rather old-fashioned concepts and issues, which could, I believe, remain useful if reformulated: lesbian and gay *sexualities*, *oppression* and '*identity*'. I do not want to replay the usual anti-humanist or poststructuralist critiques of identity which seek to displace, decentre or even destroy the notion of subjective/sexual 'identity', but to rewrite or reclaim them and, in the process, to clarify some issues that are or should be crucial to the area now known as 'queer theory'.[3] It is not simply the political history and former power of these terms that I wish to resuscitate: I am not really interested in nostalgic replayings, but in refusing to give up terms, ideas and strategies that still work, whose potentialities have still not been explored. I want to look at these terms very carefully, to see what they mean and how they are being and can be used.

Systematic Structures of Power

For notions like oppression, discrimination or social positioning to have any meaning, they must be grasped outside any particular form (whether racist, imperialist, sexual, class, religious). In other words even though we recognize that oppressions have massive historical and cultural variations, something must be shared by all the different forms of oppression, if they are to be described by the same term. Both this core, or perhaps even 'essence', and the range and variability of the term need to be addressed if one is to come to a clearer understanding of the relations and interactions between different forms of social domination, and their concrete differences and specificities. Our understanding of the term must be precise if it is to be used not only to cover a wide variety of different types of oppression, but also to articulate the interlockings and transformations effected by the congruences, convergences, points of reinforcement and/or tension among these different types. My goal, however, in attempting to render these interlocking systems of oppression visible, is not to set up a kind of hierarchy of oppressed subjects, an index of degrees of oppression,[4] nor to provide a typology which is inclusive of all types of oppression (this seems to be the current trend in much contemporary theorizing about oppressions[5]), but to understand the inflections any particular category must undergo when it is coupled with or related to other categories.

If there are general characteristics that mark the social attribution of value, the distinguishing and marking of social categories, that is, if *oppression* is to have some broad meaning, it must be minimally understood as:

1. A systematically differential production of social positions or places which function as modes of specification, constitution and valuation within a general structure that distributes benefits, power, authority and value according to those differential (usually hierarchically structured) positions. This implies that whatever skills, capacities and attributes members of the subordinated groups have, their ability to take up the privileged positions remains extremely limited if not impossible. There is always a submersion of singularities and particularities by the characteristics attributed to the group.

2. These differential positions, marked by inequities of value and power, distribute benefits to those in privileged positions only at the expense of other, subordinated positions. This privilege is possible only because its cost is borne by subordination. This explains why structures of power and authority remain tenaciously difficult to transform: it is simply not in the interests of the dominant groups, who have benefits without actually paying for them, readily to give up those benefits without a struggle. Certainly, the impetus and motive for change cannot come from this dominant group, which stands to lose much of its privilege in any realignment of relative positions.

3. Not only are specific groups positioned in differential locations within the social structure (positions which may be interlocked or interdependent, but which serve only the interests of the dominant group), these positions are directly or indirectly linked to values, attributes, benefits, mobility, which are not specifically inscribed in but are preconditioned by these positions. Being born male, white, middle-class, Christian, and so on gives one access to wealth, decision-making and naming capacities which, while not entirely out of the reach of other groups, is made extremely difficult for them to attain, except perhaps at the cost of renouncing or overcoming their definitional link to a subordinated group. (Blacks or women, for example, can attain the benefits of the middle class, but only by leaving behind any identification with others within that group).

4. Relations of domination and subordination are characterized not simply in terms of tangible material benefits, although these are readily documented, but also in terms of the ease and ability of dominant groups to produce systems of meaning, signification and representation, which present their interests, perspectives, values and frameworks in positive terms and define their others (non-reciprocally) in terms of these interests. This ease is denied to members of subordinate groups. Here, I do not want to suggest that the capacity to change meaning, to develop new meanings and frameworks, is impossible for dominated groups, but it is none the less made considerably more difficult, and is a matter of bitter struggle and contestation.

5. The relations of domination and subordination constituting oppression are more complicated than the occupation of fixed, stable positions of power and powerlessness or centrality and marginality, respectively. While positions of domination clearly accrue privileges and benefits at the expense of the subordinated, they also have their long-term drawbacks, in so far as those who occupy these positions lose access to certain skills of self-determination, skills acquired through struggle, resistance and the necessary ingenuity of those in subordinated positions. While positions of subordination require the loss or absence of many of the rights and privileges of dominant positions, they also produce certain skills and modes of resourcefulness, the capacity precisely for self-sustenance and creativity which are lost to the dominators. These become complacent and self-satisfied, while the subordinated must sharpen their wits and continuously develop themselves or succumb to their oppressed positions. It is only through the engagement, the encounter between the dominators and the dominated, through the resistances posed by the dominated to the dominators that social change follows a certain direction (even if that direction and the rates of progress to any pre-given goal cannot be guaranteed by members of either or both groups).

The notion of oppression is clearly linked to power, to the relations, impulses and forms that power may take. But perhaps since the work of Michel Foucault in the mid-1970s, notions of power and, indeed, oppression have undergone relatively major transformations, so that the relations between power, domination and subordination are no longer rendered quite so clear-cut and unambiguous in their status. The subordinated are implicated in power relations even if they are not complicit in them: they are implicated because, as a mobile set of force relations, power requires structural positions of subordination, not as the outside or limit of its effectivity, but as its very internal condition, the 'hinge' on which it pivots. In spite of its well-documented problems in feminist terms,[6] the work of Foucault has at least one insight (but no doubt also many more) to offer feminist and lesbian theorists. It has rendered the notion of oppression considerably more sophisticated; it has taught us that those who are assigned inferior social values are not automatically made passive and compliant victims or sufferers; those occupying subordinate social positions cannot be stripped of all capacities and all modes of resistance. These positions are not simply subordinated to a singular schema through a universally enforced operation; rather, resistance is engendered and engenders its own kinds of strategy and counter-strategy, exerts its own kinds of force (which are not simply the opposite or inverse of the dominators), its own modes of ingenuity, its own practices, indeed its own knowledges, which may themselves, depending on their socio-cultural placement, and the contingencies of the power game that we have no choice but to continue playing, be propelled into positions of power and domination. Foucault, in short, and by no means on his own, has provided a sense of hope, a signal of the possibility, indeed necessity, of a certain (subjective but non-intentional) agency and efficacy for those classified as oppressed.[7] He has problematized megalithic understandings of capitalism, patriarchy, racism and imperialism as systematic, coherent, global programmes and this made it more difficult to assert hard-and-fast allegiances and interlockings between these great systems. These interconnections now appear more expedient, less programmed and cohesive, and thus more amenable to realignment and transformation, even if they are now murkier, less clear-cut, less easy to read than any simple assertion of good (politically correct) or bad.

Given this understanding of relations of power and domination, we can wrench notions of oppression and social valuation from a humanist history and make them reveal the issues of difference that undergrid them. When theories of oppression remained embedded in the framework of a universalizing, individualizing humanism, which sought to recognize all subjects (or, more commonly, most subjects) on the model of a bare or general humanity, difference disappeared into categories of the pre-, proto- or non-human. Otherness could enter at best, if at all, as a secondary modification of this basic human nature, a minor detail, and not as a fundamental dimension or defining characteristic, which alters with it all the other general capacities attributed to 'human' existence. Feminism, along with anti-humanism, launched the most direct assault on that humanism that took as its standard of the human form the presumptions, perspectives, frameworks and interests of men.

Sex and Sexuality

Are the characteristics I have outlined above adequate for characterizing what I will call 'sexual oppression', the disqualification, devaluation and misrepresentation of subjects and practices on the basis of either (or both) their sex and their sexuality? Do they encompass the specific modalities of oppression experienced by women in general, by lesbians and gay men, by various perverts, transsexuals, transvestites, drag queens, butches, cross-dressers and all the other variations of sexual transgression? This is the anti-humanist question: do the apparently universal characteristics of all modes of oppression, independent of their particularities, in fact refer equally to all types of oppression? If they do, then in what ways do they help to explain misogyny and homophobia in their concreteness and difference from other forms of oppression? If they only serve to characterize oppression, but not to specify its homophobic dimension, then what needs to be added or modified to make them appropriate? These questions give rise to others: Is there such a thing as homophobia? Do lesbians experience the same forms of homophobia as gay men? Does the fact that one is a woman or a man (however one chooses to define these terms) alter the forms of homophobia one experiences? Moreover, does the very category of sex/sexuality differ sexually, that is, according to the sex and the sexuality of the subject under question?

Here I want to reconsider the terms 'sex' and 'sexuality' in the light of, but at variance with, the theory of Foucault. For him – and this is one of his major innovations – sex can no longer be understood as the ground, the real, the (biological/natural) foundation to which the superstructures of 'gender' and 'sexuality' can be added. There is no biological substratum available as support for some discursive and cultural overlay. For him, the very notion of sex as given and as fundamental to subjectivity, to identity, is itself the product or effect of a socio-discursive regime of sexuality. An often cited passage makes this clear:

> Sex – that agency which appears to dominate us and that secret which seems to underlie all that we are, that point which enthrals us through the power it manifests and the meaning it conceals, and which we ask to reveal what we are and to free us from what defines us – is doubtless but an ideal point made necessary by the deployment of sexuality and its operation. We must not make the mistake of thinking that sex is an autonomous agency which secondarily produces manifold effects over the entire length of its surface of contact with power. On the contrary, sex is the most speculative, most ideal, and most internal element in a deployment of sexuality organized by power in its grip on bodies and their materiality, their forces, energies, sensations and pleasures.[8]

In *Gender Trouble: Feminism and the Subversion of Identity*, and in more recent texts, Judith Butler seems largely to affirm Foucault's understanding of sex as an artificial, conventional or cultural alignment of disparate elements linked together, not through nature, reason or biology, but through historical expedience – the kinds of alignment produced by and required for the deployment of discourses, knowledges and forms of power. Butler, however, adds a third term to the Foucauldian pair sex/sexuality: the notion of gender, which is, I believe, more antithetical to Foucault's account than she admits. For gender *must* be understood as a kind of overlay on a pre-established foundation of sex – a cultural variation of a more or less fixed and universal substratum – and this fact is captured by the notion of performance in so far as the body that performs, however much Butler insists it is produced by the performing itself, must nevertheless abide in between performances, existing over and above the sum total of its performances. For Butler, performance is the term that mediates between sex and gender: gender is the performance of sex. This notion of gender, as I have argued elsewhere, following the work of Moira Gatens,[9] now seems largely irrelevant or redundant, a term that is unnecessary for describing the cultural variability in the ways we live, give meaning to and enact sex. While not wishing to deny this variability, I am reluctant to regard gender as the expression of sex, as Butler suggests, in so far as sex is itself always already an expression, which does not require (or forbid) a second-order expression:

> The notion that there might be a 'truth' of sex, as Foucault ironically terms it, is produced precisely through the regulatory practices that generate coherent identities through the matrix of coherent gender norms. The heterosexualization of desire requires and institutes the production of discrete and asymmetrical oppositions between 'feminine' and 'masculine', where these are understood as expressive attributes of 'male' and 'female'. The cultural matrix through which gender identity has become intelligible requires that certain kinds of 'identities' cannot 'exist' – that is, those in which gender does not 'follow' from either sex or gender.[10]

As I understand it, the term *sex* refers, not to sexual impulses, desires, wishes, hopes, bodies, pleasures, behaviours and practices: this I reserve for the term *sexuality*. *Sex* refers to the domain of sexual difference, to the question of the *morphologies of bodies*.[11] I do not want to suggest that sex is in any sense more primordial than or exists independently of 'sexuality'. With Foucault, I agree that sex is a product of regimes of sexuality (which is another way of saying that the inscription, functioning and practices of a body constitute what that body is: a body *is* that which it is capable of doing; the body cannot be understood as a pre-inscriptive surface on which culture writes its norms, for such an understanding ignores the constitutive productivity of inscription itself: the inscription actively and retrospectively creates the surface on which it writes). With Butler, and against Foucault, I want to argue that both sex and sexuality are marked, lived and function quite differently according to whether it is a male or female body that is being discussed. Sex is no longer the label of both sexes in their difference as in Foucault's writings, a generic term indicating sexed, as opposed to inanimate, existence: it is now the label and terrain of the production and enactment of sexual difference. Gender, it seems, is a redundant category: all its effects, the field that it designates, are covered by the integration of and sometimes the discord between sexuality and sex.

Butler enjoins us to 'Consider gender, for instance, as a *corporal style*, as "act", as it were, which is both intentional and performative, where "performative" suggests a dramatic and contingent construction of meaning.'[12] She herself needs the category of gender to mark the discontinuity, the alarming and threatening disjunction, between gender and sex, the possibility for the masculine behaviour of a female subject and the feminine behaviour of a male subject, the point of tension and uneasiness, separating heterocentric demands from the subversive transgressions of the queer subject, the subject in drag, the subject performatively repeating but also subverting heterosexual norms and imperatives, the site of radical disconnection. But the force of her already powerful arguments would, I believe, be strengthened, if instead of the play generated by a term somehow beyond the dimension of sex, in the order of gender, she focused on the instabilities of sex itself, of bodies themselves. Isn't it more threatening to show, not that gender can be at variance with sex (which implies the possibility or even social desirability or necessity of the Stollerian solution of realigning the one, usually sex, with the other, gender, of forcing their conformity through psychical or surgical means), but that there is an instability at the very heart of sex and bodies, that the body is what it is capable of doing, and what anybody is capable of doing is well beyond the tolerance of any given culture?

Affective Bodies

In order to provide an account of the production of sex through the regimes of sexuality, I am less interested at this moment in invoking Foucault than Gilles Deleuze and Félix Guattari. I am interested in understanding the differences and the connections between an ontology – what a body is – and a pragmatics – what a body can do. Since Deleuze and Guattari are not very explicit about questions of sexuality, sex and sexual identity, my forays into their work will be more speculative and tenuous than the readings offered by feminists working with psychoanalytical or Foucauldian theory, which is more easily recuperable for the project of understanding the ways in which erotic and pleasurable practices help constitute the specificities and cultural particularities of sexed bodies. Because Deleuze's work unsettles the notion of a stable subject, he thus also problematizes the assumption that sex is the secret or truth of the subject. Whether or not this unsettling has positive effects for feminist and queer theory will depend on what it enables us to do, to change. If a body is what a body does, then lesbian and gay sexualities, and above all, lifestyles, produce lesbian and gay bodies, bodies distinguished not just by sex, race and class characteristics, but also by sexual desires and practices.

Deleuze's reading of Nietzsche[13] stresses his privileging of affect, force, energy and impulse over depth, psychology, interiority or intention. Nietzsche not only corporealizes knowledge, the arts and indeed all cultural production, he also reconceptualizes the ways in which these are now judged: philosophy, theory, knowledge are now understood in terms of movement, action, production.[14] Philosophy is best performed as dancing, with joyous bodily affirmation, with revelry and delight. Knowledge is the effect or product of bodies which have – through habits, errors of grammar and cultural imperatives – been misconstrued as conceptual or purely mental. But not only an effect of bodies, knowledge also enables bodies to act, or prevents them from acting, overcoming themselves, becoming.

To be brief: while Nietzsche is often read for his distinction between noble and base impulses, between the moralities of the aristocrat and of the slave, Deleuze reads in him a distinction between active and reactive forces. Systematizing Nietzsche's openly chaotic writings, Deleuze links the will to power to the functioning of differential forces (both in an individual body and in social or collective bodies) that can be described as either (or, variously, both) active or reactive, depending on their quality. These qualities are a function and effect of the differing quantities of excitation or force of impulses. It is not the case that only active forces exhibit the will to power, while reactive ones are those that have somehow succumbed to the will or given it up; rather, both forces are equally products of the will to power. Where *active* and *reactive* are terms that express force, corresponding to them, at the level of the will to power (the level of interpretation rather than affect), are the terms *affirmative* and *negative*: 'Affirming and denying, appreciating and depreciating, express the will to power just as acting and reacting express force' (p. 54). Affirmation clearly functions in some alignment with action, just as negation is reactive, but these alignments are tenuous. They do not define entities but processes: 'Affirmation is not action but the power of becoming active, *becoming active* personified. Negation is not simply reaction but a *becoming reactive*' (p. 54).

Deleuze makes the distinction between active and reactive forces in terms of the links between them and affirmation and negation. Active forces affirm or assert themselves, revel in their differences, develop in their own positive directions; reactive forces, by contrast, function to limit and contain activity. They function to negate, dampen or restrict activity, to neutralize it and prevent its effects. According to Deleuze, reactive forces function primarily by way of decomposition, by introducing a decisive break between active force and what it can do. (p. 57) Reactive forces, then, do not steal the activity from active forces; rather, they convert active forces into the forces of reaction, they separate a force from its effects, through the creation of myth, symbolism, fantasy and falsification. In a certain sense, reactive force can be regarded as seductive, enticing, luring: it ensnares active force for its own purposes and procedures, for its own falsifications and rationalizations.[15]

In short, active force is that which stretches itself, takes itself as far as it can go (a limit that cannot be known in advance), moves along its own path without regard for anything other than its own free expansion, mindless of others. It is guileless, open, perhaps even naive; it is open to what befalls it. Reactive forces, on the contrary, are cunning, clandestine, restricting, intervening, secondary, mindless, diligent and obedient. They function ingenuously, dwelling in modes of sensibility and sentiment (nostalgia, self-justification and hatred of the other are their primary features). Where active forces affirm, produce and stretch, reactive forces judge, pontificate, produce ideologies and modes of explanation, devise ingenious theories, compromise. They can be identified with the production of religion, morality and law, with the systems constrained to endless reproduction of the same, without affirming the infinite nature of chance, change and transformation. Although affirmative judgments and active force are commonly described as aristocratic or noble, and negative forces as servile and base – that is, although affirmation is seen as the domain of the powerful, of those *in* power, and negation and *ressentiment* as attributes of the oppressed and the powerless – this description oversimplifies Nietzsche's more sophisticated understanding of these as microforces, alignments and interactions *within* individuals as much as *between* them.

Although neither Nietzsche nor Deleuze ever discusses the question of sexual orientations and lifestyles, it seems to me plausible to suggest that those forces, activities and impulses governed by the regime of compulsory heterosexuality (in which we all participate, since none of us can remain free of this imperative, even as we may choose to defy it or transform it) could be understood on the model of slavish or reactive forces, forces that act to separate a body from what it can do, that reduce a body to what it is rather than what it can become; while gay and lesbian sexual practices and lifestyles, in so far as they risk a certain stability, a certain social security and ease, in so far as they refuse the imperatives of heterosexuality, can and should be seen as a triumph of active and productive forces. We are prevented, however, from too ready a generalization, too black and white a characterization of straights as crippled emotional slaves, and gays, lesbians and other queers as transgressive sexual radicals if we refrain – as we must – from the simplistic assumption that there exist singular impulses directed solely to conformity or subversion. In each of us there are elements and impulses that strive for conformity and those that seek instability and change: this is as true for heterosexuals as it is for queers of whatever type (although it may well be that there is less external impetus for expansion, development and change for those – heterosexual men, primarily – who reap the rewards and benefits of conformity). Indeed, one of the avowed reasons why many have adopted the term 'queer' was to set themselves outside, not only the heterosexual but also the gay communities, which, many claim, function as coercively, as judgmentally as their heterosexual counterparts. It is a question of degree, of more or less, rather than of type, a matter of varying investments which all of us have, one way or another, in a certain type of complicity with stability and social imperative.[16]

This is not, however, to say that all of us – from the suburban couple whose rate of copulation is at least once a month, to the queerest of queers – are the same.[17] Of course not. But simply that it is a matter of degree, of location, and of will. The heterosexual can, I believe, remain a heterosexual but still undertake subversive or transgressive sexual relations outside the copulative, penetrative, active/passive, stereotyped norm (but does so only rarely); and lesbians and gays can, of course, engage in sexual relations that duplicate as closely as they can the structures, habits and patterns of the straightest and most suburban heterosexuals (but succeed only rarely). So simply *being straight* or *being queer*, in itself, provides no guarantee of one's position as sexually radical: it depends on how one lives one's queerness, or one's straightness, one's heterosexuality as queer.

Regimes of Sexuality

If we return to Foucault and his distinction between sex and sexuality, his claim that the discursive regimes of sexuality produce as their historical effect the phenomenon called sex, we see that, although he is at great pains to deny it elsewhere, he does in fact distinguish between the functioning of power (the deployment of sexuality) and a somehow pre-power real, a real that he describes in terms of a set of timeless 'bodies and pleasures'. In a notorious passage from *The History of Sexuality*, one which Judith Butler has also taken as a significant site of tension in his works,[18] Foucault discusses a game called 'curdled milk' (which today we would have to regard as a case of child sexual abuse), between a simple-minded farmhand and a young girl:

> At the border of a field, he had obtained a few caresses from a little girl, *just as he had done before* and seen done by the village urchins round him . . . What is the significant thing about this story? The pettiness of it all; the fact that this *everyday occurrence* in the life of village sexuality, these *inconsequential bucolic pleasures*, could become, from a certain time, the object not only of a collective intolerance but of a judicial action, a medical intervention, a careful clinical examination, and an entire theoretical elaboration.[19]

Foucault seem to imply here that there are certain activities, 'inconsequential pleasures', that are somehow below the threshold of power's reach: these pleasures are relatively innocent, disinvested and pedestrian. They are everyday occurrences which only became objects of power's ever-intensifying scrutiny relatively recently. He makes a similar claim, though perhaps with less sinister effects, in one of his more inciting and direct statements:

> It is the agency of sex that we must break away from, if we aim – through a tactical reversal of the various mechanisms of sexuality – to counter the grips of power with the claims of bodies, pleasures and knowledges, in their multiplicity and their possibilities of resistance. The rallying point of the counterattack against the deployment of sexuality ought not to be sex-desire, but bodies and pleasures.[20]

To remain within the domain of sexuality (as, Foucault implies, much of sexual liberationist politics does), is not only to remain complicit in the functioning of power – for there is a constitutive complicity between power and resistance, he insists – but also to support and extend power's operations. But, he seems to be arguing, in the multiplicity of possibilities for bodies and pleasures that are somehow bound up with the functioning of the regime of sexuality, we have now opportunities for a non-complicit resistance to power. This means that even if sexual liberationists remain within the folds of power, gay and lesbian (though he certainly does not mention the latter) bodies, pleasures, practices and lifestyles may not.

This assertion cannot be made without some explanation of the status and political position of bodies and pleasures. Bodies and pleasures cannot be understood as somehow fixed or biologically given constants, somehow outside or beyond the constraints of power, no matter how much Foucault may have yearned for a disinvested ground, a datum onto which the operations of power could be directed, no matter how much he believed, in spite of himself, in harmless yet timeless pleasures, and bodies as yet unmarked, uninscribed by power. What Foucault means, in the most generous reading, is that bodies and pleasures are themselves produced and regulated as distinct phenomena through, if not forms of power as such, at least various interlocking 'economies', libidinal, political, economic, significatory, which may congeal and solidify into a sexuality in 'our' modern sense of the word, but which also lend themselves to other economies and modes of production and regulation. A different economy of bodies and pleasures may find the organization of sexuality, the implantation of our sex as the secret of our being, curious and intriguing, rather than self-evident.[21] It is this reorganization of this libidinal structure, which Foucault nowhere discusses, that does not seem to be adequately addressed by psychoanalysis.[22]

Thus, Deleuze's distinction between active and reactive forces, and between affirmative and negative judgments or interpretations, may prove useful in filling this gap, in rethinking the issue of a different libidinal organization, a mode of living and of using bodies and pleasures in ways that escape the regimes of sexuality which establish heterocentrism (and its mode of ideological validation, homophobia) as the regulative norm of subjectivity.

Pleasures

In devising a theory of queer pleasures and their relations to the straight, we cannot, in fact, rely only on the works of Foucault and Deleuze, no matter how crucial these have been to our conceptualization of the present limits of various theories of sexual politics. Because we are dealing with sexual specificities, differences between the sexes, and those differences that constitute each sex, I can no longer afford to generalize about 'queerness'. For this term, which covers a vast range of sexual practices, partners, aims and objects (heterosexual as well as homosexual), is basically a reactive category, which sees itself in opposition to a straight norm and thus defines itself in terms of this norm. It collects all sorts of deviant sexual practices, without asking what they share and without taking into account the profound tensions and contradictions that may exist among these practices. I do not find it useful to talk about queerness, or even gayness, when trying to theorize sexed bodies and their sexual relations without specifying at least broadly the kinds of bodies and desires in question.

I will, then, concentrate on lesbian desire and sexual relations between women, an area that still remains largely untheorized – though this may function to the advantage rather than the detriment of lesbians. It is clear that, especially in the era of the AIDS crisis, there is an ever more detailed analysis, observation and theorization of gay and bisexual men's sexual practices, while lesbianism remains, among the sexual 'perversions', one of the least analysed. It is significant, too, that while gay men's sexual practices have been under the scrutiny of the law for over a century, in Australia at least there have never been laws specifically prohibiting lesbianism. Legally, it went unrecognized until recent equal opportunity and anti-discrimination legislation. I do not want to suggest that lesbians are either more or less oppressed than gay men, that it is better or worse to be recognized or not recognized in the eyes of the law; arguments could be made both ways. My point here is simply that there is no representation of lesbians *as* lesbians in certain key discourses deeply invested in power relations.

This underinvestment in the theorization of lesbian sexual practices is only partly illustrated by the status of lesbianism in the discourses of law and medicine. A similar underrepresentation characterizes erotic discourses, particularly visual pornography, where only a certain form or, better, fantasy of lesbianism – sanitized, safe, figured in male-oriented terms – is representable. There is a manifest inadequacy of erotic language to represent women's sexual organs, sexual pleasures and sexual practices in terms other than those provided either for male sexuality or by men in their heterosexual (mis)understanding of the sexualities of their female partners. All the terms for orgasm, for corporeal encounters, for sexual exchanges of whatever kind are not only derived from heterosexual models, but, more alarmingly, from the perspective of the men, and not the women involved in these relations. The very terms for sex, for pleasure, for desire – *fucking, screwing, coming, orgasm* and so on – inscribe this male perspective.

But perhaps the solution to this problem is not simply the addition of a new set of terms, new labels to describe 'things' that, while they exist as such, are not yet named. For this solution presumes a female sexuality, and especially lesbian sexuality, which is readily designatable as distinct entities, objects and organs;[23] it implies that one knows in advance what one wants to designate by the new terms, that the sexual pleasures, desires, organs and activities of women are a known or knowable quantity, and that, like the new discoveries of science, they only need appropriate names. Before opting for this solution, we must first ask ourselves why given the enormous investment of knowledges in the codification and control of sexuality, lesbianism has been so decidedly ignored. Does this neglect represent a lapse in the regime of sexuality, a sign of its imperfections and its capacity to create sites of resistance; or is it a mode of further delegitimizing lesbianism, a ruse of power itself? This is not an idle question, for whether one reads it as a shortcoming of power or as one of its strategies will dictate whether one seeks to retain the indeterminacy of lesbianism and of female sexuality – my present inclination – or seeks to articulate lesbianism as loudly and as thoroughly as possible, which Marilyn Frye seems to advocate.

Frye seems to believe that the silence that obscures the details of lesbian sexual relations is an effect of the obliteration or subsumption of women under heterosexist sexual norms. Thus, in her largely phenomenological reflections on lesbian 'sex', she yearns for a language and a mode of representation of lesbian sexual practices. She implies that without an adequate language, without appropriate terms, women's experiences are themselves less rich, less rewarding, less determinate than they could be:

> I once perused a large and extensively illustrated book on sexual activity by and for homosexual men. It was astounding for me for one thing in particular, namely, that its pages constituted a huge lexicon of *words*: words for acts and activities, their sub-acts, preludes and denouements, their stylistic variation, their sequences. Gay male sex, I realized then, is *articulate*. It is articulate to a degree that, in my world, lesbian 'sex' does not remotely approach. Lesbian 'sex' as I have known it, most of the time I have known is, is utterly *in*articulate. Most of my lifetime, most of my experience in the realms commonly designated as 'sexual' has been pre-linguistic, non-cognitive. I have, in effect, no linguistic community, no language, and therefore in one important sense, no knowledge . . . The meaning one's life and experience might generate cannot come fully into operation if they are not woven into language: they are fleeting, or they hover, vague, not fully coalesced, not connected, and hence, not *useful* for explaining or grounding interpretations, desires, complaints, theories.[24]

While I certainly have sympathy for this claim and recognize that certain delegitimated social and sexual practices may require adequate modes of representation to affirm and render these practices viable, it is not clear to me that representability is in itself always a virtue: the most intense moments of pleasure, their force and materiality, while broadly evocable in discourse, are never captured discursively. A distinction must be drawn between discourse and experience even though one understands that language is the prior condition for the intelligibility of experience. Moreover, it is ironic that the very terms Frye uses to characterize the failure of representation to specify lesbian relations and experiences, the accusation that it renders them *fleeting, vague, unconnected,* accord precisely with the more positive characterization accorded to these concepts and to female sexuality itself in the writings of Luce Irigaray.[25] For Irigaray female sexuality is itself not self-identical, not enumerable, not made of distinct and separate parts: not one (but indeterminately more than one).

Here we must be careful not to erect a new ontology based on what woman *is*, in and of herself. Irigaray, and other theorists of female sexuality (either heterosexual or lesbian), do not provide an account of female sexuality in its essence or in its fixed form, but rather expose the paradoxes and consequences that attend female sexuality within forms of knowledge and representations that can only ever take it as object, as external and alien to the only set of perspectives presenting themselves as true: men's. Female sexuality, lesbian desire, is that which eludes and escapes, that which functions as an excess, a remainder uncontained by and unrepresentable within the terms provided by a sexuality that takes itself as being straightforwardly what it is.

Part of the reason that there is such an explosion of sexual terminology regarding details, distinctions, nuances, phases, modalities, styles, organs, practices in gay male literature, and especially in pornography and in personal columns in newspapers, is that male sexuality, both straight and gay, continues to see itself in terms of readily enumerable locations defined around a central core or organizing principle. When sexuality takes on its status as phallic, entities, organs, pleasures and fantasies associated with it become definitive, distinguishable from their environment or context, separable, nameable and capable of being reflected on, fantasized and experienced in isolation from one another. Distinct organs, separable bodily regions, with distinct states, definitive and readily measurable goals, are possible only when one has the capacity to assume a reflective and analytic relation to one's own body and experiences, to distance oneself as a knowing subject from oneself as the object known. Any experience, any organ, any desire is capable of categorization and organization, but only at the expense of its continuity with the rest of the body and experience, and only at the cost of separating oneself from immersion in its complexity and intensity. To submit one's pleasures and desires to enumeration and definitive articulation is to submit processes, becomings, to entities, locations and boundaries, to become welded to an organizing nucleus of fantasy and desire whose goal is not simply pleasure and expansion, but control, and the tying of the new to models of what is already known, the production of endless repetition, endless variations of the same.

This fact is borne out most clearly in the fascination that sexology has had in the various long-term debates surrounding female sexuality (debates that in a certain sense logically precede discussions of lesbianism, in so far as lesbianism in its broadest sense must be understood as female sexual desire directed to other women): a clitoral versus a vaginal location of female orgasm, the existence or non-existence of the legendary 'G spot', the homology or lack of it of female stages of sexual excitation and orgasm with male excitation and orgasm, and so on. I continue to find it astounding that these debates exist at all, that there is such confusion not only among male researchers, but also among the female objects of investigation, that there continues to be such mystery and controversy surrounding the most apparently elementary features of female sexuality. Male sexuality, by comparison, *seems* to be completely straightforward, completely uncontentious, knowable, measurable, understandable. This manifest asymmetry depends, of course, on the assumption that one already knows what female sexuality is, but it also depends on the imposition of models of knowing, of identity, distinctness and measurability, which are in some sense alien to or incapable of adequately explaining female sexuality. Instead of assuming it to be an inherent mystery, an undecipherable enigma, we must continue to think of it as potentially knowable, even if it must wait for other forms of knowledge, different modes of discourse, to provide a framework and the broad parameters of its understanding. But before asking *how* we might come to know woman (what theories, concepts and language are necessary for illuminating this term), we must ask: what are the *cost* and *effects* of such knowledge, what do various processes of knowing *do* to the objects they thereby produce?

One thing remains clear, however: whenever the same models are used to discuss female and male sexuality, whenever sexuality is conceived in generic or human terms, we surrender our capacity to assess the particularities, the differences that mark female sexuality as other than male sexuality. Clearly, lesbianism remains the site of the greatest and most threatening challenge to the phallocentrism that subsumes the female under the generic produced by the male in so far as it evidences the existence of a female sexuality and sexual pleasure outside male pleasure and control.

Pleasure and Subversion

I asked a series of questions at the beginning of this chapter, which have thus far remained unanswered. Is oppression still a politically and theoretically useful term, in the light of postmodern and anti-humanist assaults on the category of identity? Can heterosexism or homophobia be understood as a regional variant of a generic oppression, an oppression that also characterizes racial, ethnic, religious and ability differences? Does homophobia have any particular characteristics that serve to distinguish it from other forms of oppression, that give it distinctive features? Does the term *homophobia* gloss over different kinds of oppression experienced by gay men and lesbians? Does it efface the specificity and particularity of, say, the oppression lesbians experience as both women and lesbians? These are, of course, the crucial questions facing current gay and lesbian struggles. While we cannot pretend to provide any definitive answers to them, we can, by using the works of Foucault, Deleuze, Butler, de Lauretis and others, at least sketch the broad outlines of some possible answers.

It seems to me that the general features characterizing the notion of oppression I outlined in the first section of this chapter, if they are valid at all, are also appropriate for describing the oppression of lesbians and gay men. But they do not seem particularly appropriate for distinguishing the oppression exerted by homophobia from other modalities of oppression. How might we *distinguish* the oppression of lesbians and gays from that of other groups, bearing in mind of course that many lesbians and gays also suffer from these other modalities in such ways that it may not be possible always and easily to separate the features of their homosexual oppression from those which attend their racial, class, religious or ethnic identity?[26]

I would argue that all other forms of oppression are based primarily on what a person *is*, quite independently of what they do. Or rather, what they do is inflected and read through who they are. People of colour, women, Jews, are discriminated against at least in part because of the fact that whatever they do, it is as people of colour, as women or as Jews that they do it. Prejudice dictates that the qualities and achievements of members of most oppressed groups are interpreted to mean something different from the qualities and achievements of the privileged group, even when they are ostensibly the same. Their racial, religious, sexual and cultural characteristics, characteristics that are in some sense undeniable (although their meanings and significances are the objects of considerable contestation) are used against them, used as an excuse or rationalization for their being treated inequitably, and for their own phenomenological realities being discounted or unvalued. Sartre argues that this form of oppression is, fundamentally, a gesture of bad faith; the very opposite, in his understanding, of a scientific attitude.[27] The oppressor refuses to accept anything as counter-evidence to his prejudices. For example, the anti-Semite believes that all Jews are mean with money. On being shown the example of a generous Jew, he will argue that the generosity is feigned, that it has an ulterior motive, that it is really corruption or bribery, that it is the product of a guilty conscience or a scheming mind. Nothing will count as evidence of a generous Jew. No amount of persuasion will sway the anti-Semite from his prejudice, because the subject, as Jew, has certain a priori characteristics, an essence, a knowable, unchangeable, stable being. The only thing that may change the anti-Semite's mind is the claim that the subject isn't really Jewish. This description seems to me broadly to account for all forms of oppression, except that which attaches to lesbians and gay men.

In the case of homosexuals, I believe that it is less a matter of who they *are* than what they *do* that is considered offensive.[28] This explains the quite common 'liberal' attitude of many straights who claim something like: 'I don't care what they *do*, I just wish they would do it only in the privacy of their own

homes!' Or 'What you do in your bedroom is your own business.' Which more
or less means, 'As long as you don't do queer things, as long as your sexuality is
not somehow enacted in public, I don't mind who you are.' That is, these
straights are content as long as they can assume you are the same as they are. It
is this split between what one is and what one does that produces the very
possibility of a notion like 'the closet', a notion which hinges on a separation
between private and public and which refuses integration. Moreover, it also
accounts for the very possibility of coming out – after all, a quite ridiculous
concept in most other forms of oppression. This is what enables homosexuals
to 'pass' as straight with an ease that is extraordinarily rare for other oppressed
groups. Homophobia is an oppression based on the *activities* of members of a
group, and not on any definitive group attributes.

This is precisely why the forces of cultural reaction are so intent, in the case
of homophobia more than in other forms of oppression, on separating a body
from what it can (sexually) do. Such an assumption, on the one hand,
presumes that lesbian and gay sexual practices and lifestyles are active and
affirmative, that they progress and develop according to their own economies
and not simply in reaction to the constraints provided by heterosexism; on the
other hand, it shows that the forces of reaction have themselves made lesbian
and gay sexuality both immensely difficult and enticingly attractive. The
constraints of heterosexism are not simply reacted to but are obstacles whose
overcoming is itself self-expanding and positive. Homophobia is an attempt to
separate being from doing, existence from action. And if what homosexuality
is is not simply a being who *is* homosexual, who has a homosexual personality,
a 'natural inclination' towards homosexual love objects (the 'persona of the
homosexual', which, Foucault claims, is an invention of the nineteenth
century), but is a matter of practice, of what one does, how one does it, with
whom and with what risks and benefits attached, then it is clear that forces of
reaction function by trying to solidify, to congeal, a personage, a being who is
permeated through and through with deviancy. This reduces homosexuality
to a legible category in the same way as women (of whatever colour) and
peoples of colour (of either sex) are presumed to be, and in a certain way
minimizes the threat that the idea of a labile, indeterminable sexuality, a
sexuality based on the contingency of undertaking certain activities and
subscribing to certain ideas, has on the very self-constitution of the heterosexual norm.

Lesbianism, for example, attests to the fundamental plasticity of women's
(and also presumably men's) desire, its inherent openness not only to changes
in its sexual object (male to female, or vice versa), but to the forms and types of
practice and pleasure available to it; in other words, to the more or less infinite

possibilities of becoming. It attests to the rigidity, the fearfulness, the boring, indeed endless, repetition of form in stable male/female Western sex roles, the roles to which stable relationships often become accustomed and to the possibilities of change inherent in them, possibilities that need to be ignored or blotted out in order to continue these roles. The threat homosexuality poses to heterosexuality is that of its own contingency, and open-endedness, its own tenuous hold over the multiplicity of sexual impulses and possibilities that characterize all human sexuality. Its own unnaturalness, its compromise and its reactive status. Queer pleasures demonstrate that one does not have to settle for the predictable, the formulaic, the respected – that these, too, are not without their cost.

This is both the power and the danger posed by lesbian and gay sexual relations: that what one does, how one does it, with whom and with what effects, are ontologically open questions, that sexuality in and for all of us is fundamentally provisional, tenuous, mobile, even volatile, igniting in unpredictable contexts with often unsettling effects: its power, attraction and danger the fundamental fluidity and transformability or liquidity of sexuality and its enactment in sexed bodies. In separating what a body is from what a body can do, an essence of sorts is produced, a consolidated nucleus of habits and expectations takes over from experiments and innovations; bodies are sedimented into fixed and repetitive relations, and it is only beyond modes of repetition that any subversion is considered possible (this is Butler's position, and its limitation: that subversion is always only a repetition and never in any straightforward way an innovation, a production of the new).

I am interested instead in the ways in which homosexual relations and lifestyles,[29] expelled from and often ignored by the norms of heterosexuality, none the less seep into, infiltrate the very self-conceptions of what it is to be heterosexual, or at least straight. The rigid alignments of sexual stimuli and responses, the apparently natural coupling of male and female lovers are all unstuck by the existence of lesbians and gays; further, the very existence of a mode of lesbianism not dependent on the phallus or even on mediated relations with a male sexual subject demonstrates that sexuality as such does not require the phallus as function or as organ. But more than this flow-on effect, which effects a certain loosening or contagion of the sphere of sexual 'normality', it seems to me that rather than endlessly theorizing, explaining, analysing, reflecting on, reconstructing, reassessing, providing new words and concepts for sexuality, we need to experiment with it, to enjoy its various modalities, to seek its moments of heightened intensity, its moments of self-loss where reflection no longer has a place. This is not, I hope and believe, either an anti-intellectualism or a naive return to a 1960s-style polysexualism, which sought pleasure with no responsibility, and which, moreover, lived out only men's fantasies of sexual freedom while subsuming women's under their imperatives. Rather, it is a refusal to link sexual pleasure with the struggle for freedom, a refusal to validate sexuality in terms of a greater cause or a higher purpose (whether political, spiritual or reproductive); it represents a desire to enjoy, to experience, to make pleasure for its own sake, for where it takes us, for how it changes and makes us, to see it as one, but not the only, trajectory or direction in the lives of sexed bodies.

Notes

1. The first part of this trilogy, 'Lesbian Fetishism?' appeared in *Differences*, vol. 3, no. 2 (1991), pp. 39–54; reprinted in *Fetishism as Cultural Discourse*, ed. Emily Apter and William Pietz (Ithaca, NY: Cornell University Press 1993), pp. 101–15; the second part, 'Refiguring Lesbian Desire', was presented at the MLA, San Francisco, 1991; a longer version of this text is forthcoming in *The Lesbian Postmodern*, ed. Laura Doan (New York: Columbia University Press). A short version of this chapter was presented at the MLA, New York, 1992; and a longer version at the Queer Sites conference held at the University of Toronto in May 1993.

2. This generic term emerged as a term of dismissal, a mode of categorization, which homogenized and labelled in a ready and disposable form a variety of disparate, possibly even contradictory positions, which share very little besides a cultural geography and inherited history. In my understanding, the term actually means 'French theory since around 1968 which is too distressing to take seriously'. Not used by its own practitioners, except in so far as they have encountered it reflected in the discourses and practices of others reading their texts, it is a label encountered only in the United States. Often it seems a shorthand dismissal of Derrida and deconstruction in particular; but it also commonly includes Foucault, Lacan, Lyotard, Baudrillard and Deleuze. 'Postmodernism' seems to function, in the hands of its critics (commonly those committed to humanist or Enlightenment conceptions of modernism), as a way of lumping together, and thereby not bothering to distinguish between, these very disparate and sometimes antagonistic thinkers; or at best, as a marketing device which serves to signal the up-to-dateness, the contemporaneity, of that which is being marketed – a book, an anthology, a conference or seminar. The problem seems to be that the term now has the general currency of a label one must take on if one is working with any of these French theorists, even though it functions to obscure and neutralize the particular projects and texts being developed or read.

3. The history of this term is also problematic, though it remains an appealing label. What is crucial in it is the ambiguity of the term *queer*: it refers not only to the objects of speculation – lesbian, gay and other forms of sexuality intolerable to the heterocentric mainstream – but perhaps more interestingly, to the ways in which they are treated, and the knowledges that deal with them. 'Queerness' thus challenges epistemological and ontological forms as much as moral and political norms.

   But there is also a cost in using this term, a certain loss of specificity, and a capacity for co-option and depoliticization. In her introduction to the 'Queer Theory' issue of *Differences* (vol. 3, no. 2, 1991), Teresa de Lauretis provides a useful account of the genesis and function of the label 'queer', its own self-understanding as distinctively defiant, transgressive, postmodern:

   > Today we have, on the one hand, the terms 'lesbian' and 'gay' to designate distinct kinds of life-styles, sexualities, sexual practices, communities, issues, publications, and

discourses; on the other hand, the phrase 'gay and lesbian', or more and more frequently, 'lesbian and gay' (ladies first), has become standard currency . . . In a sense, the term 'Queer Theory' was arrived at in the effort to avoid all of these fine distinctions in our discursive protocols, not to adhere to any one of the given terms, not to assume their ideological liabilities, but instead to both transgress and transcend them – or at the very least problematize them. (p. v)

De Lauretis is, of course, perfectly correct in her claim that the phrase 'lesbian and gay' by now has a pre-designated and readily assumed constituency and a correlative set of identities as well as a series of easy presumptions and ready-made political answers. The label 'queer' does problematize many of these presumptions; but its risks are greater than simply remaining tied to a set of stale and conventional assumptions, assumptions which now carry the weight of given truths. 'Lesbian and gay' has the advantage of straightforwardly articulating its constituency (as straightforwardly as the terms, to be analysed here, allow), while 'queer' is capable of accommodating, and will no doubt provide a political rationale and coverage in the near future for, many of the most blatant and extreme forms of heterosexual and patriarchal power games. They, too, are in a certain sense queer, persecuted, ostracized. Heterosexual sadists, pederasts, fetishists, pornographers, pimps, voyeurs also suffer from social sanctions: in a certain sense they, too, can be regarded as oppressed. But to claim an oppression of the order of lesbian and gay, women's or racial oppression is to ignore the very real complicity and phallic rewards of what might be called 'deviant sexualities' within patriarchal and heterocentric power relations. It is of the same order as the claim that men, too, can be the victims of 'female chauvinism': such a claim rests on the denial of a relentless and systematic distribution of values and benefits.

Moreover, underlying the incipient distinction between the labels 'lesbian and gay' and 'queer' is a series of often unspoken ontological and political assumptions. For example, the question of sexual difference is at the very heart of lesbian and gay theory and politics (the marking of 'homosexual' irreducibly designates a specific type of love object, male or female); while the proliferation of 'queer' sexualities is bound to include bisexuality (a position that I have always believed both wants to have its cake and eat it, anguishes and cries oppression at the impossibility of doing so), heterosexual transvestism and transsexualism, sado-masochistic heterosexuality. The proliferation of sexualities beyond two (the assertion of these two has been difficult enough!) seems to underlie the rapidly expanding domain and constituency of queerness (and sexes). While I do not want to prevent this proliferation, or to judge the transgressiveness or conservatism of these multiple sexualities, this field of queerness, it seems to me, can only ignore the specificities of sexed bodies at its own peril: it still makes sense that even if we are all composed of a myriad of sexual possibilities, and fluid and changeable forms of sexuality and sexual orientation, these still conform nevertheless to the configurations of the two sexes: a male sado-masochist does not function in the same way or with the same effect as a female sado-masochist. It *does* make a difference which kind of sexed body enacts the various modes of performance of sexual roles and positions.

4. How one could ever, in fact, compare different articulations of oppressive structures in order to find out who is more oppressed than whom is entirely unclear to me, particularly in view of the fact that, with the exception of a relatively small minority of white, middle-class, hetero, Anglo, young men, all of us can in some sense or other understand ourselves as oppressed.

5. In a whole series of current lesbian feminist texts, there seems to be a curious imperative to provide an account of lesbianism, or feminism, from which no category of women is excluded, in which all women are able to find some self-representation. This is partly a consequence of what I would call the 'me too' syndrome, a drive to all-inclusiveness, the common claim that this or that particular account of lesbianism or feminism does not include 'me too', does not represent me in my context and specificity, as black, as working-class, as non-Anglo, as non-Christian, as old, as disabled. This has had the consequence, on the one hand, of creating discourses that naively and self-contradictorily claim to speak only for me, not representing anyone, and thus not coercing anyone into accepting a self-

representation which is mine alone (see, for example Joyce Trebilcot, 'Dyke Methods', in *Lesbian Philosophies and Cultures*, ed. Jeffner Allen, (Albany, NY: SUNY Press, 1990), pp. 15–29. This kind of position not only refuses to accept the responsibility for the fact that no discourse or cultural production simply reflects the intentions of its author, in so far as they are read, responded to and are of interest to others, but cannot, moreover, provide an explanation for its own existence. If what I write is true only for myself, it is not true at all: the notion of truth can in fact have no relevance to it ('true for me' is self-contradictory). On the other hand, the opposite extreme is found in many feminist texts, which either become embedded in and crippled by their own hyphenization and hybridization as lesbian-feminist-anti-racist-anti-classist-anti-ageist . . . their own aspiration towards all-inclusiveness, or reduced to the kinds of generalization which, while including everyone, have very little to say about anyone's specificities and differences. A choice has to be made either to refuse to efface specificity (in which case clearly not everyone can be included); or to refuse to efface generality or universality (in which case, no particular form of oppression can be adequately accounted for in its differences, in its concrete articulations). For a particularly acute analysis of the difficulties of these two extremes, and the political necessity of acknowledging that all subjects are in fact placed in a position (whether they recognize it or not) of speaking on behalf of others, even if their words cannot express or include valid universal claims, see Linda Alcoff, 'On Speaking for Others', *Cultural Critique*, 20 (1992), pp. 5–32.

6. Most notably, Foucault's inability to acknowledge that the institutions whose genealogies he so well documents – prisons, the insane asylum, the discourses on sexuality and self-production and so on – are distinctively male-dominated sites, and the privileged subjects whose histories of subordination and insurrection he documents are men. See Irene Diamond and Lee Quinby's *Feminism and Foucault* (Boston, MA: Northeastern University Press 1988), and my 'Contemporary Theories of Power', in Sneja Gunew, *Feminist Knowledge, Critique and Construct* (London: Routledge 1990).

7. The well-known lament among feminists, Marxists and particularly humanists that postmodernism, in particular in the work of Lacan, Foucault and Derrida, destroys the notion of agency and thus the possibilities of revolutionary social change, seems to me to be a misguided after-effect or carry-over from a nineteenth-century notion of determinism, which occupies very little, if any, place in the work of these postmodern thinkers, in so far as they advocate neither free will nor determinism. Lacan is perhaps most explicit on this point, showing that the notion of free will itself is certainly no guarantee of any kind of political or subjective agency in so far as it posits the possibility of random events, events which have *no* cause, and thus over which subjects can exert no control. Similar, and in terms that are perhaps more widely recognized as in tension with the notion of agency, is the notion of strict determinism. Lacan's anti-humanist assertion of the notion of overdetermination (not multiple causation) – a fundamentally indeterminable and thus necessarily interpretable grounding, a set of multiple pathways from any set of psychical conditions to their effects – is neither determined nor undetermined. There are certainly 'causes' of symptomatic behaviour, but psychoanalysis is more interested in reasons. 'Overdetermination' remains one of a number of Freudian concepts whose logic befuddles the binary opposition of free will and determinism. It is the intrinsic possibility of many pathways between a set of ideas or impulses and their psychical or behavioural effects. It is this kind of understanding that is necessary for any politically viable understanding of agency: agency is the functioning of options, decisions and choices from within a given context which may effect a transformation of that context but which is not guaranteed nor simply a function of intentions or choices alone, the acting of events whose effects are fundamentally open-ended.

8. Michel Foucault, *The History of Sexuality*. vol. I: *An Introduction*, trans. Robert Hurley (London: Allen Lane 1978), p. 155.

9. See in particular, Moira Gatens, 'A Critique of the Sex/Gender Distinction', in *Interventions Beyond Marx*, no. 2 (1983); reprinted in *A Reader in Feminist Knowledge*, ed. S. Gunew (London and New York: Routledge 1990).

10. Judith Butler, *Gender Trouble: Feminism and the Subversion of Identity* (New York and London: Routledge 1990), p. 17.

11. On the question of morphologies and the redundancy of the category of gender, see my *Volatile Bodies: Towards a Corporeal Feminism* (Indiana University Press, forthcoming).

12. Butler, *Gender Trouble*, p. 139.

13. Here I will rely primarily on Deleuze's *Nietzsche and Philosophy*, trans. Hugh Tomlinson (London: Athlone Press 1983). Subsequent references to this book will be made in the body of the text.

14. See my paper 'Nietzsche and the Stomach for Knowledge', in *Nietzsche, Feminism and Political Theory*, ed. Paul Patton (London and New York: Routledge 1993).

15. Reactive force is: (1) utilitarian force of adaptation and partial limitation; (2) force that separates active force from what it can do, which denies active force (triumph of the weak or of slaves); (3) force separated from what it can do, which denies or turns against itself (reign of the weak or of slaves). And, analogously, active force is: (1) plastic, dominant and subjugating force; (2) force that goes to the limit of what it can do; (3) force that affirms its difference, which makes difference an object of enjoyment and affirmation (Deleuze, *Nietzsche and Philosophy*, p. 64).

16. Deleuze's reading of Nietzsche makes it clear that the forces of the body are only ever a matter of more or less, a question of differential quantities, and that through the differential relation between two quantities, there is a production of qualities. Nietzsche says:

> The attempt should be made to see whether a scientific order of values could be constructed simply on a numerical and quantitative scale of forces. All other 'values' are prejudices, naiveties and misunderstandings. They are everywhere reducible to this numerical and quantitative scale. (F. Nietzsche, *Will to Power*, trans. Walter Kaufmann and R. J. Hollindale (New York: Random House 1968), p. 710)

Deleuze's gloss is as follows:

> qualities are nothing but the corresponding difference in quantity between two forces whose relationship is presupposed. In short, Nietzsche is never interested in the irreducibility of quantity to quality; or rather, he is only interested in it secondarily and as a symptom. What interests him primarily, from the standpoint of quantity itself, is the fact that differences in quantity cannot be reduced to equality. Quality is distinct from quantity, but only because it is that aspect of quantity that cannot be equalised, that cannot be equalised out in the difference between quantities . . . Quality is nothing but difference in quantity and corresponds each time forces enter into relations. (Deleuze, *Nietzsche and Philosophy*, pp. 43–4)

17. In her intriguing and brilliant paper 'Lesbian "Sex" ' in *Lesbian Philosophies and Cultures*, ed. Jeffner Allen (Albany, NY: SUNY Press, 1990), Marilyn Frye quotes some of the statistics of the sex researchers Philip Blumstein and Pepper Schwartz from their text *American Couples* (New York: William and Morrow Co 1983) on rates of frequency of sexual activity among married, de facto heterosexual, gay and lesbian couples. Their statistics suggest that 47 per cent of lesbians in a long-term relationship had sex once a month or less, while only 15 per cent of married couples had sex once a month or less. Frye's profound insight in her commentary on these statistics is that it is not clear what 'having sex' actually means, especially when it emerges that the 85 per cent of married couples who 'had sex' more than once a month on the average take less than 8 minutes for such activities. I will return to this crucial paper later in my discussion.

18. Butler argues that Foucault seems to want to say *both* that the regimes of sexuality are what produce sex; and at the same time, that there are bodies and pleasures that are somehow outside the law and the discursive apparatus, there as 'raw materials' for the functioning of power. She claims that there is

> an unresolved tension within the *History of Sexuality* itself (he [Foucault] refers to 'bucolic' and 'innocent' pleasures of intergenerational sexual exchange that exists prior to the imposition of various regulative strategies). On the one hand, Foucault wants to argue that there is no 'sex' in itself which is not produced by complex interactions of discourse

and power, and yet there does not seem to be a 'multiplicity of pleasures' *in itself* which is not the effect of any specific discourse/power exchange. (Butler, *Gender Trouble*, p. 97).

19. Foucault, *The History of Sexuality*, p. 31. Emphasis added.
20. Foucault, ibid., p. 157.
21. Hence the final paragraph to Foucault's text in which he counterposes the reorganization or realignments of bodies and pleasures to the regime of sexuality:

> we need to consider the possibility that one day, perhaps, in a different economy of bodies and pleasures, people will no longer quite understand how the ruses of sexuality, and the power that sustains its organization, were able to subject us to that austere monarchy of sex, so that we became dedicated to the endless task of forcing its secret, of exacting the truest of confessions from a shadow. (Foucault, *The History of Sexuality*, p. 159).

22. It seems stuck within a model which can do nothing but endlessly vary itself around a central core which itself remains inviolable: the domination of the phallus, the structure of power accorded to the position of the father at the expense of the mother's body, the impossibility of a viable position for women as autonomous and self-defining subjects. I have discussed this in further detail in my paper 'Refiguring Lesbian Desire'.
23. This is the underlying assumption in the writings of an earlier generation of feminist and lesbian theorists, including most notably perhaps those of Mary Daly.
24. Frye, 'Lesbian "Sex" ', p. 311.
25. Most notably in *Speculum of the Other Woman*, trans. Gillian Gill (Ithaca, NY: Cornell University Press 1985) and *This Sex Which is Not One*, trans. Catherine Porter with Carolyn Burke (Ithaca, NY: Cornell University Press 1985), but also in her more recent writings:

> she does not set herself up as *one*, as a (single) female unit. She is not closed up or around one single truth or essence. The essence of a truth remains foreign to her. She neither has nor is being . . . The/a woman can sub-sist by already being double in her self: both the one and the other. Not: one plus an other, more than one. More than. She is 'foreign' to the unit. And to the countable, to quantification. Thus to the more than, as it relates to something already quantifiable, even were it a case of disrupting the operations. If it were necessary to count her/them in units – which is impossible – each unit would already be more than doubly (her). But that would have to be understood in another way. The (female) one being the other, without ever being either one or the other. Ceaselessly in the exchange between the one and the other. With the result that she is always already othered but with no possible identification of her, or of the other. (Luce Irigaray, *Marine Lover of Friedrich Nietzsche*, trans. Gillian C. Gill [New York: Columbia University Press 1991], p. 86)

26. Incidentally, there need be no commitment to the presumption of an homogeneity of the objects or victims of homophobia – lesbians and gays may be as varied in these characteristics as any individuals, indeed, are likely to be members of more or less every constituency, every social category or group; but simply to the fact that whatever 'identity' is bestowed on lesbians and gay men is the product of relentless forms of oppression, for they produce the homogeneity necessary to single out and define the objects of revulsion and inequity.
27. Jean-Paul Sartre, *Anti-Semite and Jew* (New York, Schocken 1961).
28. Indeed, there is always the common reaction that when someone comes out or is 'outed' they will not be believed – a reaction that is pretty well unimaginable in the case of other oppressions. If someone confessed to being Jewish or Moslem, there could be no disbelief!
29. After all, this experimental and innovative mode cannot be simply reduced to sexual relations alone. The possibilities of an entire lifestyle, revolving not simply around who one is sleeping with or how, but around a set of identifications with what is domestic, familial, suburban or their opposites must also be included in the category of the transgression of heterosexual norms.

8 THE *ROLE* OF GENDER AND THE *IMPERATIVE* OF SEX

CHARLES SHEPHERDSON

Role and Imperative

In contemporary discourses on sexuality, the transsexual is sometimes referred to as the most radical example of the 'malleability of gender'. The distinction between the transvestite and the transsexual is often presented in this way: if the *transvestite* is able to play with gender identity through the masquerade of clothing, demonstrating the 'symbolic' character of identity through the mimetic adoption of behaviour, the *transsexual* would assume the even more radical position of altering the body itself, changing the very material of the flesh, as if the body itself were another 'constructed' phenomenon, subject to manipulation (displacement and substitution) in the same way that clothing is, as if it too were 'fashionable'. This argument implies a sort of continuum linking the transvestite and the transsexual, as two examples of the 'construction of gender', one at the level of clothing, the other at the level of anatomy. The idea has been widely accepted today that 'the subject', and thus 'gender' as well, is historically produced; why should we not also expect that the *subject's embodiment*, like the *subject's role* in the symbolic order, would shift with the 'fashions' of history? The power of modern technology would join hands here with the historicist thesis according to which 'subjectivity' has no essential form, but is a 'product' of history.

In her discussion of transsexuality, *Horsexe*, Catherine Millot argues on the contrary that we must not confuse the transvestite and the transsexual as two examples of a common enterprise, two instances of a similar demonstration of the 'constructed' character of gender.[1] Millot's book aims to introduce a Lacanian perspective to the specifically clinical literature on transsexuality. In spite of its references linking transsexuality to religious practices of sacrifice, castration and doctrines of divine *jouissance* (one recalls Schreber's conviction that God required his transformation), as well as a few passing remarks – though important ones – on the legal questions raised by transsexuality (the right to change one's name, to keep one's previous identity private, to marry after surgery, to adopt children, and so on, and different national positions on these matters), *Horsexe* is fundamentally concerned with the clinical task of determining which subjects seeking an operation will in fact benefit from surgery, and which will not. Such a discussion may seem to some readers a rather marginal one, concerned either with a very specific and limited clinical problem, or else with 'extreme cases' of identity, cases that will not shed much light on the more general theoretical issues of gender and sexuality. But although Millot's book is principally a contribution to a specific clinical issue, the theoretical implications of her work are in no way confined to the 'exceptional' case.

As always with Freud, the 'abnormal' instance, the 'deviation', turns out to have a more decisive function, implicating the norm itself. In this sense, the categories of 'the normal and the pathological' discussed by Georges Canguilhem as fundamental to nineteenth-century thought, and taken up again by Michel Foucault in *The Order of Things*, are displaced by Freudian thought.[2] This was already the case in the *Three Essays*, for example, where Freud's analysis of 'perversion', in which the purportedly 'normal' sexual object was replaced by a substitute, eventually turned out to demonstrate that the sexual drive is intrinsically 'perverted'.[3] Thus, as Freud's analysis proceeded, the model of a 'normal' or 'natural' sexual object with which he began had to be dropped, in view of the discovery that the sexual 'drive' is *constitutively* denatured, that it does not follow the automatic machinery of the 'instinct' in nature, passing through stages of adolescence and reproductive maturation, culminating in procreative sex by arriving at its 'proper object'.[4] The sexual 'drive' in the human animal is thereby *originally detached* from what might otherwise be its natural foundation. Although the *Standard Edition* translates *Trieb* and *Instinkt* with the same Latinate word (*drive* does not appear in the index; see also 1: xxiv–vi), Jacques Lacan always insisted on Freud's terminological distinction, whereby the drive is distinguished from the instinct precisely in so far as sexuality in the human animal is *intrinsically bound to representation.* It is this link between the drive and representation which separates human sexuality from the natural function of instinct – not only in the occasional or 'perverse' instance, but in its very constitution. Will we not find then that, if Millot refuses to regard transvestism and transsexuality as two instances of the malleability of gender, the question of the difference between them, in spite of its apparently esoteric or merely clinical character, will have consequences for the theory of sexuality as a whole?

The radicality of this distinction between the instinct and the drive has not been sufficiently grasped, as is clear from the fact that we still hear many commentators speak of a supposedly 'natural' sexuality, an 'id' that would be subjected to the 'constraints of civilization', like so many historical conventions or taboos imposed upon an original, organic 'urge'. That framework, as Slavoj Žižek has argued, provides the foundation for political theories (from Hobbes and Kant to the present, perhaps) which oppose 'appetite' to 'law', positing an innate human aggression or self-interest which must be ordered by the imposition of cultural convention (submission to the moral law) – that artifice by means of which humans transcend the 'state of nature' and enter into 'history'.[5] But it is precisely this conceptual framework, in which nature and culture are opposed, that is refused by Freudian theory. Clearly, this refusal also amounts to a rejection of the idea that a natural sexuality is constrained by the imposition of *external* taboos. In this sense, Freud's position coincides with Foucault's rejection of the 'repressive hypothesis'. This point is avoided by those who continue to read Freud as though 'desire' were a natural fact regulated by cultural prohibitions, but the problem is not confined to that misreading. In so far as current discourse is still organized around a cultural category of 'gender,' which we regard as 'historical', opposing it to the 'natural' category of 'sex' – do we not remain within the framework that Freud sought to contest?

We have indicated the most fundamental issue by distinguishing between the terms *role* and *imperative*. If we often hear today that gender is 'constructed' – that it is a matter of convention, or is in some way a 'symbolic' phenomenon (I put the word in quotation marks to suggest that Lacan's use of the term is quite different from its use in cultural studies, where 'the symbolic' simply designates those historically diverse conventions that various cultures produce) – it must nevertheless be acknowledged that *sexual embodiment* is not a purely 'symbolic' phenomenon. In contrast to what we call 'gender roles', sexual difference is not a human convention, like democracy or monarchy, a social form that was invented at some point in historical time, a contingent formation that one culture produced, but that might be replaced by another form, as socialism might be said to replace capitalism. Obviously, this is not to claim that sexual embodiment *escapes* historical inscription, as if it could be reduced to a simple 'fact of nature'. The distinction between the instinct and the drive already indicates that we are not concerned with a naturalistic conception of the body, or of sexual diffference. The point is rather that we cannot treat embodiment as though it were simply one more human institution, another convention invented (in the course of time) by human beings, like agriculture or atomic weapons.

To speak of the drive as *constitutively* detached from nature ('always already') is thus to stress the *imperative of inscription*, the structural inevitability of representation which characterizes human sexuality in all its diversity – indeed, as the very condition for the possibility of this diversity, which would otherwise be reduced to the 'natural diversity' discussed by evolutionary theory, in which the symbolic order is eliminated. Obviously, such an imperative does not directly contradict the idea that sexual difference has a history, in spite of the popular polemic according to which we are encouraged to choose 'psychoanalysis *or* history'. But it does suggest that we cannot (psychoanalysis does not) situate embodiment or sexual difference *in the same way* that we situate the human conventions that are developed historically, as particular responses to the 'law' of inscription. This difference between the *contingent*, historically constituted forms of life, and the *inevitable* dimension of sexually marked embodiment, is what we have indicated by distinguishing between *the role of gender* and *the imperative of sex*.

Psychoanalysis and History

The 'law' of sexual difference, then, is not a human law; like death (that other imperative), it is not a human invention, and should not be situated at the same level as the 'social roles' that concern contemporary discussions of 'gender'. This imperative is, of course, taken up and 'symbolized' differently by different cultures, and therefore enters into history, but it would be a mistake to reduce 'sexual difference' to one more human convention, as though it were synonymous with what we usually mean by 'gender'. As Joan Copjec puts it, particular contingent institutions, such as the family, are efforts to give some kind of consistency to a sexual division which is not organized in advance by the 'laws of nature', submitted to the regulative function of instinct.[6] Historicist accounts can describe the development of such institutions in their various forms, but what concerns psychoanalysis is a rather different problem, namely the fact that every construction such as the family is a 'failed attempt', a symbolic integration that comes at a cost, and often at the expense of women. As Copjec points out: 'The problem with believing . . . that the subject can be conceived *as* all of those multiple, often conflicting, positions that social practices construct, is that the ex-centric, or equivocal, relation of the subject to these discourses is never made visible' (Copjec, p. 13).

Psychoanalysis is distinguished from historicism not only by 'the insistence that the subject's essential conflict with itself cannot be reduced by any social arrangement' (as when 'man and woman' are transformed into 'man and wife'), but also by its recognition that 'attempts at such a reduction are the source of some of the worst ethical misconduct'. If feminist-oriented historicism needs to be 'supplemented' (Copjec, p. 12) by psychoanalysis (not 'replaced', for again this would engage in a superficial opposition that does not do justice to the complexity of the relation between psychoanalysis and history), this is because, 'in the attempts to structure the relations between men and women as a resolution of conflict, as a cure for it . . . we will find the greatest injustices against women' (Copjec, p. 17).[7] The question of *the subject* in psychoanalysis is therefore distinct from the constructed *subjectivity* of historicism, understood as a discursive formation, precisely to the extent that the subject in psychoanalysis is conceived in relation to this 'cost', this traumatic residue that remains, even in not belonging to the symbolization that seeks to pacify and regulate it.

It should, therefore, be clear that the 'subject' is not to be understood as a sort of 'ahistorical' foundation, a 'pre-discursive *cogito*', which would supposedly underlie all cultural differences, any more than sexuality is a 'natural urge', which would resist cultural inscription, according to a familiar schema (the id and the superego, as popularly conceived). The crucial point, repeatedly stressed by Lacan, is that this residue 'outside' symbolization, far from being a 'natural' fact, or some sort of 'reality' of the subject that underlies all historical forms, is on the contrary an effect of the symbolic order, a kind of 'by-product' or 'residue'. We can see here why the 'trauma' in psychoanalysis does not have the status of a 'real event', an 'event in reality', in the sense in which historical description usually employs this term.[8] The trauma is not an origin but rather a residue, a surplus effect of symbolization itself, which explains why, when a new interpretation appears, certain aspects of the past that were never previously noted suddenly take on a traumatic status (as the wars over the canon should suggest). The trauma thus obliges us to distinguish ordinary, sequential time from the temporality of the signifier.[9] 'When we spoke of the symbolic integration of the trauma', Žižek writes,

> we omitted a crucial detail: the logic of Freud's notion of the 'deferred action' does not consist in the subsequent 'gentrification' of a traumatic encounter [what we called a 'real event'] by means of its transformation into a normal component of our

symbolic universe, but in almost the exact opposite of it – something which was *at first* perceived as a meaningless, neutral event changes *retroactively*, after the advent of a new symbolic network . . . into a trauma that cannot be integrated. (Žižek, *For They Know Not What they Do*, pp. 221–2)

The difference between historicist accounts of various 'symbolic' formations and the psychoanalytic focus on the relation between the symbolic and this traumatic residue, this surplus effect of 'the real' (understood, moreover, as a structural inevitability or 'imperative'), should therefore be clear. When the term *symbolic* is used, not to describe the law of the signifier, the peculiar logic by which the human animal is detached from nature and subjected to symbolic regulation (at a cost), but rather to designate those social formations, the various 'symbolizations' which this detachment from nature generates, then one is faced with a collapse, by which the specific questions of psychoanalysis concerning the *constitution of the subject* are lost, having been confused with the historicist task of describing the *historical formation of subjectivity*.

The further problem which such a confusion entails can now be clarified accordingly. Like death, sexual difference is not a human institution, and if in our theories we pretend that it is simply one more social construction, invented by a particular society (like democracy or Christianity), do we not unwittingly sustain the humanistic (narcissistic) notion that 'man is the maker of all things'? Do we not remain committed to a familiar theory of 'man', to the same conception of the 'subject' in which sexual difference has always been foreclosed? As Constance Penley says, the effacement of sexual difference

can be seen quite clearly in the recently renewed will to purge feminism of psychoanalysis [which] takes the form of a call to substitute 'gender' for 'sexual difference' as an analytic category for feminist theory – thus displacing the role of the unconscious in the formation of subjectivity and sexuality – or to substitute a theory of a *socially divided and contradictory subject for one that is psychically split*.[10]

What is more, this shift in terminology amounts to a *return* to certain aspects of humanism that the analysis of gender was intended to surpass (as Parveen Adams puts it, 'the essentialism that is being attacked . . . often returns even if in a more sophisticated form').[11] Marjorie Garber, from a position well outside psychoanalysis, nevertheless observes that the idea of 'Renaissance self-fashioning' may owe some of its popularity to the fact that it sustains a theory in which 'gender' is discussed, while sexual difference quietly disappears in favour of a *return* to a humanist historicism in which 'man invents himself'.[12] Is it possible that historicism, in treating the contingent formations of 'gendered subjectivity', unwittingly obliterates the question of sexual difference?

Luce Irigaray, too, from a rather different perspective, nevertheless sees precisely this erasure of sexual difference in our current appeal to categories of 'gender', an appeal that, she says, unwittingly maintains a covert commitment to 'the mastery of the subject'. Her formulation also indicates that, in the current climate of opinion, any reference to 'sexual difference' – as distinct from 'gender' – will be immediately misconstrued as a return to 'natural' categories (the so-called 'essentialism').[13] In addition, she allows us to return to the question of technology, which is closely bound up with transsexuality:

> The human spirit already seems subjugated to the imperatives of technology to the point of believing it possible to deny the difference of the sexes. Anyone who stresses the importance of sexual difference is accused of living in the past, of being reactionary or naive . . . Some men and women really do live in the past. But as long as we are still living, we are sexually differentiated. Otherwise, we are dead. The question of whether language has a sex could be subtitled: Are we still alive? alive enough to rise above the level of a machine, a mechanism, to exert an energy that escapes the mastery of the subject?[14]

The point we would add is that this effacement of sexual difference in favour of the category of gender is itself due to our commitment to a very specific, and perhaps inadequate, conception of history. Foucault saw very clearly that historicism is a recent invention, a nineteenth-century phenomenon, the central mechanism by which the theoretical edifice of post-Enlightenment 'man' was built. His thesis on the 'death of man' was not only directed against a particular conception of the 'subject', or to expose the contingent foundations upon which the 'human sciences' had been built; it was clearly an argument regarding the collapse of nineteenth-century historicism. It is one of the ironies of our present theoretical moment that Foucault has been claimed by a 'new historicism' which sustains the very conception of the subject that Foucault sought to dislodge. Could it be that, in so far as Foucault's work has been taken up as a renewal of historicism, this is strictly an indication of the *compulsion to repeat* (manifested in the term '*new* historicism')? The symptomatic cost of this compulsion to repeat (on the part of the concept 'Man') would be clearly revealed in the fact that the 'new historicism' easily coincides with the effort to demonstrate the social construction of gender, but in the process the question of *sexual difference* has disappeared, having been replaced with forms of analysis inherited from the nineteenth century.[15]

One can see from this where a genuine encounter between Foucault and Lacan would have to begin – not with the familiar, polemical opposition between history and psychoanalysis, but with the following proposition: to think sexual difference is to think the end of historicism. It would therefore be a mistake to engage in the familiar polemic between 'psychoanalysis or history' – not only because psychoanalysis is in no way simply *opposed* to history, as though psychoanalysis were simply 'ahistorical', or as though there were a contradiction between them, obliging us to choose one or the other (one wonders what logic produces the popular, 'economic' account, according to which it is always necessary simply to take sides, thereby confirming an opposition at the cost of recognizing the real complexity of the relation); but also because, in the absence of psychoanalysis, our concept of history itself remains truncated, conceptually impoverished, bound to nineteenth-century models that have lost their power without being reconceived, and are consequently condemned to repeat themselves, returning like the dead who have not been properly buried. (This is what Heidegger says too: at the 'end of metaphysics', metaphysics does not come to an end – what it does is repeat.) Thus, in much of our current literature, there is no clear distinction between the constitution of the subject in psychoanalysis, and the social construction of subjectivity. As a result 'sexuality' is regarded as a 'construction' at the same 'historical' level as 'gender', thus testifying to a difficulty that remains largely unconfronted by current discussions of history, like a traumatic element that remains to be encountered.

Having distinguished between the historicist *construction of subjectivity* and the psychoanalytic *constitution of the subject*, by reference to the terms *role* and *imperative*, we must consider one final point. We have suggested that current accounts of the social construction of subjectivity *replace* 'sexual difference' with the category of 'gendered subjectivity', thereby confusing two different conceptions of 'the subject', while remaining bound to a specifically historicist conception of history, one that avoids the question of the body, and particularly the question of sexed embodiment, treating 'subjectivity' as a historical invention. According to the historicist view, however, any reference to 'sexual difference' will be taken as an appeal to naturalism. Any reference to terms such as *imperative*, or the *law*, or *embodiment* will be regarded as a return to the 'ahistorical' category of 'sex' – a 'natural' category which must then be resisted or denounced.

But the psychoanalytic emphasis on sexual difference is not a 'return to nature', nor is it a refusal of history, as the distinction between the instinct and the drive should already indicate. To speak of embodiment and sexual difference as something other than a 'social construction' is immediately to invite, in today's context, the misunderstanding that 'the body' is being construed as a 'biological fact', and that psychoanalysis amounts to a return to that 'essentialism' of which it has so often been accused. But it is precisely this opposition between 'biology and history', 'nature and culture', 'essentialism and historicism', that psychoanalysis rejects. It should be recognized that phenomenology, too, begins by rejecting precisely this conceptual framework.[16] In this respect, the appeal to 'historicism', as a cure for the 'universalist tendencies' of the tradition, remains bound to a conceptual network that psychoanalysis does not support. When commentators debate whether psychoanalysis is 'genuinely historical' or just 'another essentialism', one has a clear indication that the most basic theoretical challenge of psychoanalysis has been obliterated.

Our final point is therefore clear: if the contemporary discussions of sexual difference still tend to be split between two concepts, 'sex' and 'gender' (the biological argument and the argument for social construction), we may say that current discussions are strictly pre-Freudian. This is the great enigma, but also the theoretical interest, of psychoanalysis: what Freud calls 'sexuality' is neither 'sex' nor 'gender'. As we shall see, one consequence is that the 'body', from the point of view of psychoanalysis, is neither a natural fact nor a cultural construction. One can see why French psychoanalytical feminism has had such a difficult and conflicted reception in the United States, where it is acclaimed as an argument on behalf of the 'symbolic' or historical character of gender, and simultaneously denounced as another form of biological essentialism. Both views amount to a confusion whereby the question of 'sexuality' is either collapsed into the historicist argument or rejected for its purportedly biological determinism. In both cases, and whether it is affirmed or repudiated, the psychoanalytical dimension of this work is avoided, and the entire question of sexuality is displaced into a familiar paradigm, governed by the terms *sex* and *gender*, which are themselves inscribed in an opposition between nature and culture inherited from the nineteenth century. It is this entire configuration that psychoanalysis contests.

The larger issues of this chapter will now be clear: in so far as contemporary French theorists who have taken up psychoanalysis are read as though they were engaged in a form of cultural studies, a form of new historicism, an argument about social construction – in so far as they are read, in other words, without an adequate sense of what is particular to the psychoanalytic conception of 'the subject' – the distinction between the psychoanalytical argument and the argument for social construction will tend to disappear. It is possible, and even necessary, to speak of the social construction of subjectivity, to show, for example, how sexuality is organized in the Renaissance or the nineteenth century, or how masculinity and femininity are historically produced in contingent and conventional forms. Psychoanalysis is not *opposed* to this view; it is not directly in conflict with it, as though one had to choose between the *historical construction* of subjectivity and a supposedly *ahistorical* psychoanalysis. But there is a significant difference between the two, which perhaps only becomes clear when the specifically clinical dimension of psychoanalysis is recognized.

The Organism and the Body

In order to clarify the particular way in which psychoanalysis situates 'the body', as distinct from both biological accounts and socio-historical analyses, let us now consider the concept of the symptom, and the vocabulary (*energy, force, cause, product, law*) that such a concept entails. As we have seen, there is no doubt, from the point of view of psychoanalysis, that sexuality is subject to historical formation and deformation. If the constitution of the subject in relation to the signifier means anything, it means that the identity of the subject is not given at birth, but has to 'come into being'. Even 'sexuality', which is still often understood as a biological substratum (something that may be shaped by cultural prohibitions, but is essentially a 'natural force' or 'biological urge') cannot be understood as natural, according to Freud – not because of 'external' prohibitions (the 'repressive hypothesis', which coincides with the socio-historical account), but because of intrinsic, 'internal' considerations, which we have called its 'original deformation'. Thus, sexuality is not governed by *the laws of nature,* or reducible to an instinctual force; on the contrary, the sexual drive departs from the natural pathway of instinct precisely in so far as the drive is *subject to representation,* which Freud speaks of in terms of 'displacement', 'condensation', 'substitution', and so on. The *energy* of human sexuality is therefore not a purely biological energy, a 'physics of libido' governed by natural laws – chemistry or biology or mechanics – but is rather an energy regulated by *the laws of the language,* the laws of representation.

Let us consider this decisive point of departure for psychoanalysis, its very origin, the dramatic rupture that separates it from organic medicine. In an early paper entitled 'A Comparative Study of Traumatic and Hysterical Paralyses' (1888), Freud distinguishes between those symptoms that are caused by an injury (what he calls here a 'trauma', in the sense of a physical accident), and those symptoms that are present in hysteria. Freud proceeds in this paper as a neurologist, whose training lay in the central nervous system. He expects to find a problem in the cerebral cortex, a 'lesion' that will explain the hysterial paralysis according to the same mechanical principles that operate in traumatic paralysis (1: p. 168).[17] But he finds that, in hysterical paralysis, the model of natural science does not appear to function.[18] *The laws of cause and effect* do not explain the symptom. Instead, the hysterical symptom appears to confront us with what Freud calls 'the force of an idea' – what Lacan will later call desire and its peculiar causality – which is governed not by nature but by another law, the law of the Other.

In this paper, Freud points out that hysterial paralysis does not correspond to the anatomical organization of the nervous system. The arm, he says, is paralysed 'as far up as the shoulder'. It is paralysed, not according to the organic structure of the body, but according to 'the common idea of the arm', or in accordance with what we commonly designate by the word *arm*. Hysterical paralysis, he writes, 'takes the organs in the ordinary, popular sense of the names they bear: the leg is the leg as far as its insertion into the hip; the arm is the upper limb as it is visible under the clothing' (1: p. 169).[19] There is an ambiguity here that Freud will work out only later, namely: when we speak of 'the body' as organized beyond the laws of nature, when we speak of 'the body' as subject to representation, *what is representation?* When Freud says that the arm is paralysed *up to the point where one sees* it join up with the shoulder, or that the paralysis follows *the common idea* of the arm, *what we commonly designate by the word arm*, are we dealing with a symptom governed by *the image* or *the word*? Is the 'hysterical body' the visible body, or the body as divided by the signifier?

Indeed, when Freud speaks of 'the force of an idea' in order to explain the basic distinction between psychoanalysis and organic medicine, every reader of Heidegger will note that this ambiguity characterizes a long philosophical tradition, and is internal to the very term *idea*: as many commentaries on Greek philosophy have pointed out, the classical term *eidos* means both the 'concept' or 'idea' and something 'seen'. Seeing and knowing are thus constitutively linked, and easily confused, but this should not conceal the fact that the logic of the concept has a very different structure from the logic of the image, understood as a supposedly immediate, 'physiological' perception.[20] Where the image provides us with an illusion of immediacy and presence, supposedly available in a 'physiological' perception, the symbolic confronts us with a play of presence and absence, a function of negativity by which the purportedly 'immediate' reality (the 'natural' world) is restructured. This is the difficulty Lacan takes up with the concepts of the imaginary and the symbolic, thus rendering the ambiguity less of a mystery.

But the initial ambiguity in Freud should warn us against repeating familiar slogans about 'Lacan's thesis on the imaginary body'. We are often told that 'the body', for Lacan, is constituted in the mirror stage as an 'imaginary body', but this is clearly insufficient: for the closure of the body, the integration that comes with the establishment of a (perpetually unstable, but yet relatively secure) difference between inside and outside, is not given with the image, but only with the *first substitution*, the inscription of the void, the intrusion of nothingness, around which the 'body' is structured.[21] Even in its earliest form, the concept of the symptom in Freud introduces a distinction between the imaginary and the symbolic. When Freud says the symptom behaves 'as though anatomy did not exist' (1: p. 169), this phrase is at first focused on the 'imaginary' character of the symptom, its visual aspect, the fact that the symptom affects what Lacan will call 'the imaginary body'; but Freud's remark will soon be linked with the claim that 'hysterics suffer mainly from reminiscences' (2: p. 7), which is to say, not 'conscious ideas', but memories *that have not been remembered* and are inscribed elsewhere (in symbolic form) on the flesh. Freud is thus obliged to recognize that, in the course of an analysis, a discursive chain (a consciously spoken discourse) will intersect, at a particular point, with a bodily effect, as when a patient's 'painful legs began to "join in the conversation" during our analyses' (2: p. 148), a thesis which the 'imaginary body' will not explain. The category of the real will complicate this picture further.

Julia Kristeva addresses this problem in her discussion of the 'father of individual prehistory', where orality is linked, not simply to the breast, or to an 'object' in the usual sense, but to the 'thing' as a container of the void – an object she explicitly regards as foundational to the emergence of language. The various analytic conceptions of 'introjection', 'incorporation' and 'internalization' thus entail a confrontation with the distinctions between the 'imaginary', 'symbolic' and 'real' aspects of the object, and the intrusion of absence is regarded as primordial, as the very opening of the symbolic. In the case of the oral object, Kristeva writes, 'when the object that I incorporate is the speech of the other' (what Lacan calls the 'voice as object'), we encounter the shift from the object as psychology usually conceives it – object of need or demand – to the object marked by lack, in relation to which the 'body' finds its place: 'orality's function is the essential substratum of what constitutes man's being, namely, *language*'.[22] Again, the link with Heidegger should be apparent, in so far as, for Heidegger, the 'thing' (the jug, to take Heidegger's example) only comes into being by virtue of its capacity to enclose the void and give it a place.[23] Although the body of Dasein is distinct from the Thing, there is a general difficulty common to both, concerning the symbolic 'containment' of the void, a problem of the relation between the symbolic and the real that is all too often confused with the imaginary. It is this 'inscription' of the void which Lacan takes up with the concept of the 'object *a*'. The concept of the body, as it is understood in psychoanalysis, will therefore be completely misunderstood if it is taken for a purely 'imaginary body', or (what amounts to the same thing) if the imaginary and symbolic are treated at the same level, according to the same logic.

The consequence should now be clear: when contemporary discussions speak of 'the construction of the subject' and the 'representation of sexuality' as if there were no difference between the imaginary and the symbolic – when the historicist thesis, in other words, is developed as though 'images and words' both construct the subject in a similar fashion – then one of the most basic questions of psychoanalysis has been obscured from the very start. It is over elementary terminology such as this that an enormous gap still remains between historicism and psychoanalysis – a gap that is concealed whenever terms like *the symbolic* are used to designate *images and words* in more or less the same way.[24] It is no wonder that French psychoanalytic theory has had such a confused reception, according to which it is simultaneously accused of 'biological essentialism' and of 'reducing everything to language' – two readings which not only contradict each other, but also amount to a refusal of the very thing they pretend to discuss, collapsing the psychoanalytic 'subject' into the 'subject' of cultural studies, where the imaginary and symbolic are treated at the same level, and the question of the real is lost altogether.

In order to formulate the distinctive position of psychoanalysis, then, we may distinguish terminologically between *the organism* and *the body*. In contrast to the organism, the body is *constitutively* denatured, 'organ-ized' (if I may use this term) by the image and the word. In this sense, psychoanalysis, far from being 'ahistorical', shows how human sexuality is inevitably historical, in that the body itself cannot take form without undergoing this subjection to representation. Born as an organism, the human animal nevertheless has to acquire a body, come into the possession of its body (to be 'born again', as suggested by many rituals involving tattooing, circumcision, baptism, and so on), through the image and the signifier – the formative power of the Gestalt, and the radical dependence on the other, in the exchange of words. This is what it means to speak of *the constitution of the body* in psychoanalysis – that peculiar myth in which the little organism sets off in search of its body.

We have seen that Freud's early paper announces a radical separation between the symptom as it is understood by psychoanalysis and the model of science that is used by organic medicine. One conclusion surely follows: in so far as psychiatry currently resorts to the methods of pharmacology and the model of natural science, it will no longer have anything to do with psychoanalysis. In other words, in so far as psychiatry seeks, like organic medicine, to intervene *directly upon the body*, as though the body were simply a natural fact, a bit of 'extended substance', which could be technologically manipulated like nature, psychiatry will in effect seek a shortcut round the entire domain opened up by Freud, a shortcut that would return to the 'natural body' and avoid the formative effect of the imaginary and the symbolic. The consequence, not only for our general account of the body, but for the discussion of transsexuality as well, should be obvious: whereas 'sexual difference', and the very concept of 'embodiment', is understood by psychoanalysis to entail a confrontation with the imaginary and the symbolic, organic medicine is dedicated to a model of science in which *sexual difference is foreclosed*, and the body is reduced to a 'natural phenomenon'.

Transsexuality

One of Millot's most far-reaching arguments can be situated here: science offers the transsexual the possibility of transformation, based on the application of technological advances which are administered in silence, without asking too many questions *about the subject* (the 'real work' begins with anaesthetizing the patient). Concerning itself only with the manipulation of the 'extended substance' of the organism (and perhaps, as Leslie Lothstein suggests, concerned with its own technical advancement, for which the subject is 'raw material'), medical science 'operates' by presupposing that it is a question of the 'organism' rather than the 'body', that the transsexual seeks an *anatomical change* rather than a *different embodiment*, a body that would reconfigure elements belonging to the categories of the imaginary, symbolic and real.[25] Put differently, the surgeon works with a conception of anatomy that presupposes a 'natural' version of sexual identity, thereby foreclosing the *question* of sexual difference. Since some of those who seek an operation also occupy a position which would foreclose sexual difference, we are obliged to recognize a clear homology: the very foreclosure of sexual difference which characterizes the transsexual position is also sustained by the medical community. Science, Millot says, participates in the transsexual demand, which is the demand for an exit from the question of sexual difference.

As striking as this conjunction between the transsexual and the surgeon may seem (as Millot says, the transsexual's demand, like all demands, is addressed *to the other*, and even shaped in advance *by the other*, demand being originally intersubjective), the relation between the question of sexual difference and the history of science will come as no surprise to those who have recognized in the metaphysical tradition a conception of the 'subject' that forecloses sexual difference, and who see the history of technology as based on an interpretation of being as 'presence-at-hand', according to which the body would be precisely a 'fashionable' extended substance. In short, this focus on the body as material substance coincides with a shortcircuit of the symbolic order, which brings the entire medical apparatus, in spite of its cultural centrality, into close proximity with psychosis. To the extent that a smooth machinery is established, making surgery *available upon demand* (as the vocabulary of commodification has it), science 'may even constitute a symptom of our civilization' (Millot, p. 16).

There is consequently a historical dimension to Millot's discussion, for although transsexuality has no doubt existed since ancient times, strictly speaking 'there is no transsexuality without the surgeon and the endocrinologist; in this sense, it is an essentially modern phenomenon' (Millot, p. 17). Here, technology seems to coincide with a certain historically developed interpretation of the body as present-at-hand, a material substratum inhabited by a 'spiritual substance', an animated 'subjectivity' who – in keeping with certain tenets of liberal tradition – should be 'free' and have the 'right to choose'. And after all, on what grounds would one argue that 'the psychoanalyst knows best' and should stand as the gatekeeper of the law?[26] Paradoxically, however, Millot argues that the position of absolute mastery is in fact claimed by the legal apparatus and the medical community, in so far as they, like the transsexual, seek to eliminate the imperative of sexual difference, to replace the real of embodiment with a fantasy body that would be fully manipulable, unmarked by the limit of the real, a body that would pose no limit to the mastery of the subject:

> Such, in any case, is the dream of doctors and jurists whose vocation it is to deal in the fantasy of seemingly unlimited power – the power to triumph over death (that other *real*), the power to make laws [laws that would demonstrate the superiority of human law over the imperatives of sex and death], the power to legislate human reality flawlessly, leaving nothing to chance. Transsexuality is a *response to* the dream of forcing back, and even abolishing, the frontiers of the real. (p. 15; emphasis added)

What then, according to Millot, distinguishes the position of the analyst from this position of mastery ascribed to the lawyer or scientist who would 'legislate human reality . . . leaving nothing to chance'? What distinguishes the analyst from the 'gatekeeper of the law', legislating who may enter, or stating (more democratically) that 'anyone may enter freely', though the gate be narrow? We are faced here with the difference between knowledge and ignorance, between the certainty of the law which provides in advance the set of possibilities offered to a neutral (and neuter) subject – 'anyone' – and the ignorance of the analyst who, not knowing who is speaking, finds it necessary (and obligatory: a different 'law') *to listen*. A distinction is thus drawn between the *question* posed by the analyst, or more precisely opened for the analysand in the analytic situation, and the *answer* that is *given in advance* by science and the law, a distinction that could also be stated by contrasting the *certainty* of the transsexual (which coincides with the mastery of the doctor), and the *doubt* that inheres in every symbolic formulation of sexual difference. This is a clue to

Millot's claim that *the certainty of the subject who claims a transsexual position, like the certainty of science* (which, after a few words have been exchanged, has 'nothing more to say'), is a sign that the symbolic order has been foreclosed.

Millot notes further than the 'preliminary interviews' that 'prospective candidates' undergo are organized by criteria that reinforce the most 'conformist' sexual stereotypes. After hormonal treatments, a male-to-female transsexual is obliged to live 'like a woman' (whatever that means) in order to demonstrate (and test out for herself) whether this identity truly 'fits':

> Like the doctors, psychiatrists, endocrinologists, and surgeons whom they consult, transsexuals gauge femininity in terms of the conformity of roles. Hand in hand, they construct scales of femininity, and measure them with batteries of tests.[27] Permission to undergo sex-change surgery is contingent on the results of these tests, which also enable transsexuals to train for their future roles. (Millot, p. 14)

Thus, Gender Identity Clinics, under the guise of 'freedom of choice', and admitting an apparent diversity, from the 'exotic' to the 'mundane' (but all under the regulation of pre-ordained 'types'), are in fact 'in the process of becoming "sex control centers"' (Millot, p. 14) – a fact that is hardly surprising in a culture where standardization is essential for the regular administration of free trade and smooth international exchange:

> Transsexuality involves an appeal, and especially a demand, addressed to the Other. As a symptom it is completed with the help of this Other dimension – more especially, with that of the function of the Other's desire. Lacan said that the neurotic symptom is completed during the analytical treatment, due to the fact that the analyst lends consistency to the desire of the Other, an enigma with which the symptom is bound up. (Millot, p. 141; translation modified)

If the Other takes the form of a science for which there are no limits, a form of omnipotence (or, in Millot's terms, if the desire of the Other is absolute, a position of omnipotent *jouissance*, outside the law), the subject who comes to this Other with a demand – a demand that is also a symptom – will find this demand 'completed' by the Other. If, on the contrary, the Other takes the form of one who is lacking, one who wants-to-know (who desires, which is precisely the opposite of absolute *jouissance*), then the symptom will be completed only by a discursive articulation in which the subject, having run up against the limit in the Other, encounters the question of his or her desire – a question the demand seeks to evade.

In the context of these psychological measures and obligatory performances (a sort of 'test drive' in which it is determined whether one can live 'in' the new model body), it should be noted of course that candidates for surgery have often read as much of the 'psychological profile' material as their clinicians, and are very well prepared for these tests (like candidates for advanced degrees, who must take LSAT or GRE entrance exams, they have taken 'primer' courses in order to 'pass'), and, as Lothstein points out, they often have a degree of expertise in the performance of their role that makes it difficult (for all parties) to discover *who they really are*. It would perhaps be fashionable to argue that there is no subject there, no 'authentic personality', but only the product of various performances, and in some respects this is precisely the case, given that 'the subject' is not constituted at birth, but formed in the course of a singular historical experience. But again, the question arises of the *relation between*, on the one hand, the subject who performs for these trials of identity, who seeks to 'correspond' to a given (or apparently 'chosen') role, or who has somehow come to demand surgery as a solution to the enigma of sexual difference; and, on the other hand, those ideals, those images, those stereotypes or performances with which the subject has come to comply (again, like the prospective 'lawyer' or 'professor'). Truly a 'correspondence theory' of (sexual) truth.

The difficulty Millot addresses here – it is the clinical difficulty, the diagnostic question, of distinguishing which candidates are likely to benefit from surgery and which are not– may be put in terms of *demand* and *desire*: when the 'who' that chooses has been brought to this choice by the 'mortifying exigency' (Millot, p. 59) of a demand in which the future is shut down, a demand in which desire is lost, a demand that the subject appears to make, but which has come from the Other, and with which the subject has complied, then perhaps the analyst has a responsibility to open for the subject a passageway that would lead from absolute submission to this demand, a pathway that would lead to the possibility of desire, which also means the possibility of a future. For it is a question of ethics here, a question that is clearly *avoided* when the clinical machinery simply stands ready to operate upon demand – in an economic circuit of 'supply and demand' which presupposes that the subject 'knows what he or she desires', when in fact desire may be lacking altogether, having been eclipsed by compliance with a punishing identification, the adoption of a role with which, however 'mortifying' it may be, the subject has come to comply.

One sees here where the family structure, and the desire of the parents, would have to be considered, according to Millot.[28] But in focusing on the character of modern science, Millot's main point is different here: the readiness of the medical community to answer all demands amounts to confusing desire and demand, to failing to distinguish between them, whereas the task of the analyst is precisely to make such a distinction – neither to answer the demand nor simply to prescribe, to tell the client what is permissible, to lay down the law, but rather to listen, in order to discover whether, behind the demand addressed to the surgeon, there is a desire, or whether there is not, rather, an effort to escape desire, by complying with this 'mortifying exigency' that compels the subject to 'choose' a solution to embodiment that would in fact have the character of a punishing imprisonment, an exit from desire as such.

In so far as medical terminology and the transsexual coincide and 'complete' each other, we may speak of a mutual relation between demand and *jouissance*, which Millot would contrast with the relation to desire. For Schreber, too, it was the absolute *jouissance* of God that Schreber's transformation was supposed to satisfy, as though he himself were being offered up as a divine sacrifice, which had become necessary in order to fill the void that threatened to appear in the universe, and that Schreber alone was able to circumvent. The 'opposition between desire and *jouissance*' noted by Millot (p. 99) is stressed by Lacan, at the end of *Seminar XI*, where he speaks of Freud's references to the spectre of Nazism in his *Group Psychology*: there is always the possibility that a group will find a solution to the fracture of the symbolic order, the intrusion of lack within it, by offering up a sacrifice in hope of satisfying the *jouissance* of an obscure god, who has become incarnated in the figure of an Other. 'That is why I wrote *Kant avec Sade*,' Lacan says.[29]

The point may also be made in terms of identification: Millot argues that whereas some subjects who present themselves for surgery have a relation to sexual difference, are identified with 'the other sex', and will consequently benefit from an operation, fashioning a future for themselves on the basis of this identification, other subjects, by contrast, are not in fact identified with 'the other sex', but are rather *horsexe*, 'outsidesex'. *This* identification is not a symbolic, but a phallic identification, in which desire has become impossible. To celebrate the transsexual as a 'free' subject, the most avant-garde instance of the 'malleability of gender', is to disregard the virtually transfixed character of this identification, and the suffering it entails.[30] These subjects, as much of the secondary literature acknowledges, are structurally close to psychosis, and Millot argues that for them, it is not a question of identification with the other sex, but, to be more precise, of a fantasy of the other sex, in which *the 'other sex' is regarded as not lacking*.[31] In short, within the group of those who present themselves for surgery, Millot distinguishes two forms of identification, one oriented in relation to sexual difference (identification as 'a man' or 'a woman', with all the ambiguity, uncertainty and symbolic mobility this entails), and another oriented by a simulacrum of sexual difference, a fantasy of 'otherness' which, in fact, amounts to the elimination of sexual difference, its replacement by the fantasy of a sex that would not be lacking. This identification is marked by *certainty*, by a demand that seeks to eliminate the symbolic ambiguity that accompanies sexual difference, replacing it with the immobility of a 'perfected' body, a body which would put an end to the agony of historical ex-sistence, and bring time itself to a halt, as it did in the case of Schreber's apocalyptic narrative.[32]

This distinction between two forms of identification may be expressed in three ways, according to three periods of Lacan's work. First, it is explained as the difference between the establishment of an ego-ideal (which is always associated with the future in Freud's thought, and the temporality of language) and the position of primary narcissism, a position in which the differential structure of language, and the relation to the other, can be eliminated. These two positions are situated in schema R, as point 'I' (the ego ideal) and point φ (a phallic identification, which amounts to a denial of sexual difference, a position outside the symbolic):

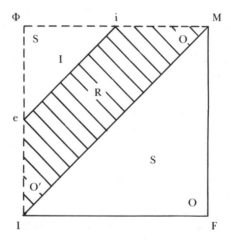

Second, these two identifications may be expressed in terms of the formulas of sexuation diagram found in *Seminar XX: Encore*: on the 'masculine' side, as the difference between 'a man' and 'the Father', and on the 'feminine' side, as the difference between 'a woman' and 'La Femme'. As Millot points out, the 'true transsexual', in the case of the male-to-female transsexual for example, is not properly defined as 'a man who wishes to become a woman', but as 'a woman born into a man's body that she wishes to be rid of'. Such a formulation replaces anatomical classification (which would then be susceptible to 'trans-formation' – from one to the other) with 'identification'. But in the case of a phallic identification, an identification with a simulacrum of the other sex (with

'La Femme' or 'The Father'), which Millot calls an identification 'outsidesex', the symbolic is shortcircuited: 'the subject is compelled to *incarnate* the phallus in the form of a narcissistic image, if nothing can show that this is impossible' (Millot, p. 59). For these subjects, the demands to occupy the position of 'the other sex' (which is not so much the 'other' sex, in a relation to alterity, as a position outside sex, a 'perfection' attributed to the other and then sought as a possibility to be obtained for oneself) is the demand, not for a sexed position, but for a position in which nothing would be lacking, a position that will be filled, in one case, by 'La Femme' and in the other case by the 'Primal Father' – each of which amounts to a foreclosure of sexual difference.

In short, what schema R designates as the phallus is later elaborated in the formulas of sexuation as equally (a) the Primal Father, the 'immortal' figure in *Totem and Taboo* who stands as the *exception to the law* ('All men are castrated'), a position impossible to occupy (which does not keep it from being sought), and (b) 'La Femme', the incarnation of 'the woman who does not exist', the 'spectacular' figure of a supposed 'femininity' incarnated by some of the clients Millot discusses. 'La Femme' represents herself as '*The* Woman', the figure who would put an end to the question 'what is a woman' (with emphasis on the *indefinite* article, by seeming to provide an answer for all. Expressed in terms of set theory, the formulas of sexuation distinguish 'women' as an open set (this one and that one and the next . . . without totality or essence), from 'the one' ('La Femme') who seems to incarnate the totality, to close the set of 'all women' by representing 'Woman' as such.

The crucial point here is the *contradictory relation* between 'La Femme', who undertakes to represent the whole, and the open set of 'women', which cannot be totalized by reference to a single essence. This contradiction between 'women' and 'La Femme' (a contradiction which runs parallel to the opposition, on the masculine side, between the set 'All men are castrated', and the exception to the law, 'the one who escapes castration', the father of the primal horde) is crucial if we are to understand the peculiar (non-dialectical) logic by which identification with 'La Femme' paradoxically amounts to a foreclosure of the position of 'a woman'. This paradox, by which an incarnation of 'The Woman' amounts to an exclusion of 'women', is clearly expressed by the client cited by Janice Raymond, who says:

> Genetic women cannot claim to possess the courage, compassion and breadth of vision acquired during the transsexual experience. Free from the burdens of menstruation and procreation, transsexuals are clearly superior to genetic women. The future is theirs: in the year 2000, when the world is exhausting its energies on the task of feeding six billion souls, procreation will no longer be held to be an asset. (Millot, pp. 13–14)

Sixty pages later, Millot quotes one of her own clients who says:

> The conviction [has come to me] that the nearest humanity approaches to perfection
> is in the persons of good women – and especially perhaps in the persons of the kind,
> intelligent and healthy women past their menopause, no longer shackled by the
> mechanisms of sex . . . . In all countries, among all races, on the whole these are the
> people I most admire; and it is into their ranks, I flatter myself, that I have now
> admitted myself. (Millot, p. 70)

As Millot explains, such an identification places itself not only outside the
symbolization of difference in an effort to circumvent desire, but also
expresses a demand which the subject *seems to make* (to 'choose freely') but
which in fact *comes from the Other*. This apparent 'choice' of identification is thus
regarded as an 'exigency' with which the subject has agreed to comply: 'The
Other's logical position, since unmarked by castration, can be replaced in the
imaginary by the myth of the father of the horde as much as by the phantasy of
the phallic woman. It is the place of absolute *jouissance*, which can be expressed
by the formula $\exists \; x \; \bar{\Phi} \; x$' (Millot, p. 58). This is why Lacan writes that 'The
Woman' is one of the names of the father. Thus, among those who request
what in the United States is called 'sexual reassignment surgery' (SRS), some
are not identified with the other sex, but hold together a precarious identity by
means of a fantasy of totalization, ascribed to the other sex. The subject who
seeks such a position is thus regarded as seeking to move, not to another sexed
position, but to a position in which his or her lack might be eliminated.

This allows Millot to make a further clarification, distinguishing these
subjects in turn from psychotics. For in much of the clinical literature, debates
hinge on the question of whether or not the transsexual is pyschotic. Millot
enters this debate in the following way: having distinguished the 'true
transsexual', who is identified with the other sex (as 'a man' or 'a woman'),
again, with all the uncertainty this entails, from the subject who maintains (or
rather seeks to occupy) a phallic identification, she distinguishes further
between *these* latter subjects and psychotics. She argues that the subjects who
maintain this relation of fantasy to the 'other sex' as not lacking, found their
subjective consistency on the basis of this relation, this quasi-symbolic link, this
relation to alterity. The consequence is decisive: for these particular subjects,
an operation would deprive them of the one *point of reference* in relation to
which they have established a subjective consistency. For them, an operation
would replace a *relation to the other* (a symbolic link), however precarious, with a
condition of 'being' that is 'outside' the symbolic, so that surgery, far from
liberating them for a future, would, on the contrary, imprison them once and
for all in a position of foreclosure which had been kept at bay only by this

fantasy of the other sex. For these subjects, surgery would precipitate a psychotic break.

The third account of transsexuality in Millot's book formulates the point we have just made in terms of knot theory: arguing, on the basis of Lacan's later work, that in some cases the three orders, imaginary, real and symbolic, are not knotted together, but are nevertheless kept in something like a semblance of consistency by means of a symptomatic formation, Millot suggests that the transsexual demand plays the part of such a symptom. In other words, this demand provides a consistency, and a symbolic relation, for the subject, such that if the subject were *in fact* allowed to undergo surgery, the symptom would be resolved, but in such a way that the three orders, the three rings of the knot, would fall apart. The proper course of action in this case would therefore be to work with the demand, rather than to answer it directly with a 'hands-on' operation.

Transvestite and Transsexual

How, then, are we to understand the difference between the transvestite and the transsexual, if it is not just a matter of degree, but a more decisive difference? Cross-dressing, and other instances of the 'instability' of the subject, its 'constructed' character, have gone far towards illuminating the symbolic mobility of gender, and the transsexual is sometimes enlisted to serve as a more radical example of this mobility. But perhaps the question of the body cannot be situated at precisely the same level as clothing, conceived as another fashionable, 'symbolic' phenomenon. Whereas the transvestite already 'has' an identity that he or she is able to orchestrate and enjoy, the transsexual that concerns Millot is in limbo, waiting for the operation that will one day make possible the assumption of an identity which has hitherto been lacking. Recent research on literary forms has shown us the great variety of functions that cross-dressing can perform; but the transsexual we find in Lothstein and Millot does not play a role, or adopt a disguise, for purposes of seduction or deceit, or to appropriate the power and privileges of the other sex, in a scheme that aims at someone's gratification or at social leverage (one thinks of *Dangerous Liaisons*, *M. Butterfly* and *The Crying Game* as recent examples). In Millot's account, the transsexual does not have the same grounding, the same identity or the same relation to sexuality, to 'being sexed', which one sees in the transvestite. In some sense, the transvestite already 'has' a body with which to perform, while the transsexual lives a time of suspension in which the body has not yet been constituted. The question of identity, as it arises at the level of sexed embodiment, is not equivalent to what we usually understand by the term *gender role*.

There is a different relation to the social order as a result. Cross-dressing can always be a technique of social criticism; it can organize the forces of laughter or defiance against the stultifying boredom and routine of hetero-sexuality; it can be enlisted to demonstrate the arbitrary, artificial convention-ality of a social standard which tries to pass itself off as 'natural', or to expose through parody the excess of a type which takes itself as the measure of all things. Millot would seem to suggest that the transvestite not only has a body to dress, but is an individual with a relation to society, as might be confirmed through the fact that so many precise names can be given to the figures of impersonation, all of them functional and socially located: the 'vamp', the 'sex goddess', the figure of 'Elizabeth Taylor dressed as Cleopatra', the 'dyke', the 'Amazon', or the 'brother-at-arms', 'one of the guys', or the woman who takes her place on the factory line, and is in it, not for sexual subterfuge, but for a wage. The diversity of this language is clear enough from the variety of genres that have been developed by literature: burlesque, satire, farce, travesty, and so on. In this sense, the great variety of forms of cross-dressing are all socially subversive acts, and can function as critique, even if the dominant culture subjects them to criticism in turn, limits their visibility and their recognition to controlled places – certain neighbourhoods, houses or cabarets. As a critical force, the transvestite is also subject to satire and victimization.

But the transsexual Millot describes does not have this same disruptive relation to society, this same position of defiance. The transvestite has a position, however marginalized and oppressed, that would seem to be denied to the transsexual, who does not yet have, on Millot's account, what the transvestite takes for granted. The transsexual, one might say, has instead a relation primarily to his or her body: if *this* relation could be settled to some extent, then a relation to society could be mobilized. In some sense, the acquisition of a body – which is not automatically given with the 'fact' of embodiment, but has to be accomplished – would seem to be a prerequisite to the subjective act of dressing or undressing. The constitution of the body, Lacan would say, is the condition for the possibility of the act of a subject. Perhaps we could say that cross-dressing is the act of a subject who plays with what we call 'gender roles', while the transsexual is someone whose capacity to act (in the sense not only of 'performance', but of speech-act theory) waits on (an idea of) embodiment. There is perhaps a difference here between 'gender role' and 'embodiment', which remains to be understood, a difference that cannot be reduced to biological terms or answered by the shortcut of technology. If, among those who come to the clinic, hoping to be referred to a surgeon, some turn out not to be identified with the other sex, but to be confined to a punishing identification Millot calls phallic, a position from which (if it could only be occupied) nothing more would need to be said, we are perhaps led to encounter what Freud called 'the silence' of the death drive: these individuals stand out, not as proof of the ultimate freedom of the subject (which is what many would like to see, in celebrating the figure of the transsexual, perhaps from the distance of fantasy); rather, they articulate in their being that symptom of a social order in which it is possible to look for a solution to suffering in the most stereotypical fantasy of the 'other' – a solution that amounts to a 'no-exit'. According to Millot, these subjects are not in a position to take up a sexual body, because they are engaged in a fantasy of totalization regarding the 'other sex'. One can only wonder if the medical technology that comes to the supposed aid of these subjects, without asking them very much about who they are (time being a precious commodity), is not in fact a force of liberation but, on the contrary, the accomplice of a society that sustains this fantasy of 'the other sex'.

Notes

1. Catherine Millot, *Horsexe: Essay on Transsexuality*, trans. Kenneth Hylton (New York: Autonomedia 1990). References will appear henceforth in the text.
2. Georges Canguilhem, *The Normal and the Pathological*, intro. Michel Foucault, trans. Carolyn R. Fawcett and Robert S. Cohen (New York: Zone Books 1991); and Michel Foucault, *The Order of Things: An Archaeology of the Human Sciences*, trans. Alan Sheridan (New York: Random House 1970), esp. pp. 356–61. These books were both published in French in 1966.
3. *The Standard Edition of the Complete Psychological Works of Sigmund Freud*, trans. and ed. James Strachey et al. (London: The Hogarth Press 1953), 24 volumes. Works will be cited by volume and page number. In this case, 7: pp. 125–243, esp. pp. 135–60.
4. In *Life and Death in Psychoanalysis* (trans. Jeffrey Mehlman, Baltimore, MD: The Johns Hopkins University Press 1976), Jean Laplanche writes: 'Are we suggesting, since deviance is necessarily defined in relation to a norm, that Freud himself would rally to the notion of a sexual instinct? . . . Such is not the case, [for] the *exception* – i.e. the perversion – *ends up taking the rule along with it*' (p. 23). See Freud, 7: p. 160. In his *History of Sexuality*, Foucault contrasts psychoanalysis with the theories of 'degeneration', which were used at the turn of the century not only to account for the 'regressive' character of homosexuality, but to establish pseudo-evolutionary models of racial 'advancement' and 'primitivism'. According to Foucault, the distance Freud took from such models, which aimed at a developmental ranking, made it possible for psychoanalysis more than other theories of the time to avoid the fascist movements and eugenics programmes which were contemporaneous with it. See *The History of Sexuality: An Introduction*, trans. Robert Hurley (New York: Vintage 1990), p. 150.
5. Slavoj Žižek, *For They Know Not What They Do: Enjoyment as a Political Factor* (New York: Verso 1991). Further references will appear in the text.
6. Joan Copjec, 'm/f, or Not Reconciled', in *The Woman in Question*, ed. Parveen Adams and Elizabeth Cowie (Cambridge, MA: MIT Press 1990), pp. 10–18. References will henceforth appear in the text.

7. A similar claim is made by Parveen Adams in the same volume, in her discussion of Nancy Chodorow's proposal that the psychic constitution of men and women would be different if men and women shared equally in the task of parenting, so that women would not be confined to the position of maternity, and men would not be excluded from this position. Such an argument, Adams points out, is a 'sociologized' version of psychoanalysis, one that situates contingent historical formations at the same level as psychic structure; but more important for our present discussion is Adams's concern with the danger of such a recommendation, which, however desirable for other reasons, proposes to 'manage' or institutionalize a 'correct' form of parenting, to resolve what Lacan calls the 'impossibility' of the sexual relation by recourse to a social arrangement. Chodorow thus would seem to risk advocating the same kind of normalizing function that has classically characterized the great humanitarian and philanthropic reforms of educational psychology in the past. Psychoanalysis remains wary of the cost that such normalization would entail – however laudable such a solution may be in its spirit and intentions, and however useful it might be as an improvement over other arrangements.

8. Elizabeth Grosz suggests that in stressing the 'symbolic' aspect of the trauma, Freud may have been covering up actual facts of empirical abuse, treating them as 'mere fabrications'. One is surely right to be wary on this point, but it would be a mistake to argue that psychoanalysis regards the trauma as merely 'fictional', in the trivial sense of reducing it to a matter of indifference. It would be a mistake, that is, to refuse the specific difficulty psychoanalysis seeks to address, in the name of restoring a pre-symbolic 'reality', as though any discussion of the effect of language amounted to a simple dismissal of such things as child abuse. See *Jacques Lacan: A Feminist Introduction* (New York: Routledge 1990), pp. 51–9.

9. The case of 'Emma' is probably the most famous example. Here, two scenes overlap: an early experience of molestation by a shop owner, which at the time 'meant nothing' to the child, in the sense that it did not produce any traumatic response; and another scene which occurred several years later in the same place, when the young woman, now at the age of puberty, was laughed at by adolescent boys, the later scene being it itself not traumatic, just a 'normal' unpleasant experience, but yet functionig in such a way as suddenly to confer meaning retroactively on the earlier scene, and producing in the young woman a phobia whose unconscious character is evident from the fact that she said she did not understand why she had a phobia and could not enter shops. This overlapping is a structure given only with the action of the signifier: the status of the trauma thus has to be understood as belonging, not to either event in itself, but in their relation. For three of the most useful texts on this subject, see Freud, 'Studies on Hysteria' (2: pp. 48–105); Laplanche, *Life and Death*, pp. 38–44; and Michèle Montrelay, 'The Story of Louise', in Stuart Schneiderman, *Returning to Freud: Clinical Psychoanalysis in the School of Lacan* (New Haven, CT: Yale University Press 1980), pp. 75–93, a case excerpted from *L'Ombre et le nom* (Paris: Minuit 1977).

10. Constance Penley, 'Missing *m/f*', *The Woman in Question*, ed. Parveen Adams and Elizabeth Cowie (Cambridge, MA: MIT Press 1990), p. 7.

11. Parveen Adams, 'A Note on the Distinction Between Sexual Division and Sexual Differences', *The Woman in Question*, ed. Parveen Adams and Elizabeth Cowie (Cambridge, MA: MIT Press 1990), p. 102.

12. Marjorie Garber, *Vested Interests: Cross-Dressing and Cultural Anxiety* (New York: Routledge 1992), pp. 75–7, 93.

13. The best account of the history underlying the terms 'sex' and 'gender' in the reception of French feminism is Tina Chanter, 'Kristeva's Politics of Change: Tracking Essentialism with the Help of a Sex/Gender Map', *Ethics, Politics, and Difference in Julia Kristeva's Writing*, ed. Kelly Oliver (Bloomington, IN: Indiana University Press, 1993), pp. 179–95.

14. Luce Irigaray, 'The Female Gender', in *Sexes and Genealogies*, trans. Catherine Porter (New York: Columbia University Press 1993), p. 107.

15. To be precise, we would have to distinguish between *various forms of historicism*. For an excellent example of the difference between a 'humanist' historicism (in which 'sexual

difference' is not made problematic, but simply presupposed, in favour of a historical
analysis of 'gender'), and a more radical historicism, see the essays by Isaac Balbus and
Jana Sawicki in *After Foucault: Humanistic Knowledge, Postmodern Challenges*, ed. Jonathan
Arac (New Brunswick: Rutgers University Press 1988). Sawicki argues convincingly that
one can see such a 'return of essentialism' in Balbus's article. Judith Butler's recent book is
clearly another effort, on the part of what might be called a radical historicism, to
encounter precisely this problem, that is, not simply to demonstrate the constructed
character of gender, but to think through the impasses of the historicist tradition, to follow
through the implications of sexual difference for the theory of history, rather than taking
for granted a conception of 'history' which can then simply be put to use in the analysis of
various constructions of 'gender'. See *Bodies That Matter: On the Discursive Limits of 'Sex'*
(New York: Routledge 1993).

16. See the essays collected in *Poststructuralism and the Question of History*, ed. Derek Attridge,
   Geoff Bennington and Robert Young (Cambridge: Cambridge University Press 1987),
   especially Rodolphe Gasché, 'Of Aesthetic and Historical Determination', pp. 139–61.

17. In *The Birth of the Clinic*, Foucault gives an extremely useful account of the emergence of
   the term *lesion* and its role in the rise of modern medicine, the independent formation of
   'organic medicine' from the 'science of diseases' that had governed the Enlightenment.
   Foucault points out that the concept of the 'lesion', in what was apparently a merely
   technical discussion of 'the seat of disease', in fact reveals the decisive elements that
   organize the concept of the 'body' in organic medicine. Freud then would seem to break
   with this organic model described by Foucault. See *The Birth of the Clinic: An Archaeology of
   Medical Perception*, trans. A. M. Sheridan Smith (New York: Vintage 1975), pp. 186–91.

18. For a useful discussion of the way Freud's theory disrupts the available models of scientific
   reasoning (on hypnosis, hysteria, animal magnetism, cathartic medicine, and so on), see
   Léon Chertok and Isabelle Stengers, *A Critique of Psychoanalytic Reason*, trans. Martha Noel
   Evans (Stanford, CA: Stanford University Press 1992).

19. For two different discussions of this and similar passages, see Chertok and Stengers, *A
   Critique of Psychoanalytic Reason*, pp. 26–45; and Monique David-Ménard, *Hysteria From
   Freud to Lacan: Body and Language in Psychoanalysis*, trans. Catherine Porter (New York:
   Cornell University Press 1989), pp. 1–16.

20. For further development of the difference between the *presentation* of the image and the
   logic of the symbolic in Lacan and Aristotle, see my 'Vital Signs: The Place of Memory in
   Psychoanalysis', *Research in Phenomenology*, vol. 23 (1993), pp. 22–72.

21. For an excellent account of this 'inscription of the void' and its role in the constitution of
   the body, see Michèle Montrelay, 'The Story of Louise', in *Returning to Freud: Clinical
   Psychoanalysis in the School of Lacan*, ed. Stuart Schneiderman (New Haven, CT: Yale
   University Press 1980); see also Julia Kristeva's discussion of metaphor in 'Freud and
   Love: Treatment and its Discontents', in *The Kristeva Reader*, ed. Toril Moi (New York:
   Columbia University Press 1986). I have discussed this inscription of lack in 'On Fate:
   Psychoanalysis and the Desire to Know', in *Dialectic and Narrative*, ed. Thomas Flynn and
   Dalia Judowitz (New York: SUNY Press 1993), pp. 271–302, esp. pp. 294–302.

22. Kristeva, 'Freud and Love', p. 244.

23. See, for the two most often discussed examples, Martin Heidegger, 'The Origin of the
   Work of Art' and 'The Thing', in *Poetry, Language, Thought*, ed. and trans. Albert
   Hofstadter (New York: Harper & Row, 1971).

24. A similar difficulty obtains with the term *negation*, as Joan Copjec has clearly shown. See
   her discussion of Brentano and Foucault in '*m/f*, or Not Reconciled'.

25. Leslie Martin Lothstein, *Female-to-Male Transsexualism: Historical, Clinical, and Theoretical
   Issues* (Boston, MA: Routledge & Kegan Paul 1983).

26. A similar difficulty appears in the legal context when, as discussions of Jack Kevorkian
   have made clear, it is said that subjects should have the right to die, *if they are mentally
   competent* – which means that in certain cases, someone else will decide upon the subject's
   competence, that someone else will (and 'ought to') protect the subject against the choices

that subject might make, and that a person's free choice may not be in the person's own interest.

27. The recent, popular book *Brain Sex* provides a good example of such a test, without the slightest ironic distance, a test designed to reveal through some 'twenty questions' the degree of intra-uterine hormonal testosterone to which one was exposed, and to rank the respondent on a sliding scale of masculinity and femininity. Anne Moir and David Jessel, *Brain Sex: The Real Difference Between Men and Women* (New York: Dell 1989).

28. See also Moustapha Safouan, 'Contribution to the Psychoanalysis of Transsexualism', in *Returning to Freud: Clinical Psychoanalysis in the School of Lacan*, ed. Stuart Schneiderman (New Haven, CT: Yale University Press 1980), pp. 195–212.

29. Jacques Lacan, *The Four Fundamental Concepts of Psychoanalysis*, ed. Jacques-Alain Miller, trans. Alan Sheridan (New York: W. W. Norton 1981), p. 276.

30. Lothstein relates a series of cases that are illuminating in this regard.

31. It should also be plain from this that Millot's position clarifies what often remains unclear in the secondary literature, namely, whether transsexuals are homosexual or not. Excessive focus on 'behaviour', without sufficient attention to structural positions (that is, to the structural difference between phallic and symbolic identification), has led clinicians to orient themselves by reference to what a subject 'does' – which in fact reveals very little. Millot's argument would suggest that whereas the homosexual position is the 'normal' one, in which there is desire, a relation to the other, and so on, the *horsexe* position is structured by a demand in which desire is eclipsed.

32. As Jacqueline Rose points out, Lacan became more and more concerned with the terms *certainty, knowledge* and *belief*, as he developed his account of sexual difference. See *Feminine Sexuality: Jacques Lacan and the école freudienne*, ed. Juliet Mitchell and Jacqueline Rose (New York: W. W. Norton 1982), p. 50. Irigaray has taken up precisely these terms in 'La Croyance Même', an essay on 'belief' and sexual difference addressed to Derrida (in *Sexes et Parentés*, Paris: Minuit 1987), pp. 37–65. Derrida has responded (to Irigaray and others) in *Memoirs of the Blind: The Self-Portrait and Other Ruins*, trans. Pascale-Anne Brault and Michael Nass (Chicago: University of Chicago Press 1993), a text which opens with the question, 'Do you believe?' (p. 1).

9 FATHER, CAN'T YOU SEE I'M FILMING?

PARVEEN ADAMS

What does it mean to watch a film about perversion? Does such a scenario invariably call up the scopophilia of the spectator? Indeed, does a perverse scenario have an advantage over others in setting up a scopophilic relation? Clearly, much of cinema thinks so and plays with a repertoire of incitement, not just to look, but to look at a perversion. It is in general a supplementary feature of any perversion to incite a spectator, as if the aura of the perversion is made up of a consumption of vision, which demands that a spectator restore the visual energy that is exhausted in the scene. 'Look at me,' says any representation of perversion in a structure of fascination. One's eye does not fall on such a representation; it is seized by it. It is clear that our horror and enjoyment go hand in hand. If we turn away because the scene is 'too much', we have to ask, 'Too much of what?'

Film theorists have argued that the enjoyment of the film spectator is perverse in so far as it obeys a regime of scopophilia and, conversely, that perversion is enjoyable in so far as it can be compared with the pleasure of the spectator. But it seems to me that this argument fails to distinguish between pleasure and *jouissance*. In order to try to sustain these distinctions I shall discuss just one film, Michael Powell's *Peeping Tom*. It concerns a young man, Mark Lewis, who films women as he kills them. At the time it was made, the film constituted something of a scandal; one reviewer suggested that it should be flushed down the sewer. But since then it has acquired a certain critical status. Linda Williams has even called it a 'progressive' horror film, in so far as the woman is permitted a look.[1] And indeed, the regime and the economy of 'looking' within the film and for the spectator is the central issue I shall explore. How are we as spectators incorporated into the structure of looking which constitutes the story of the hero?

I want to situate the question of looking within the question of perversion and its relation to *jouissance*. An alternative title for the film might have been 'Father, Can't You See I'm Filming?' for, as I shall argue, the deadly filming of Mark Lewis is a defence against and a fulfilment of the *jouissance* of the Other. The film, which starts by including us within the perverse scenario, gradually creates a separation between us and that scenario by representing the sight and looks of two women. Yet as this very representation of the women separates us from the perversion, it simultaneously hastens Mark into the enactment and culmination of perversion's logic.

I have already referred to the Lacanian category of *jouissance*. *Jouissance*, of course, is not something that exists; or rather, it exists as that which is not there, is lost and gone forever. It is the real, that which Lacan famously announced is impossible. But that does not mean that it is irrelevant. It irrupts and disturbs the life of the symbolic order. That which comes to the symbolic from the real, Lacan calls *objet petit a*. It functions both as a hole and as the cover for a hole; to describe it is to chart the vicissitudes of the lost object. The lost object constitutes the very connection between the symbolic and the real, and its stake is *jouissance*. The symbolic and the real are two heterogeneous orders, and yet the real appears in the symbolic; this means that although there is no direct relation to *jouissance*, we still have to deal with the object which is the remnant of *jouissance*. I shall add that that *jouissance* isn't very nice, and unlike Mark Lewis's mother, your own should have warned you against it.

Now *objet petit a* can be misrecognized and can be sought for in different ways. You can hanker after the object, believing you can have it, in which case you fail to understand that the object comes *before* desire, that it is the cause of desire. Or you can hanker after the object, believing that the Other has it, which can be seen in the analysand's expectations in the analytic situation. Or, instead of desire the relation to the object may be one of identification, as in the perversions, most clearly exemplified by masochism, where the masochist becomes – *is* – the object that ensures the *jouissance* of the Other; in perversion, in other words, the subject is that which ensures that the Other has the object. This is where analysis comes in; one may be led to recognize, at the end of analysis, the lack of the object in the Other; in other words, that the Other is incomplete and does not have the object either. En route to this conclusion, one may identify with the fall of the object, as in the *passage à l'acte* such as was performed by the young homosexual patient of Freud when she jumped onto the railway cutting. Or by contrast, in acting out, one may seek direct access to the object and to *jouissance*, seeking to have the object in reality. This differs from merely hankering after the object in reality because it partakes of that strangeness that made Lacan identify the presence of the real in the symbolic.

All this is meant to demonstrate that the subject is partially determined by the particular relation it assumes towards the object. Hopefully, analysis will undo many of these relations to the object and permit a separation from it. Perversions such as that which the film unfolds resist such a separation, so the spectator may well be placed in an interesting relation to the object.

First, let me tell you something about the film. *Peeping Tom*, as I stated, is the story of Mark Lewis. He works in a studio as a focus puller; but he also has his own cine camera, from which he is never separated; it is for him a special object. With it he can film the scenes that he cannot put into words. In these scenes the camera is used to film a murder and as a murder weapon, for one of the tripod legs has a concealed blade in its tip. A victim is filmed as the blade approaches her, the subject being a study in terror. The expression of terror is amplified by the addition to the camera of a reflector, a concave mirror in which the victim watches her own terrified, distorted image, which fixes a look on her face. As the detective investigating the case remarks, this distorted image far surpasses the terror normally found on the victim's face. Yet this act of filming never quite works; *something* is not captured which would guarantee Mark's own assumption of the role of director. Such a triumphant documentary eludes him; 'the lights always fade too soon'.

This partial and schematic summary will readily support your worst fears about the kind of film *Peeping Tom* is. But is it, as Mary Ann Doane asked a decade ago, the kind of film in which, to the detriment of women, 'the dominant cinema repetitively inscribes scenarios of voyeurism, internalising or narrativising the film–spectator relationship'? In this characterisation the man looks and the woman isn't allowed to look. Presumably the man looks at the woman and presumably he finds satisfaction in the target. Mark, however, is looking for a *look* which will satisfy his looking, and yet this look will not give him this satisfaction. Certainly, his looking is inscribed in scenes of voyeurism and exhibitionism, but there are other scenarios of looking which are narratively constitutive of the film. In these it is the woman's look that counts. Or rather, the woman's relation to the look. For the look in question is the object-look and it is the vicissitudes of this object that I want to follow through the film.

The title of the film, *Peeping Tom*, and the appearance of a psychiatrist who speaks of scopophilia, are both necessary and misleading. If anything, at the beginning, it is the film that peeps; we peep; Mark is primarily an exhibitionist. This has partly to do with his murderous camera with its phallic blade, but has also to do with the fact that what he aims to do is produce and steal a look. For what is the terror he produces? What does it do? It effects the division of the other in order to show that the Other has the object. That is to say, the scene ensures the *jouissance* of the Other, which is the aim of all perversion. Now, in exhibitionism and voyeurism the object at stake is the look. When a peeping Tom looks, the circuit of the drive closes only when, by a rustle or a movement, he finds *himself* surprised as pure look. By contrast, the exhibitionist forces the look in the *Other*, through the division of the other. In the end, in the Lacanian doctrine, the exhibitionist, too, identifies with the object. But its mechanism allows us to make sense of the distorting mirror in Mark's scenario and of two crucial scenes later in the film.

It is important, whether it concerns exhibitionism or voyeurism, that the pervert's partner has an eye that is complicit in the production of the perversion, a fascinated eye. This reminds us of a story of a failed exhibitionist act told by Theodore Reik in which the woman, confronted by an exhibitionist, exclaims: 'My good man! Won't you catch cold?' She looks and refuses. But what happens when the look is captured? For in seeking to divide the other, the pervert is mounting a challenge to castration. The lack that would appear in the Other will be filled with the object. The exhibitionist's partner with the fascinated eye is complicit with this denial of castration; the look completes the Other, it secures the *jouissance* of the Other. It doesn't work, however, with the woman in Reik's story and, as we shall see, it doesn't work with one woman in *Peeping Tom*.

So Mark Lewis, in his exhibitionist murder scenarios, attempts to experience *jouissance* directly, and in this the film invites our participation. As he stalks his first two victims, we are enclosed within his camera's point of view. At this point we are one with a thousand horror films relishing the threat to the victim at the very moment we identify with her. Then the film veers away from this filmed documentary; it cuts before the murder and it repeats the images we have just seen as a film projected in Mark's darkroom. But he has not captured what he had hoped to capture. The film shows us that, as indeed in sado-masochism, what is at stake is something quite different from pain as the simple opposite of pleasure. Mark's aim is to document what Lacan calls the *angoisse* of the other, that anxiety that touches the real and places it in relation to the barred subject. This is what positions the film at the level of *jouissance* rather than the imaginary system of pleasure and unpleasure. We as spectators are implicated in this scenario, since we are put in the position of wanting to see what it is that Mark wants to see, though we do not know what he wants to do. Not only do we see through his viewfinder in the first two murder scenes, we also watch with him as he screens the film in his darkroom. Usually we are first presented with his broad back; only then do we see what he sees: his documentary film. This sets up a relay of looks by which we come to look together at our shared victim. Sometimes, however, an image of his back dominates the screen again as the documentary ends. Thus, at the moment when he recognizes that he has not captured the ultimate look he wants, his body functions to block off the prior scene of perverse anticipation; it operates as the block on perverse seeing. In the replay of the second murder, another figure is added, and a second block is set up. This second figure produces the blocking effect for another reason: she is blind.

The film shows us not only Mark's unfinished documentary, but another related one as well. Old footage reveals Mark as a boy filmed by his father who was also a maker of documentaries. Strong lights awaken the boy who is deprived of sleep and privacy by being filmed in states of fear. The boy's father, it turns out, was a scientist whose study of fear led him to film his own child – awakening to find a lizard in his bedclothes; grieving at his mother's deathbed; watching a courting couple. The old footage ends with an image of the father leaving home with a second wife, having bequeathed to his son a gift: a camera. Obviously, the camera can only shoot the father's film, and the son sets off to document a scene that essentially repeats the scene his father filmed. The scene that Mark Lewis tries to film, his own primordial *mise-en-scène*, has nothing to do with the primal scene in the usual sense, but with intolerable *jouissance*. The promise is that this scene will free him once he has captured it on film. But each murder can only be a rehearsal, since the lights always fade prematurely.

In effect, Mark wants to make a documentary that will free him from the torment of his own life. If he can capture something on film, he will free himself. He wants to document the look of terror that someone about to be murdered would exhibit if she were to face not only death, but her own face at the *momento mori*. In this scenario we can see the promise of looking and its impossibility; it rests upon the notion of the *completion* of terror in which the subject and the Other, killing and being killed, seeing and being seen, would be incarnated in a single object, in a single impossible moment. Mark's murders rest on the hypothesis that by killing his victim he will have enacted a sufficient sacrifice. But this is impossible and the documentary is only a simulacrum of the documentary that awaits *him* as its completion. The attempt to mimic, in order to flee, the Other returns Mark to the place of victim in these sacrifices to the Other. The final scene can only be completed when it is correctly cast, when Mark himself finally takes the lead.

The final drama concerns the fulfilment of this logic. A daughter and her blind mother live in the flat below. They precipitate a crisis in the narrative and in the spectator's relation to the object-look. The daughter (in so far as she mobilizes a romantic wish which is split off from his primordial scene) produces the wish in him *not* to make a victim of her; he must not see her frightened or her fate would be sealed. It is that wish that highlights the inescapability of his perversion and it makes us finally look differently. Meanwhile, Mark's encounter with the mother propels him to suicide and allows a break in the relay of looks which the perverse scenario had set up. I will begin by speaking about the daughter and her first meeting with Mark in order to show how this meeting produces something new, the new wish which will eventually expose the inescapability of his perverse desire. Since the film is not explicit about how this comes about, I shall try to elucidate the implications of what we are given to see.

So, the first meeting. We find ourselves witnesses to a birthday party in full swing and to Mark looking in at it through a window. The daughter, Helen, whose twenty-first birthday party it is, rushes ingenuously into the hall to invite him in, but he excuses himself because of his work and goes upstairs. We watch him as he screens part of his unfinished documentary (the film of the first murder, which we have already seen). There is a knock at the door; Helen has arrived with a piece of cake for him. She comes in, accepts a glass of milk, and precipitously asks to see the films he's been watching – as a birthday present. She and Mark go into his darkroom and there she learns more than she bargains for from this stranger: not only that he is the landlord of the house, but that the house previously belonged to his father and that his father was a scientist who studied the development of fear in the child. In fact, in *his* child, in Mark. Helen is shown black and white documentation of the father's research: the scene with the lizard. She is frightened and demands to know what the father was trying to do. Finally, a party guest comes to take her back, leaving Mark staring at the slice of cake on the table.

Something has happened, of which this description gives no idea. Visually, the scene, set in Mark's darkroom, is quite remarkable. It is dimly lit, with high contrast between shadowy, blurred spaces and the sudden violence of spotlights; deep reds and yellows and a certain grainy quality predominate. Our eyes scan it uncertainly, much as Helen stumbles uncertainly in the dark, and we, too, react to the lights Mark focuses on her with sudden violence. The scene plays on the machinery of lighting and filming, the elements producing an echo of his scenario and a faint threat.

This is far from his intent. He sits her down in the director's chair which has his name on it – Mark Lewis – to watch the films of his childhood. Something makes it hard for her to be his victim; something that this scene itself produces. Despite the threatening echo, something other than a threat is taking shape: a mutation among the partial outlines, shapes, dim spaces and volumes. This mutation has to do with what is happening to Mark, which we register through what is happening to us. As in a dream, our position is, as Lacan says, 'profoundly that of someone who doesn't see'. Which is to say that we merge with this scene just as Mark merges with Helen within it. We could say that this identification founds Mark's ego and saves Helen from his perverse scenario.[2]

Helen is associated with a matrix of things that has to do with his mother. There are clues scattered about – the milk which figures again, the knowledge that Helen's room was his mother's – but they only fall into place when we take other things into account, things that are less obviously about the mother and that refer to what we might call the 'time of the mother'. This time is that of the reflection in the mirror, before triangulation, the time when a nascent relation to others and its promise of tenderness emerge. Let us call it the promise of the humanization of this monster, Mark Lewis.

These disparate clues include the image of Mark looking in through the groundfloor window of his own house, looking in at the party – at what is so familiar to all and so desperately foreign to him – looking in at chatter, laughter, gaiety. He is looking into his childhood home and there he finds Helen. She is literally and symbolically in the place of his childhood. But more explicit still is the gesture with which Mark, caught up in the scene in front of him, seems suspended in a response from the past. It occurs twice: once during the second meeting when he gives Helen a birthday present, a dragonfly brooch, and again, on his way to dinner with her, when he stands transfixed before a couple kissing in the street. The gesture is a strange one: he slowly and tentatively touches his chest almost without knowing it, caught up in another world. In the first scene this gesture occurs as a mirroring of Helen's movements as she holds the brooch up in one place and then in another to see where it should go (It is in the middle of this scene that he strangely asks the question, 'More milk?') It is a gesture that includes the breast, feeling and some fledgling relation to others, a gesture that gives us the little there is of Mark outside his compulsive and near-psychotic perversion.

So, Helen has a special place. He risks killing her if he photographs her and it is a risk he cannot take. It is not just that she is linked to the dim recollections of his mother; it is that these have been incorporated into something new. The romantic wish does not emerge in a direct way from these links but from an identification with Helen, an identification which founds his ego. This is the type of identification that is made with someone who has the same problem of desire as oneself. This is true here in so far as the Other is absent in both cases. Helen and her mother, two women and the absence of the father, on the one hand and, on the other, Mark and his father, two men without the mother.

The film conveys something of this founding identification of the ego by situating Helen at the point of intersection of the imaginary and the symbolic. Helen functions as the place of demand, first for a birthday present, then for an explanation of his childhood films and also for help with photographs for the children's book she has written. She is curious and full of questions about him. This is an appropriate place for the intersection of the imaginary and the symbolic. It is a place where Mark might try to tell his story, dividing himself between his ego-ideal, which is the place of the camera, and this alternative place in which his nascent ego might flourish.

In this way Helen stands for the normality, the release from the constant repetition of his scenario, the peace for which Mark longs. He risks killing her and destroying this promise of peace if he photographs her. He risks losing that little part of himself that he has built, through her, alongside the perverse structure. Despite this, the project of making the documentary is not abandoned. Rather, the effect of the encounter with Helen is that a sense of urgency is added to the task of finishing the documentary. It remains the only way Mark can conceive of finding peace. So we must note that Helen is not the place of Mark's desire. His desire remains elsewhere, coordinated with the camera and with fear, his master signifiers. Helen kisses him goodnight after dinner; he stands there and slowly raises his camera till the lens touches his lips and his eyes close. Helen kisses Mark; Mark kisses the camera.

What of the spectator in all this? These scenes with Helen work in a quite different way to capture the spectator in a play of perverse looking. As Helen watches the films of Mark that his father made, it is her voyeuristic pleasure and her own recoil from it that implicate the spectator. Reynold Humphries has pointed out that when we see the father handing his son a camera:

> The child immediately starts filming those who are filming him, i.e., he points the camera at their camera and, by extension, at the camera of the *enonciation*: at Helen, at us. For her it is too much and she asks Mark to stop the film. Her voyeuristic status is even more clearly revealed to her than at the point where he started to set up his camera to film her. Now the screen is doing what it is not meant to do: it is looking back at her/us, returning her/our look.[3]

Which is to say that the object-look falls. The mechanism that produces this fall is just one of the number of ways in which Michael Powell harasses us throughout the film into a certain spectatorial vigilance. While this vigilance concerns the separation from the object, a final intervention in the relay of perverse looks is necessary and it is Helen who will figure narratively in the film's definitive intervention.

If Helen is the motive behind Mark's hastening to complete the documentary, her blind mother is the one who is the determination of its suicidal form. This mother is in herself quite frightening; she produces a panic in Mark as is clear in two uncanny scenes on which I will comment. The first is her initial meeting with Mark when he calls to collect Helen for dinner. I say 'uncanny' because in dwelling on it, we dwell on Mark's dwelling, his home from which he is estranged and yet in which he continues to live. It is the uncanny of the maternal presence re-presented within his madhouse. It is worth focusing on the opening moments of this scene, which Powell has organized with great care. We see Mark's face in the hall and are semi-aware that a veil in front of the camera is being lifted at the top right-hand side of the screen, revealing first the mother in focus on the sofa on the bottom left of the screen and then Mark, standing on the right. If the film is slowed, something very interesting is revealed: through the veil we see the face of Mark in the hall on which is superimposed an image of the mother seated on the sofa in the living room. It is astonishing; it is there and yet one can hardly see it in real time. There follows a handshake and paced heartbeats on the soundtrack as she holds onto his hand and the beats continue even after she releases it. Again, before leaving, he looks at the back of her head knowing that she knows that he is looking at her. She troubles him deeply, but we've seen nothing yet.

In his projection room, Mark watches the film of Viv's murder; he hears a sound and he switches on the spotlight to reveal the blind mother standing against the wall with her stick. This provocative presence in his inner sanctum is threatening. Mark panics in front of this woman, castrated by her blindness but armed with her weapon with its pointed tip. This much is fairly obvious. But what can we say of the look? It is too simple to say that the blind cannot look. What makes the mother a terrifying figure is that she also stands for the object-look. For it is not the look the pervert seeks. The aim of the pervert is to make vision and the look coincide; here, we have instead the blind woman as the look, the look from which vision has been subtracted. This look is not locked into the Other; it falls from the Other. This, of course, is the Lacanian idea of separation.

Now, the spectator does not remain unaffected by this woman who stands for castration and the fall of the look. She interrupts our desire to see what Mark wants to see by threatening us just as she threatens him. In or out of the perverse structure, we too are threatened by castration and the non-coincidence of vision and the look. Usually, as Lacan remarks in *Seminar XI*,[4] the look is the object that most completely eludes castration. Here, the separation of the look unveils castration.

This woman knows and 'sees'. She has 'seen' the darkroom through the nightly visits as she lies in her room below, and Mark says at one point that she would know immediately if he were lying. Her 'seeing' is the screen of knowledge that he must pierce through in order to attain his *jouissance*. When she taunts him about what it is he watches all the time, he switches on the film of Viv's murder which her abrupt entry had interrupted. Following the injunction 'take me to your cinema', he leads this blind woman towards the screen. Perhaps this is a test: will she see his secret or will the murder documentary bring reassurance of the truth of *jouissance* and the lie of castration? The test fails him. For the documentary reveals the failure of another 'opportunity' and he moans that the lights always fade too soon.

But this test also fails the spectator, though not for the same reasons. Remember, we have just seen Mark take the blind woman to his 'cinema'. We are there as before, looking at him looking at the screen. Usually, the image of his broad back gives way to the images of the documentary he is replaying, but in this scene this does not happen; the space of perverse seeing does not unfold before our eyes. His unseeing back continues to occupy a large area of the screen and the usual relay of looks is interrupted. Moreover, this time there is one more spectator, for we are in fact also looking at the blind woman's back as she faces the image of the second victim at the point of death on Mark's film screen. So what do we see? On the upper part of our screen we see the upper part of the victim's face with its staring eyes, on the lower left Mark's back, and on the lower right the large coarsely patterned cardigan and hair of the blind mother. It is with this image that the object falls. Paradoxically, we are too much in Mark's place – the victim is looking straight out at us, since we are positioned in the very spot where the camera originally stood. Yet Mark himself is no longer in that place, since we continue to see him on the screen. Moreover, we see the woman who cannot see, but whose head is turned towards the documentary screen. The circuit of the look is then doubly disturbed. We do not occupy the place from which Mark now seeks to see what he wants to see and the blind woman *cannot* occupy that space. The look falls and releases us from the perverse loop of seeing by disrupting our identification with the two viewers on the screen. They become the blind spots in our wish to see. *The position of the object affects the nature of our desire.*

One cannot but recall the famous analysis of Holbein's *The Ambassadors*, in which Lacan develops the notion of the fall of the look. In this painting, according to Lacan, the anamorphotic spot allows us to catch a glimpse of the reality beyond the illusion of the painting. At the moment we turn away from

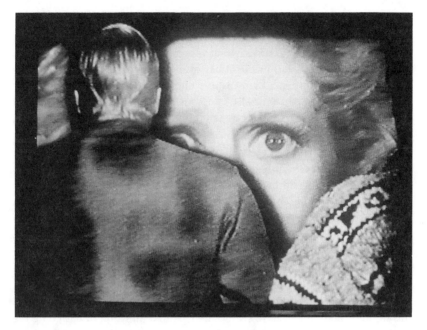

Peeping Tom, Michael Powell, 1960

the painting of worldly success, the strange shape in the foreground suddenly takes on the aspect of a skull, a reminder of our mortality and the vanity of things. The painting is shown to be merely a representation; for a moment it fails to elude castration. Now for Lacan, anamorphosis always concerns a certain stretching and distortion but, as I have argued elsewhere, the phallic metaphor which underwrites this unnecessarily restricts the conditions under which the reality beyond the signifier is indicated.[5] Here there is no question of a perspectival distortion of any kind, but none the less the look falls, the separation of the look unveils castration for us.

But our knowledge and Mark's do not coincide; Mark does not see what we have just seen. Having failed once more to document the murder scenario he panics and grabs the only available victim, which is, of course, the mother. He begins by unsheathing his blade, but it won't work. He cannot put this woman into his exhibitionist scenario; her blindness refuses inclusion in the documentary that he continuously seeks to complete. In her case the lights have always already failed. Yes, she is frightened, but he cannot get a blind woman to *see* her own terror. How can he escalate the terror and produce the ultimate division without being able to obtain a response to his distorting reflector? She will always be the incomplete Other, who is not invested with the object. This is the moment when Mark recognizes that all future opportunities will end in failure. One could say that he realizes that the object will not be realized, that the *jouissance* of the Other cannot be guaranteed.

On leaving, the mother talks of 'instinct' and notes dryly that it is a pity that *it* can't be photographed. She tells him, 'All this filming isn't healthy', and suggests that he get help, talk to someone.

What is the consequence of all this? The encounter with the mother alters only one detail of his project. The urgency of his need to finish his documentary is not diminished, but this encounter determines him to put into operation something he had known he would have to do for a long time, namely, to include himself in the film as victim. I have not mentioned that part of the narrative that involves the police who are investigating the murder of the stand-in at the studio. It is clear, psychically as well as narratively, that Mark commits suicide not because the police are closing in on him, but rather that he ensures their closing in when he decides to commit suicide. The police are to be included in the final documentary.

The mother and daughter have interrupted the logic of looks that prevailed throughout the film and have served the narrative function of hastening the final suicide scene. But what about Mark? Is his last act different from the preceding ones? Does he not stop the chain of murders, the endless series of failed 'opportunities' by sacrificing himself? Does he not bravely turn the cameras and the blade point on himself to face what he has hitherto avoided, his own division? Does his suicide represent some psychical shift, or an ethical decision?

My thesis is this: there is no drama of separation from the object here, only an acting out that by itself changes nothing and serves merely to complete a scenario already begun. Mark does not extricate himself from his dilemma by giving up hope that his documentary act will finally work. He just makes sure that this time, the last time, it does work. Now, in acting out, as it is understood by psychoanalysis, a particular relation to the object obtains. There is at one and the same time an acting *out*, outside, the scene of analysis and an acting *for* the Other, that is the analyst. Something in the analyst's discourse propels the analysand's acting out. A break in the analyst's discourse results in his no longer being there as analyst and occasions what Lacan, in his seminar on anxiety, calls wild transference. Acting out is transference without an analyst; when there is no one to speak to, there is only the Other to act in front of. When the analyst *qua* object leaves the analytic scene, the analysand looks for the object in the real.

Lacan elaborates the concept of acting out in relation to a patient of Ernst Kris who thinks he is a plagiarist. Kris reads the patient's book and assures him he is not; upon leaving this session, the patient goes straight to a restaurant where he eats cold brains and returns to tell the analyst about it. This is a bit of acting out directed at the Other; it takes place in the real and is only secondarily put into language. The only point I want to emphasize here is that Lacan reads this as the patient's comment to the effect that everything Kris is saying is true but beside the point; for what concerns him, the patient, is cold brains, the remainder, the *objet a*. Acting out can also take the form of smelling your analyst. Lacan alludes to smell as object. What is happening if you smell your analyst is an acting out, for the Other, as Jacques-Alain Miller has pointed out, has no odour.

The question of whether Mark is acting out or not in the suicide scene is a complex one. One could argue that all perverse scenarios are actings out and that Mark's last scenario is not essentially different from all the others. Certainly, acting out in analysis can produce innumerable transitory perversions. Acting out is similar to perversion not only in its relation to the object but also in its relation to knowledge. Miller, in his unpublished seminar *Extimité*,[6] speaks of acting out as the shortcircuiting of the discourse of the analyst. You will recall the diagram of this discourse with its four places, agent, other, product and truth, occupied respectively by the analyst as object, barred subject, S_1 the master signifier, and S_2 unconscious knowledge. The discourse is shortcircuited when the analysand tries to obtain the object directly, in reality, without any reference to knowledge (S_1 and S_2). So acting out is by definition acting outside knowledge and it involves a real object.

The pervert also pierces the screen of knowledge, and in a more constant way. For the disavowal that is at the heart of all perversion, as Freud showed, is not just a disavowal of the fact that the mother does not have the penis. It is also a disavowal of the lack of knowledge that preceded the sight of that absence. Jean Clavreul elaborated this scenario of disavowal in 'The Perverse Couple'. There he argues that a lack of knowledge causes the child to look in the first place; a lack of knowledge is the cause of the scopophilic drive. What is disavowed in perversion is this period of not knowing and wanting to know. This means, in turn, that the father is not recognized as having the knowledge before the child. The pervert thus occupies the position of one who will never again be deprived of knowledge, particularly knowledge about eroticism. As Clavreul says, 'This knowledge about eroticism feels assured of obtaining the other's *jouissance* under any circumstances.'[7]

We saw earlier that what the pervert seeks is an eye complicit with his own, one that will turn a blind eye to what is happening and will remain fascinated and seduced. This is made possible precisely by the shortcircuiting of the dimension of knowledge that is coordinated with the Other.

In a sense, then, the pervert is always already in the place of the analysand who acts outside the Other and yet for the Other. The final scene is therefore not distinguished from the others by virtue of its being a bit of acting out. Mark maintains his perverse position until his deadly end. If anything distinguishes the final scenes, it must be their *difference* from acting out. Now, if the suicide scene is pure acting out, the scene with Helen that immediately precedes it is quite different. In this scene the distorting mirror is revealed, and not just to Helen, but to us for the first time. Mark's encounter with Helen alters his desire concerning his relation to knowledge. In the scene of this encounter, Mark, at the limit of temptation, and while wielding the very instruments of his enjoyment, does not seek complicity from Helen. Hers is an eye that he wishes *not* to fascinate and seduce. He reveals his perverse secret, knowing she will not turn a blind eye. There is no threat to Helen in this scene even when he holds the blade at her throat. What is new is his *telling* of his story – fitfully and in large part through images and actions – but it is a telling all the same, just as the blind mother had bade him do. So, in addition to the documentary he is about to complete, he also leaves this narrative behind. The pity of it is that it in no way diminishes his own disavowal of his lack of knowledge. His acting out has set him outside the symbolic, with no means of return. If he learns anything at all, it is simply that his documentary can never be the means of his return. The interventions of the women represent the fact that his act, killing, is only a postponement of his destiny. So he goes to meet his death, and thus his Maker, his father. As the screen darkens, a small voice says: 'Goodnight, daddy; hold my hand.'

These are the last words in the film; mine, however, must be about Helen and her part in the scene where she is told Mark's story and confronted with her own distorted reflection in the mirror. Clearly, she survives castration. The mirror is like the Medusa's head, and though Helen has to look at it, she can also turn away. The fascination of the image fails; Helen is not petrified. She does not become stiff with either terror or enjoyment. She declines to be the pervert's partner and thus effects a separation from the perverse scenario. The way in which this is achieved also ensures that we, as spectators, are freed from it. Once again, this is accomplished through the fall of the object. Helen awaits Mark in his darkroom and, curious, turns on the projector. We realize what she is looking at as her face registers first disbelief, then dawning horror and finally a choking fear. Mark enters and fiercely demands that he not see her fear. He agitatedly turns on a whole bank of sound tapes to satisfy her curiosity with his cries and screams when he was five, seven . . . This is the first time that the sound that complements his father's documentary footage is referred to; it is also at this point that we learn that all the rooms in the house

were and still are wired for sound. Then, on her insistence, he shows her the
secret instrument of his scenario – not just the blade, but the concave mirror in
which we clearly see Helen's grotesquely distorted image. And simultaneously
we hear a dreadful cry such as his first victim had emitted. But Helen is mute
and the cry resounds as his own childhood terror in the father's 'scientific'
scenarios. It is in the gap between her terror and his, between her grotesque
reflection and his bloodcurdling cry, that the object falls. A space bursts open
in the seamless scenario which is too close, too present, too full. Our drama is
over. Mark Lewis no longer threatens Helen or the spectator. What is left is his
enactment of the remnants of the perverse scenario, starring an old Mark
Lewis.

Notes

1. Linda Williams, 'When the Woman Looks', in Mary Ann Doane, Patricia Mellencamp and
    Linda Williams, eds., *Re-Vision* (Washington: American Film Institute 1984). [Throughout
    this chapter the focus is on the 'look' referred to here. For the most part, the term could
    have been better translated *gaze*, since it is the Lacanian concept that is at issue in the
    analysis. But because this is not always so – some ambiguity of reference is intended – and
    because the language of the essay is woven with that of the commonsense film-theoretical
    notion, the term *look* has been retained – Ed.]
2. I am grateful to Gerry Sullivan for drawing my attention to the passages on André Gide
    and his choice of love-object in Lacan's unpublished seminar on anxiety.

3. Reynold Humphries, '*Peeping Tom*: Voyeurism, the Camera and the Spectator', *Film Reader*, vol. 4 (1980).
4. Jacques Lacan, *The Four Fundamental Concepts of Psychoanalysis*, trans. Alan Sheridan, ed. Jacques-Alain Miller (London: The Hogarth Press and the Institute of Psycho-analysis 1977).
5. See 'The Three (Dis)Graces', in *The Point of Theory*, ed. Mieke Bal and Inge Boes (Amsterdam: University of Amsterdam Press and Crossroads 1994).
6. Jacques-Alain Miller's seminar was delivered in 1985–6.
7. Jean Clavreul, 'The Perverse Couple', in *Returning to Freud: Clinical Psychoanalysis in the School of Lacan*, ed. Stuart Schneiderman (New Haven, CT: Yale University Press 1980).

10 ANXIOUS NATIONS, NERVOUS STATES*

HOMI K. BHABHA

As the century nears its end – let us call it the *late* modern condition – there emerges a pervasive, even perverse, sense that history repeats itself. Circumstances compel us to regard our own contemporaneity in the language and imagery of a 'past' that turns tradition into a turbulent reality. Through the cadavers of Bosnians, we see the shadows of other 'ethnic' cleansings in Belsen and Auschwitz. The fires of Hindu–Muslim riots, in this their Hindu nationalist moment, revive memories of India's struggle for independence and the unfinished past of the country's partition. The high-tech, slow-motion record of Rodney King's beating in South Central Los Angeles revive the iconography of lynchings and whippings. In England today, Winston Churchill MP – grandson of that great British bulldog himself – echoes Enoch Powell's anti-immigrant speech of 1968, predicting 'rivers of blood' coursing down English country lanes unless 'coloured' immigration is stopped.

My imagistic collage does not seek to establish a geopolitical generality. I have resorted, briefly, to the random and the impressionistic in order to emphasize the common belief, widely repeated by scholars, politicians, and journalists over the last couple of years, that on the threshold of 2000 we are afflicted with the political/cultural agendas of the late nineteenth and early twentieth centuries: race, nation, religion. These founding ideas of

* For Joan: an anxious debt eagerly incurred.

the Age of Empire, ironically subverted in the political discourses of decolonization, now find a new destiny, and another designation, in the *fin de siècle*. At the end of the hawkish politics of the Cold War, no doves of peace fly. Nationalist aspirations turn the values of civility into forms of ethnic separatism; a sense of community is replaced by the crisis of communalism; citizenship is less the habitus of the homeland, and more frequently an experience of migration, exile, diaspora, cultural displacement.

Even a cursory look at the events I have mentioned above displays the breakdown, in a more international frame, of the national experience as a stabilizing force that establishes a consensual commonality amidst subjects of difference – a shared measure of social synchronicity. Each event focuses conflict around issues related to the construction of ethnic and racial differences embodied in the strategic formation of social minorities. The 'minoritization' of a people, no less than its 'nationalization', exceeds the language of numbers and territory, and must be seen for what it is: the 'other' side' of the phantasy of the national 'people-as-one' which disturbs the democratic dream in a process that the political philosopher Claude Lefort places at the centre of the modern experience of the social:

> Property, Family, the State, Authority, the Nation, Culture . . . the bourgeois cult of order sustained by those who are placed in the position of the *other* . . . testifies to a certain vertigo in the face of the void created by an indeterminate society . . . covering many different times which are staggered in relation to one another within simultaneity . . . definable only in terms of some fictitious future; an adventure such that the quest for identity cannot be separated from the experience of division.[1]

It is within this cleavage, or division, of national identification, articulated in the staggered, interstitial temporalities that exist between the disjunct moment of the present and the fictitious space of the future, that we must try to understand our contemporary reality, recalled in the echoes of the past. Why, in a post-Cold War, post-industrialist world, conjoined by multinational economies and electronic mass media, do we mediate *our present* as an interruption, an iteration of the shibboleths of a past age?

There is no affection that attaches more closely to the state of the nation's present than the figure of the 'past'. Like the liminal experience of memory which we live *through*, never entirely within or without, the desire of the nation's past is less a passion and more the passageway to constituting, and confronting, the problem of its modernity. In his great essay on the Janus-faced nature of national consciousness, *The Break-up of Britain*, Tom Nairn describes this temporal disjunction well: 'human kind is forced through [the nation's] strait doorway looking back into the past to gather strength wherever it can be found for the ordeal of development'.[2]

Whatever its latest modalities and mutations – multinational, transnational – please note that the passage of time is always marked in the *pre*fix, as an anteriority, something that is placed behind the sign of the nation's contemporaneity to signal its precarious progress. This moment of the turn of the nation's subjects to a past then re-turns, rushes past – indeed, projects *the past* – into a paradoxical position of futurity. The national past is never simply an archaic assertion of ethnic or racial essentialism. The directionality of the past – its political destination as well as its designation of cultural identities – participates in fetishistic forms of social relations.

The desire for the national past disavows the differentiae of culture, community, and identity. It does not 'repress' the contradictions and incommensurabilities that inhabit these social realities; nor does the nostalgia for the past 'homogenize' histories, cultures, ethnicities, as is often hastily and polemically concluded. The national past negotiates social and cultural differentiation precisely through *disavowal*: by saying, 'I know difference exists, *mais quand même* . . . '. This disavowing, split posture turns the enunciative 'present' of national discourses on temporality into rhetorics of peripherality that activate the ambivalent and indeterminate structure of Western modernity itself – what Lefort has described as the staggered temporal frames; what Michel Foucault, in *The Order of Things*, defines as the dialectic of 'man and his doubles'; and what Hannah Arendt, in *The Human Condition*, demonstrates as the problem of agency in the causal narrative of the modern public sphere. Peripherality inflects discourse of the national past by providing a containing circumference of time–space relations which functions like the *route périphérique*: it takes you to your destination by rushing you past somewhere else. When we consider the familiar ideological descriptions of the national past – the invention of tradition, or the instrumentality of national nostalgia – we realize that they do little justice to this discursive movement of the nation's time and being caught in the act of turning–returning, to the restless hesitation that articulates the contemporaneity of the past: part disavowal, part elliptical idealization, part fetishism, part splitting, part antagonism, part ambivalence.

Exploring the nation's passageway to the present through the 'peripheric' route, where the past disavows or *bypasses* the differentiae of nation, people, culture, I am drawn in the direction of Walter Benjamin's *Konvolut N*:

Comparisons of others' attempts to setting off on a sea voyage in which ships are drawn off-course by the magnetic north pole. Discover that North Pole. What for others are deviations, for me are data by which to set my course. I base my reckoning on the *differentiae of time* that disturb the 'main lines' of the investigation for others.[3]

The 'peripheric' representation of cultural difference to establish a cult of a national order through repositioning and regulating the other (in a contingent yet historical relation) is splendidly demonstrated at various points in Walter Benn Michaels's essay 'Race into Culture: A Critical Genealogy of Cultural Identity'. Discussing Willa Cather's *The Professor's Wife* (1925), Benn Michaels suggests that the importance of the difference between the white man and the nigger also begins to rewrite

> that difference as the difference between an Indian and a Jew. . . . [The] older racist structure is not perpetuated with a new content: rather it is altered. For the new valorization of the Indian points toward an interest in an essentially *pre*national America . . . Americanism would now be understood as something more and different from the American citizenship that so many aliens had achieved.[4]

Although Benn Michaels's argument is firmly located in the American 1920s, the strategic binding or 'binarizing' of cultural difference, whose very terms are exceeded and displaced in the process of its 'peripheric' performance, finds a suggestive echo in the current attempt paradoxically to 'contemporize' the Hindu–Muslim conflict by placing it in a 'pre-national' archaic past. The Muslim Babri Masjid in Ayodhya, India, torn down by Hindu fundamentalists who claimed that it was built on holy ground, the birthplace of Rama, was a religious edifice and a cultural icon found threatening by bigoted communalists because – as Alok Jain pointed out recently in *India Today* – it bore testimony to a vernacular, democratic Islam. The mosque was a hybrid, multivalent structure that embodied the 'differentiae of temporality' of an Indianized Islam. Nearer home, the British Tory war-cry against contemporary multicultural life – the patriarchal nuclear-family-based political ethics that they term 'Back to Basics' and deploy to police the state – has only released all the fissures and contradictions within that regressive, backward-looking social policy. The skeletons in the cupboards of Tory ministers have emerged, as in a carnivalesque bacchanal, to haunt the vaunted principles of the 'new' Majorite Conservatism. The affective symbol of the 'single mother/welfare-queen', pilloried at the 1993 Tory Party Conference as representative of the moral degradation of multiculturalism and 'minority rights', has become our new Boadicea. She is no longer the Labourite feminist with the flat vowels, as depicted in the Tory press. She is now, in many cases, a Conservative Party activist, half persuaded to go back to basics, who accusingly points her red-white-and-blue-rinsed bouffant at those very Conservative Members of

Parliament who have fathered, proportionately, the highest number of 'children out of wedlock' (their phrase) of the entire British population!

The invention of the national past, then, follows a 'peripheric' route: it is a turning away from the differential, disjunctive cultural present, and presence, of modern society. But in its backward glance, the present of *nationness* turns ambivalent and anxious. If the *positing* of the national past – in 1920s America or 1990s Ayodhya – is ironically both the 'atavistic' *end* of the present and, performatively, the rhetorical and affective *means* to the perpetuation of a national(ist) contemporaneity – *its means of continuance* – then the enunciative *place of the past* as it moves between temporalities, *in the interstices*, is itself subject to the Benjaminian process of 'positing' that Werner Hamacher has finely expounded in 'Afformative Strike'.

> Every positing and every law is thus subject to a more powerful law that demands that it expose itself to another positing, and another law. This more powerful law is the law of historical change and internal structural transformation, dictated by *the ambiguity of being both means and end*. (my emphasis)[5]

If the invention of tradition is an interregnum, a place-holding position constructed as the passageway to modernity, then what does the peripheral past make of that primal scene, the love of the nation? Is there another law of love that *agitates* the national fantasy, its filiation and its fealty, that emerges from its *positing* to 'overpower', and expose, the nation's ends and means?

Amor patriae satisfies the demands of a theory of nationness that is, more than nationalistic, profoundly naturalistic. In everything natural there is something *unchosen*, writes Benedict Anderson[6] in the course of an argument which suggests that the nativity of the unchosen, its familial, domestic metaphor (motherland, *Vaterland*, *patria*, *Heimat*), becomes the object of national identification: skin colour, gender, parentage. Those 'natural ties of the national sentiment and its naturalist narrative produce the "beauty of *Gemeinschaft*", a ghostly intimation of simultaneity across homogeneous, empty time, evoking an as-it-were ancestral Englishness'.

Now, this link that I am positing between nationalism and naturalism is clearly visible in the work of Johann Fichte, often credited with being the father of modern national sentiment. It is rarely remarked of *The Addresses to the German Nation*[7] (1807–8) that the central metaphor for rational, national identification is the scopic regime. It is the love of the eye – and the avoidance of the gaze – that enables 'the designation of [national] objects directly perceived by the senses; and in the beginning all human language is this'

(p. 58). It is German as a 'living language' that constitutes a national territory for the Germans after the Prussian defeats at Jena and Auerstadt in 1806. The project of a national(ist) discourse, in terms of Fichtean metaphysics, would be to insert 'The-thing-without-image in the continuous connection of things which have an image' (p. 61). It is the world of perception – the eye of the mind – that fosters a naturalist, national pedagogy which defines the *Menschenfreundlichkeit* of the German nation: 'Naturalness on the German side,' he writes, 'arbitrariness and artificiality on the foreign side, are the fundamental differences' (p. 83). The arbiter of this nationalist/naturalist ethic is the bearer of this visibility (some call it the phallus) – the familial patriarch. This position must be understood as an enunciative site – rather than an identity – whose identificatory axes can be gendered in a range of strategic ways. The instinct for respect – central to the civic responsibility for *the service* of nation-building – comes from the Father's presence which, I shall argue, is an effect of his 'peripheral' position in the family. 'This is the natural love of the child for the father, not as the guardian of his sensuous well-being, but as the mirror from which his own self-worth or worthlessness is reflected for him' (p. 173).

But amidst the metaphysics of the 'directness of national perception', the Father's image is a form of identificatory non-direction or elision – what we may call 'phallic' peripherality. For it is the absence of the Father, rather than the mother, who appears 'more directly as benefactor', which constitutes the principle of national self-identification. The national subject is founded on the trace of the Father's absent presence in the present of the mirror, whereas the mother's immanent 'over'-presentness is supplemental – marked by the overbearing shadow of the Father, but more clearly held in the line of light and vision. The orientation towards national subjectivity is caught between the reflective frame and the tain of the mirror.

The visibility of the national mirror cannot but be liminal rather than 'supersensual', as Fichte would claim. The citizen-subject is created in the splitting of the gaze: its iterative and interstitial insertion between presence/ absence reflected in the national mirror whose temporality is consequently caught in a disjunctive present-past. It is this very temporality that provided my starting point, somewhere *in between* Belsen and Bosnia; *in the midst of* the communal riots in India, the spectre of an unfinished struggle for independence.

This gendering of the nation's familial, domestic metaphor makes its naturalism neurotic. The temporality of the national present, with its elisional (rather than illusional) past in the *fort/da* games of fatherlands and mother- lands, turns *amor patriae* into a much more anxious love. Explicitly so when we realize, through Samuel Weber's[8] reading of the psychoanalytic genealogy of anxiety, that it is a 'sign' of a danger implicit in/on the threshold of identity, *in between* its claims to coherence and its fears of dissolution, 'between identity and non-identity, internal and external' (p. 154). This anxious boundary that is also a displacement – the peripheral – has a specific relevance to national identification when we realize that what distinguishes fear from anxiety is the danger of a loss of perception (a *Wahrnehmungsverlust*) attached to familiar (and familial) images, situations and representations (p. 155). The indetermi-nacy of anxiety produces, as with my reading of the Fichtean mirror, 'a traumatic divergence of representation and signification' (p. 155) at the very core of the cathexes that stabilize the I. As if further to emphasize my articulation of anxiety's 'present' and the desire for the national past as a peripherality that borders and bothers the national discourse, Lacan suggests that the structure of anxiety 'seems to be that of a twisted border' (p. 158). This structure – a twisted border – has an immediate relevance to our speculations on the national past and its challenge to the naturalism and progressivism of the matricial myth of modern progress. For, as Lacan suggests, that spatial 'twisting' is part of a profound temporal disjunction at the heart of anxiety:

> [t]hat is anxiety. The desire of the *Other* does not recognize me . . . It challenges me, questioning me at the very root of my own desire as o, as cause of this desire and not as object. And it is because this entails *a relation of antecedence*, a temporal relation, that I can do nothing to break this hold rather than enter into it. *It is this temporal dimension that is anxiety.* (p. 160; my emphasis)

If one can say that nation*ness* is the Janus-faced strait gate of modernity, and all who enter shall look backwards – in what we may now call an *anxiety of the antecedent* – then one must also point out, following Weber, that that experience 'is to be caught in the space between two frames: a doubled frame, or one that is split . . . ' (p. 167). What enters this double frame of the nation's anxiety is not the naturalized, harmonized unchosen of the *amor patriae* – which is also the love of the nation-people – but its double: those who are the 'unchosen', the marginalized or peripheralized non-people of the nation's democracy. In the discourse of nationness there is a continual reference to something resembling the process of the *peripheral*, which I described above: it is the 'unchosen', the unassimilable. In Tom Nairn's *The Break-up of Britain* the 'unchosen' is 'the complex of refractory, unassimilable phenomena linked to nationalism and its many derivatives (racism, anti-semitism, etc.) which time and time again appeared to undermine and thoroughly discredit Western rationality'.[9]

In Benedict Anderson's *Imagined Communities* the 'unchosen', once again, focuses the idea of the nation on the question of racism and anti-Semitic languages that erupt – illegitimately, extraneously in his view – into the discourse of nationness. Once more, we have peripherality: that which sets the limit and boundary of the discourse but, in a twisted temporality, becomes its displacing, disjunctive instance. Anderson writes:

> The fact of the matter is that nationalism thinks in terms of historical destinies, while racism dreams of eternal contaminations, transmitted from the origins of time through an endless sequence of loathsome copulations: *outside history*. Niggers are, thanks to the eternal tar-brush, forever niggers; Jews, the seed of Abraham, forever Jews, no matter what passports they carry.[10]

Does the 'racial' unchosen of cultural difference, then, designate something that is 'outside' nationalist histories or 'outside' rationality, modernity's avenging angel – the nation's counter-principle – or is it the peripheral perspective that reveals the fragile, anxious apparatus of national affiliation that can suddenly turn the nation's insides, or insiders, into outsiders – the enemy within? What lends support to my reading of this indeterminate, yet disastrously *determining*, 'unchosenness' lies in its double-and-split scenario of inscription. If the nation's past, contained in an image of racial and cultural difference, is relegated outside its democratic, collective history, then the signifying sign of race and its iterative, interruptive temporalities of archaism and discrimination inform the very moment of the enunciation of the nation's contemporaneity: time and time again, the sign of the complex, unassimilable phenomena and paraphernalia of racial marking emerges with its banal evil. It is as if the *Aufhebung* that sublates the nation's anteriority – its dynastic pre-democratic verticality – and raises the national idea to the level of historicity does not merely return as the repressed, but turns daemonically from *Aufhebung* into an archaic, articulatory temporality of the nation's enunciation and performativity, its everyday enactment. Time and time again, the nation's pedagogical claim to a naturalistic beginning with the unchosen things of territory, gender, and parentage – *amor patriae* – turns into those anxious, ferocious moments of metonymic displacement that mark the fetishes of national discrimination and minoritization – the racialized body, the homophobic defence, the single mother: the 'chosen' fixated objects of a projective paranoia that reveal, through their alien 'outsideness', the fragile, indeterminate boundaries of the 'People-As-One'.

In order to grasp such peripherality and ambivalence in the idea of the nation, Nairn resorts to Walter Benjamin's *Angelus Novus*, his 'angel of history' – an allegorical figure which emerges in recent discourses of the nation

to mark the complex temporality of its modernity. Nairn and Anderson end
their books with the figure of the *Angelus Novus*; the collage on the cover of
Stuart Hall's volume on Thatcherism, *The Road to Renewal*, shows Margaret
Thatcher as the angel of history sucking large numbers of the British radical
left of the late 1970s and 1980s into her catastrophic vision of progress. Let me
remind you, once more, of that sphinx-like figure, half-bird, half-man, half-
historian, half messiah, Walter Benjamin's *Angelus Novus*:

> His face is turned towards the past. Where we perceive a chain of events, he sees one
> single catastrophe which keeps piling wreckage upon wreckage and hurls it in front
> of his feet. The angel would like to stay, awaken the dead, and make whole what has
> been smashed. But a storm is blowing from Paradise; it has got caught in his wings
> with such violence that the angel can no longer close them. The storm irresistibly
> propels him into the future to which his back is turned, while the pile of debris before
> him grows skyward. The storm is what we call progress.[11]

And this is Nairn rereading the coming of the angel:

> Let us return to the real historical sources of Benjamin's single catastrophe, the home
> of the wind that has propelled [the angel of history] so far and so erratically. This
> means the history of Western-founded progress. It is only now that a distinctively
> non-occidento-centric version of the story is becoming possible, a version that will be
> something like the world's picture in which the Enlightenment, and the bourgeois
> and industrial revolutions of the West, figure as episodes, however important . . .
> (p. 361)

> The terror of [the angel's] vision comes from the original west wind of progess *as well
> as* the multiform reactions it has produced in the east and the south. (p. 360)[12]

What might the non-occidentocentric version of the story be? To allegorize
Benjamin's angel by identifying the past with the catastrophe of colonialism,
and the future with the purblind violence of the drive to modernization and
uneven development, is to miss the angel's interstitial agency. The angel's
liminal critique of historicism comes not from transcending the contradictions
of Western progress but from inhabiting a space in between the past and the
future: a melancholic midden stance that is the present. Such 'now-time', as
Peter Osborne has recently written, 'is neither wholly inside or outside history,
but faces both ways at once' (p. 86) 'in a *gestalt* of betweenness' (p. 92).[13]

The angel hovers over the discourse of the nation's anxiety at the very point
when the spectre of race and cultural difference emerges in a radical
disjunction – what I described above as the 'unchosen' – to question its modern
homogeneous temporality, and its democratic promise of social horizontality.
To contemplate the agency of the Benjamin 'temporal montage'[14] as it defines

the geopolitics of the historical present – the destiny and discourse of democracy – is no easy task. It requires a complex translation of the politics of time into the history of the event itself. Surprisingly, such an occasion was recently provided by Michael Kinsley in an essay in *Time Magazine* entitled 'Is Democracy Losing Its Romance?'. After a *tour d'horizon* of the post-communist world, he concludes that 'democracy, far from suppressing nationalist hatred, has given ferocious vent to it', and then turns a homeward glance. In the USA today, he suggests, there has emerged a populism with an anti-democratic flavour that hungers for 'a strong leader on a white horse . . . Thus Ross Perot, America's would-be Fujimori.' Then he continues:

> As the current movie *The Remains of the Day* reminds us, there was a time, not long ago, the 1930s, when openly expressed doubts about the wisdom of democracy were positively fashionable, even in established democratic societies. These days everybody at least pays lip-service to the democratic ideal. Will that change?[15]

Is it possible to read Kazuo Ishiguro's *The Remains of the Day*, centred on the very British bathos of the butler Stevens, a 'gentleman's gentleman', as a parable of the 'peripheralization' of progress, the melancholy of modernity, represented by the *Angelus Novus*? Does the temporal montage of the novel – the authoritarian populism of the Thatcherite late 1980s (the moment of authorship) restaging the Suez-centred mid-1950s with its post-imperial 'confusions' (the historical 'present' of the narrative) which, in turn, frames the country-house fascism of the fellow-travellers of the late 1920s and 1930s – do these disjunctive historical events enable us to rethink the place of national minorities?

Ishiguro's historical and narrative retroactivity works through a performative identification with an aristocratic Tory traditionalism, enacted with the customary belief in the 'dignity of service'. In the English context, 'service' has a double cultural genealogy. It represents an implication in the class structure where service normalizes class difference by extravagantly 'acting it out' as an affiliative practice, perfectly exemplified in the metonymic mimicry of the idiomatic naming of the butler as a 'gentleman's gentleman': 'A butler's duty is to provide good service', Stevens meditates, 'by concentrating on what is within our realm . . . by providing the best possible service to those great gentlemen in whose hands the destiny of civilisation truly lies'.[16] But service has at this historical moment, in the very same English context, an imperial and international connotation – the service to the ideal of Empire conducted through knowledges and practices of cultural discrimination and domination. For instance, in a 1923 essay in the proto-fascist *The English Review* titled 'The Character of a Fine Gentleman', which extols the virtues of 'Dutifulness (*pietas*) and reverence for all that deserves veneration', H.C. Irwin proposes three classes of gentleman: the 'English gentleman', our 'transatlantic cousins', and 'Anglo-Indian worthies'.[17]

The brilliance of Ishiguro's exposition of the ideology of service lies in his linking the national and the international, the indigenous and the colonial, by focusing on the anti-Semitism of the inter-war period, and thus mediating race and cultural difference through a form of difference – Jewishness – that confuses the boundaries of class and race, and represents the *insider's outsideness*. Jewishness stands for a form of historical and racial *in-betweenness* that again resonates with the Benjaminian view of history as a 'view from the outside, on the basis of a specific recognition from within'.[18]

If 'domestic service', in the figure of the butler, is that 'unchosen' moment that naturalizes class difference by ritualizing it, then the narrative's attention to Jewishness and anti-Semitism raises the issues of gender and race and, in my view, places these questions in a colonial frame. It is while Stevens is polishing the 'silver' – the mark of the good servant – that the narrative deviates to recall the dismissal of two Jewish maids at the insistence of the fascist Lord Darlington. The gleam of the silver becomes that Fichtean national mirror where the master's paternal authority is both affirmed and, in this case, tarnished by the housekeeper Miss Kenton's pressing the charge of anti-Semitism against both Darlington and Stevens. This is the ambivalent moment in the narrative, when the 'memory' of anti-Semitism and the inter-war 'English' Nazi connection turns the naturalism and nationalism of the silver service into the 'anxiety' of the past – what Lacan has described as the temporal antecedence of the anxious moment.

The preservation of social precedence, embodied in the butler's service, is undone in the temporal antecedence that the presence of the Jew unleashes in the narrative of the national present. The English silver – the mark of the gentleman – becomes engraved with the image of Judas Iscariot – the sign of racial alterity and social inadmissibility. But the anti-Semitic historic past initiates, as anxiety is wont to do, a double frame of discrimination and domination that produces a temporal montage where Jew and colonized native, anti-Semitism and anti-colonial racism, are intimately linked. For the British fascists, such as Ishiguro's Lord Darlington, argued for the Nazi cause on the grounds that Hitler's success was intimately bound up with the preservation of the British Empire. In *My Life*, Oswald Mosley, founder of the British Union of Fascists, remembers his first meeting with Hitler in April 1935 – a luncheon in Munich – during which, he recalls, Hitler claimed to want no more from Britain than its neutrality in his struggle against Russia and communism: 'in return, he would have been ready to offer all possible guarantees for the support of the British Empire . . .'[19]

E. W. D. Tennant, who was undoubtedly amongst the most prominent of Lord Darlington's guests, and had certainly basked in the afterglow of Stevens's glinting silver, had this to say in 1933, in an article entitled 'Herr Hitler and His Policy', published in *The English Review*, which surely adorned the walnut veneered tables at Darlington Hall:

> The evidence that I saw supports the idea that the burning of the Reichstag and the consequent seizing of the Karl Liebknecht house was an act of providence. The Karl Liebknecht house was set up as a printing works where Communist propaganda was prepared for distribution all over the world. There were thousands of pamphlets in many languages including thousands for distribution among the natives of India and South Africa. *Much information of the highest interest to the British Empire and particularly in regard to India and the Anti-Imperial league is available.*[20] (my emphasis)

In peripheralizing progress and the myth of modernity – of which the nation is the modal form of community – the Benjaminian angel makes the present a site of history's *intermediacy* – a theoretical concept that I have elaborated in *The Location of Culture.*[21] The present of the nation, which appears through Ishiguro's temporal montage, signifies a historical *intermediacy* intrinsic to the psychoanalytic concept of *Nachträglichkeit* (differed action or retroactivity). It is a transferential function, 'whereby the past dissolves in the present, so that the future becomes (once again) an *open question, instead of being specified by the fixity of the past*' (my emphasis).[22] This iterative time of the future as becoming 'once again open' makes available to marginalized or minority communities a mode of performative, public agency such as Judith Butler, for example, has elaborated for lesbian sexuality: 'a specificity . . . to be established not *outside* or *beyond* the reinscription or reiteration, but in the very modality and effects of that reinscription'.[23]

What is at issue in the interstitial space of the nation's 'present/past' is the regulation and negotiation of those social identities that are continually, contingently 'opening out', remaking the boundaries, exposing and endangering, *in the performative moment*, any possibility of a singular, sovereign difference – be it class, gender, or race. Is the *Angelus Novus* the guardian angel for those belated, beleaguered subjects of Western modernity in the age of anxiety – its racialized, discriminated minorities?

My emphasis on the disjunctive 'doubleness' of national identity enables us to get away from defining minority or subaltern consciousness as starkly binary: as having positive and negative dimensions. It allows for the understanding of subaltern agency as the power to reinscribe and relocate the given symbols of authority and victimage. One way of concretely envisaging such a practice is through the work of Adrian Piper. Her series *Pretend*[24] deploys the dynamic of the fetishistic gaze to replay the scenario of disavowal across the portraits of Black men – Martin Luther King amongst them – each bearing a piece of the text: *Pretend not to know what you know*. The unmarked icon at the end of the series shows three apes in the familiar 'speak no evil/see no evil/hear no evil' trio. Piper substitutes the mother figure of the Freudian fetishistic scenario with the Black father figure of the civil rights movement. The mother's overdetermined 'lack' is replaced by the ineradicable *visibility and presence* of the black skin to which Fanon drew our attention; the signifier of sexuality, with its splitting, haunts the male icon of racial victimage that seeks to constitute itself in a continuist political/prophetic tradition of patriarchal activism.

The spectator's identification with the apes incites, even excites, two forms of disavowal and its undoing – it cuts both ways, Janus-faced, across sexual difference and racial subjection. The viewer cannot but occupy an ambivalent, even incommensurable identification with the visible 'black' history of racial victimage and the struggle against it; there is, at the same time, a refusal to 'pretend' and a resistance to the disavowal, within Black patriarchal 'race' politics, of the agency of women, gay and lesbian activists. Social splittings of form and content are at the core of Piper's work,[25] as one critic has written, and she instructs us in 'Pretend', I think, that what-we-see-is-not-what-we-need-to-get-or-desire. It is by placing the viewer in a split position – an intermediacy between the ambivalent phantasmatic scene of sexuality and the more binary, heterosexist tradition of a style of race politics – that Piper makes us aware of the complex, even contradictory, relations between historical needs and political desires.

Contemporary art forces us to recognize, in the very midst of making the 'image' or constructing the discursive object, that the social context must be sought in what Walter Benjamin has described as 'the tiny spark of contingency, of the Here and Now, with which reality has seared the subject'.[26] And the use of this contingency – realized as a technique of historical recovery and a technology of representation – becomes visible in the most interesting projects as the basis for questioning the narratives of national identification.

The richness of Elaine Reichek's *Native Intelligence* lies in her exploration of the 'here and now' as the scenario of the Native American presence in the white American nationalist phantasy. It is the wildness concealed in the domestic imagination that Reichek locates in the 'everyday' detail of the American home – the cowboys-and-Indians wallpaper, the 'Home Sweet Home' runner with the desolate tepee – which she then reinscribes, acts out, through the agency of the 'domestic' arts of knitting and stitching. 'Home' now is not merely the scenario of a colonial history of extermination, or the pious celebration of nativism. It becomes quite literally a cipher – an intertexture of double writing – where the contemporary forms of white American popular culture turn into the everyday ethnographies of their own 'native' present. Having displaced the 'homey' values to display the profound cultural introjection and projection through which they are constructed in their naive (should we say native?) innocence, Reichek turns towards the more monumental histories of national self-awareness.

If I have tried to replace the displacement of identity with the agency of implementation, and the repetition of difference with a complex 'newness', then Reichek's reworking of the ethnographic photograph is an exemplary instance of this same strategy. By quite literally knitting the present into the past, mimicking the stereotypical, fixed postures of native subjects, Reichek gives them a mobility, breaks down their immediate recognizability. The Native American is photo-graphed: the familiar image of the native subject, whether resistant hero or victim, is recalled in the register of light – *photo* – and then unrecognizably reinscribed – *graphed* – in the texture of thread. What Reichek de-ciphers are two forms of the searing of the subject. The native subject seared through the domestic imaginary of white suburbia and its wild unconscious; and the native subject incarcerated in the reservations, seared through the loss of language, land, sovereignty, and rights. Reichek's double consciousness splits the American dream, at its most vulnerable point, by deploying the feminine arts of domesticity to unpick and refigure history's 'unconscious', amnesiac realities.

Time permits only a fleeting glance at another exemplary instance of the 'newness' of repetition that lurks in the past–present of our contemporary moment: what I have called history's *intermediacy* – Victor Burgin's 'Family Romance'.[27] Burgin's computer-generated graphics allow him to touch the contingency of the 'here and now' through what he calls the mess of image-fragments that coexist in a hybrid technological and social environment. In 'Family Romance' he literally rearticulates the homogenizing, universalizing *mythos* of the Hollywood film *South Pacific*. Burgin reveals how the colonizing dream of the 'family of man' is complicit with America's imperialist ambitions in the South Pacific, perpetuating a national culture which disavows forms of social difference that cannot be essentialized, biologized or individuated. Across this political, spatial argument, however, Burgin deploys phantasmatic scenarios of projection and introjection to rearticulate the sites and signs of psychic and identificatory difference. It is the virtual reality of the computer image that becomes the medium of translation. In that process Burgin opens up the historical intermediacy between the American 1950s – the moment of *South Pacific* and the 'Family of Man' exhibition – and its iterative agency in the *shape* of historical events as we experience them today.

The 'minoritization' of culture is a more radical way of emphasizing the democratic possibilities of the expression of cultural difference in a world of transnational, migratory social forces. The possibility that there is a new cosmopolitanism to be found and formed through the hybridity of cultural boundaries – on the model of great post-colonial, cosmopolitan centres – is strongly resisted. That does not prevent a Parsee journalist from Bombay writing just such a ballad to the city, over the embers of the bombings and the riots:

> A metaphor they call Bombay. Of modernity, celebrity, audacity. Cocking a snook at atavistic piety. Its idols only matinee; and Satyam-Shivam merely cinema halls. Ram is the migrant worker. As much as Rahim . . . They all came to Bombay chasing a dream. . . . *Bombaim*, they called it. The men from the far-off place and time, gliding full-sailed into the harbour. First Lisbon and London, then refugee and Non-Resident Indian, poured into the city of gold. Even if home was only the pavement . . . *Together they shaped it* . . . Citizens for Peace. Artists against Communalism. Divided over toilet blocks. United for a place in the sun. Blackmoney, blackmail. Green Bombay. Saffron Bombay. I am curious (but never yellow) Bombay. Did they think they could torch it and scorch it to the colours of death?[28]

The resistance to acknowledge a cosmopolitanism that is born from the contra-modern conditions of the post-colonial condition[29] is centred in the agonizing of those, like Robert Hughes, who are the prophets of the 'fraying' of the West.[30] They refuse to envisage a form of culture that does not ground its beliefs and values in the integrity of a consensual national 'commonality' as the matrix of cultural authenticity and communal integrity. This nation-centred-ness – with its myriad historical and institutional imperatives – becomes both the cause of cultural panic, and its panacea.

So the late-twentieth-century diasporic, exilic composition of national communities, demographically representing the real history of war, racism, famine, colonialism, political tyranny, and refugees, becomes partial cultures, marginal entities: *the cultures of complaint*. This process produces what Robert Hughes, and others on both sides of the Atlantic, consider to be the 'broken polity' of the national culture, the loss of good faith in social virtue. The solution, they believe, lies in the genius for national consensus, 'getting along by making up practical compromises to meet real social needs'.[31] But couldn't this panacea, which is superseded by the testimony of history itself, be what induces the panic and frustration rather than what calms it? For Hughes, a representative hope lies in looking at modern life as we look at mosaics, concentrating on the big picture rather than the differently coloured tiles.[32]

What if the nature of historical experience produces tiles that have incommensurable, jagged dimensions? What if different social experiences occupy disjunct spaces and divergent time-lines? What if the 'big picture' of national culture has always dominated and silenced the anxious, split truths and double destinies of those who are minoritized and marginalized by the iniquities of modern society?

It is to begin to answer these questions that I have, throughout this chapter, proposed to you the 'peripheric' path, where the anxiety of art and politics meets in the twisted borderlands of the nation's love and hate; the culture's disjunct differences make possible the reparation of the present and the revision of the past in future's fold.

Notes

This chapter is a transcription of a lecture; it is part of a larger project that will be elaborated in the book on which I am currently at work, *A Measure of Dwelling*.

1. Claude Lefort, *The Political Forms of Modern Society* (Cambridge: Polity Press 1986), pp. 304–5.
2. Tom Nairn, *The Break-up of Britain* (London: Verso 1986), p. 349.
3. See Andrew Benjamin's stimulating essay 'Time and Task', in *Walter Benjamin's Philosophy: Destruction and Experience*, ed. A. Benjamin and P. Osborne (London: Routledge 1994), p. 241.
4. Walter Benn Michaels, 'Race into Culture: A Critical Genealogy of Cultural Identity', in *Critical Inquiry, Identities*, vol. 18, no. 4 (Summer 1992), p. 667.
5. Werner Hamacher, 'Afformative Strike: Benjamin's Critique of Violence', in Benjamin and Osborne, eds. *Walter Benjamin's Philosophy*, p. 111.
6. For the citations in this paragraph, see Benedict Anderson, *Imagined Communities: Reflections on the Origin and Spread of Nationalism* (London: Verso 1983), pp. 131–2.
7. J.G. Fichte, *Addresses to the German Nation* (Chicago and London: Open Court Publishing 1922). Page references will appear in the text where appropriate.
8. All citations in the next two paragraphs (including the quotation from Lacan) are from Samuel Weber's signal contribution to this debate. See his *Return to Freud: Jacques Lacan's Dislocation Of Psychoanalysis* (Cambridge: Cambridge University Press 1991), especially Appendix A, 'Beyond Anxiety: The Witches' Letter'. All page references to this work will be given in the text.
9. Weber, ibid., p. 337.
10. Ibid., p. 136.
11. Walter Benjamin, *Illuminations* (London: Fontana 1973), p. 259.
12. Nairn, *The Break-Up of Britain*.
13. See Peter Osborne's fine reading of the angel of history towards the end of his essay, 'Small-scale Victories, Large-scale Defeats: Walter Benjamin's Politics of Time', in Benjamin and Osborne, eds, *Walter Benjamin's Philosophy*, see especially pp. 89–96.
14. The phrase belongs to Andrew Benjamin, and can be found in 'Time and Task'.
15. *Time Magazine*, 17 January 1994, p. 60.

16. Kazuo Ishiguro, *The Remains of the Day* (London: Faber & Faber 1989), pp. 115–17.
17. *The English Review*, vol. 37 (1923), p. 643.
18. Osborne, 'Small-Scale Victories', p. 93.
19. Sir Oswald Mosley, *My Life* (London: Nelson 1968), p. 365.
20. E.W.D. Tennant, 'Herr Hitler and His Policy', *The English Review*, vol. 56 (1933), p. 373.
21. H.K. Bhabha, *The Location of Culture* (London and New York: Routledge 1994). See in particular ch. 8, 'DissemiNation' and ch. 11, 'How Newness Enters the World'; also more generally for this argument that is elaborated throughout the book.
22. John Forrester, 'Dead on Time', in *The Seductions of Psychoanalysis: Freud, Lacan, and Derrida* (Cambridge: Cambridge University Press 1990), p. 206.
23. Judith Butler, 'Decking Out: Performing Identities', in *Inside/Out: Lesbian Theories, Gay Theories*, ed. Diana Fuss (New York: Routledge 1991), p. 17.
24. Catalogue for The Ikon Gallery Exhibit, 1991, p. 42.
25. Arlene Raven, 'Adrian Piper: You and Me', Catalogue, p. 18.
26. Benjamin, *Illuminations*, p. 253.
27. Victor Burgin, 'Realizing the Reverie', in *Digital Dialogues Ten-8*, vol. 2, no. 2 (Autumn 1991), pp. 8–13.
28. B. Karkaria, 'A Chasm and a Bridge', in *When Bombay Burned*, ed. D. Padgaonkar (New Delhi and Bombay: UBSPD 1993), p. 165.
29. See ch. 12, 'Race, Time and the Revision of Modernity', in Bhabha, *Location of Culture*.
30. Robert Hughes, *Culture of Complaint: The Fraying of America* (New York and Oxford 1993).
31. Ibid., p. 14.
32. Ibid.

NOTES ON
CONTRIBUTORS

PARVEEN ADAMS is a Lecturer in Human Sciences at Brunel University, where she is also Director of Psychoanalytic Studies. One of the founding editors of the feminist journal *m/f*, she edited, with Elizabeth Cowie, *A Woman in Question*, a collection of essays from the journal. She has written extensively on feminism and psychoanalysis and is now focusing on art and film.

ETIENNE BALIBAR teaches philosophy at the University of Paris I. He is the author of numerous books, including *Reading Capital* (with Louis Althusser); *The Dictatorship of the Proletariat; Spinoza et la politique; Ecrits pour Althusser; Race, Nation, Class: Ambiguous Identities* (with Immanuel Wallerstein); and *Masses, Classes and Ideas*.

HOMI K. BHABHA is a Reader in English at Sussex University. Well known for his work on post-colonialist discourse, he is the editor of *Nation and Narration* and author of *Locations of Culture*.

MIKKEL BORCH-JACOBSEN teaches in the Department of Romance Languages at Washington University. He is the author of several books on psychoanalysis and philosophy, including *The Freudian Subject; Lacan: The Absolute Master;* and *The Emotional Tie: Psychoanalysis, Mimesis, Affect.*

JOAN COPJEC is the editor of *Jacques Lacan's Television/ A Challenge to the Psychoanalytic Establishment* and *Shades of Noir* and the author of *Read My Desire: Lacan against the Historicists.* She teaches English and Comparative Literature at the University of Buffalo, where she is also Director of the Center for the Study of Psychoanalysis and Culture.

MLADEN DOLAR is a Lecturer in the Department of Philosophy at the University of Ljubljana. He has published in French, German and Slovenian, and is the author of a book on Hegel's *Phenomenology of Spirit* and of a study of fascist discourse. He is also editor of *Wo es War*, a German Lacanian journal.

ELIZABETH GROSZ is Director of the Institute of Critical and Cultural Studies at Monash University, Australia. She is the author of *Sexual Subversions: Three French Feminists*; and *Jacques Lacan: A Feminist Introduction*; and is currently editing an anthology called *Sexy Bodies: Feminism, Postmodernism, and Corporeality* with Elspeth Probyn.

JULIET FLOWER MACCANNELL is most recently the author of *The Regime of the Brother: After the Patriarchy* and co-editor of *Feminism and Psychoanalysis: A Critical Dictionary* and of *Thinking Bodies*. She is Professor and Director of the Program in Comparative Literature in the Department of English and Comparative Literature at the University of California, Irvine.

CHARLES SHEPHERDSON was recently Henry A. Luce Fellow at the Claremont Graduate School and Visiting Fellow at the University of Virginia. He writes about Kant, Derrida, Foucault and Irigaray, as well as about Freud and Lacan. His forthcoming book is titled *Vital Signs: Nature and Culture in Psychoanalysis*.

SLAVOJ ŽIŽEK'S most recent book is *Tarrying with the Negative. For They Know Not What They Do*; *Looking Awry*; *The Sublime of Ideology* are the titles of some of his books in English. He is a philosopher and researcher in the Institute of Sociology at the University of Ljubljana and was a Fulbright Fellow at the Center for the Study of Psychoanalysis and Culture in Buffalo.

INDEX